ALSO BY CAROLYN BAKER

Sacred Demise: Walking The Spiritual Path of
Industrial Civilization's Collapse

U.S. History Uncensored: What Your High School
Textbook Didn't Tell You

Coming Out of Fundamentalist Christianity:
An Autobiography Affirming Sensuality, Social
Justice, and The Sacred

The Journey of Forgiveness: Fulfilling The
Healing Process

Reclaiming The Dark Feminine: The Price of
Desire

NAVIGATING THE COMING CHAOS

[A HANDBOOK FOR INNER TRANSITION]

Carolyn Baker

Foreword by Andrew Harvey

iUniverse, Inc.
New York   Bloomington

Navigating The Coming Chaos
[A Handbook For Inner Transition]

iUniverse books may be ordered through booksellers or by contacting:

iUniverse
1663 Liberty Drive
Bloomington, IN 47403
www.iuniverse.com
1-800-Authors (1-800-288-4677)

Because of the dynamic nature of the Internet, any Web addresses or links contained in this book may have changed since publication and may no longer be valid. The views expressed in this work are solely those of the author and do not necessarily reflect the views of the publisher, and the publisher hereby disclaims any responsibility for them.

ISBN: 978-1-4502-7087-8 (sc)
ISBN: 978-1-4502-7088-5 (ebook)

Printed in the United States of America

iUniverse rev. date: 01/01/2011

Dedication

With love and gratitude to Michael Brownlee and Lynette-Marie Hanthorn who have pioneered the development of the Transition movement in the United States and taken its message to unprecedented and landmark levels.

Table of Contents

Stay near this book; it will stretch out its legs and trip you;

You'll fall into God

Hafiz, 1325 CE

Not Christian or Jew or Muslim, not Hindu,
Buddhist, sufi, or zen. Not any religion

Or cultural system. I am not from the East
Or the West, not out of the ocean or up

From the ground, not natural or ethereal, not
Composed of elements at all…

I belong to the beloved, have seen the two
Worlds as one and that one call to and know…

This we have now
Is not imagination.

This is not
Grief or joy,

Not a judging state,
Or an elation,
Or sadness.

Those come and go.

This is the presence that doesn't

When grapes turn to wine,
They're wanting this.

When the night sky pours by,
It's really a crowd of beggars,
And they all want some of this!

This that we are now
Created the body, cell by cell,
Like bees building a honeycomb

The human body and the universe
Grew from this, not this
From the universe and the human body.

~Rumi, Translated by Coleman Barks~

FOREWORD

By Andrew Harvey, Author of *The Hope: A Guide to Sacred Activism*

It is becoming increasingly clear to many of us that our culture is utterly inadequate to the enormous world crisis that is now erupting on all sides, and so is, unavoidably, doomed to an agonizing collapse on an unprecedented scale. This clarity, is of course, brutally hard-won and extremely hard to sustain since it involves accepting that we are all entering together a whirlwind of ferocious ordeal at a time when the human race is profoundly unprepared and in a state of paralysis and deep denial.

Without this clarity infusing and informing both our inner work and our outer engagement with the world, we are however doubly lost since it is only by knowing where we are and what faces us that we can begin to do what is necessary---undertake a massive inner transformation to be strong and calm and passionate and focused enough not only to endure what is now inevitable but to guide others through it and midwife, in the middle of a seismic death of all previous human agendas, the Birth of an embodied divine humanity that is also being offered us by divine grace.

Carolyn Baker in her great book *Sacred Demise: Walking The Spiritual Path of Industrial Civilization's Collapse,* challenged us all to face the coming collapse of civilization unshrinkingly; in it, she lays down, with inescapable precision, exactly why our current mindsets, addictions, and economic and political policies are doomed, and what we all must start to feel and to do to respond to such a devastating situation. Sacred demise is one of the most essential books of our troubled time, and perhaps its most important gift to us is the tone in which it is written, a tone that shirks none of the difficulty and suffering ahead for all of us but which remains steady, joyful, and resonant with the kind of profoundly grounded, wise, and down-home instruction that can help us prepare ourselves both inwardly and outwardly for what is to come.

Carolyn Baker's equally important and essential new book *Navigating The Coming Chaos: A Handbook For Inner Transition* begins where Sacred Demise ends and should be read, carefully and slowly, alongside its predecessor. In it everyone who has woken up to where we are will find the kind of guidance we now need---one that does not play down either the severity of our crisis or its potentially atrocious consequences but which still provides us with a comprehensive set of inner and outer tools, skills, and practices with which to meet it in such a way that its ferocity can help us birth a new world and a new kind of humbly empowered divine human being. In the deepest sense, *Navigating The Coming Chaos* is a handbook for midwifing the birth that is struggling to be embodied through the great death that is erupting, and like any authentic handbook of sacred midwifery, it is at once stringently unsentimental in its facing of the gritty and grueling process of birth, and loving and joyful in its depiction of what could be possible.

There are other wise books coming out that address with great intelligence the practical aspects of the transition we are going through and focus on the new kinds of community building, organic agriculture, survival skills, and revivified local culture that we are going to need to start building now with great focus and fervor to have a chance of surviving the future. What these books for all their usefulness have not begun adequately to explore--- and perhaps don't want to explore---is the vast and frightening emotional trauma which the transition ahead will inflict, a trauma that can only be healed by attention as radically directed to inner spiritual grounding and preparation as to outer actions. Carolyn Baker's *Navigating The Coming Chaos* fills this much-needed gap with rich wisdom; in it she lays before us a brilliant and vivid smorgasbord of tools and practices by which we can prepare to be strong, empowered, and joyful enough not only to endure the great shattering ahead but to use it to birth ourselves into a new dimension of spiritual depth expressed in wise action and so help birth, amidst and through, the burning chaos of the Death, a new way of being and doing everything.

Perhaps the richest aspect of Carolyn's book is her unflinching exploration of what she calls, inspired by the great psychologist Miriam Greenspan, the *alchemy of the dark emotions.* The vast trauma that the transition into a new world is inflicting and will continue to inflict will inevitably bring up all of our shadow emotions---rage, fear, grief, and potentially annihilating despair. Patiently and precisely, Carolyn Baker takes us through the demanding process by which the very emotions we are all terrified of can become, through surrendering them to compassionate consciousness, our deepest guides to a new form of being and action. Only someone who continues, at personal cost, to surrender to the mystery of this alchemy could have given us such profound and helpful instruction; this is not the work of a person who knows all the answers and poses as a new age guru of the birth but something far more valuable---the clear message from the cutting edge of our evolutionary process given to us by a being who dares to be its humble pioneer, surrendered to a mystery she knows she cannot fully predict or control or even completely understand. In being such a messenger and giving us such a message, Carolyn Baker makes us aware that evolutionary process itself is something that we co-create at each moment and which is therefore a great adventure demanding of us that we stay at all moments as responsible, clear, inspired, and humble as possible.

The other aspect of Carolyn Baker's book that I want to salute is its note of dry-eyed but insistent optimism. For everything that Carolyn knows about our situation and our current dangerous inadequacy of response to it, she is far from being in despair either about us or about the potential result of the alchemical process we are burning in. She is herself someone who has risen phoenix-like from the smoking ashes of many previous selves and psychic and conceptual deaths and knows from her own experience how the deepest crises birth the most astounding and transformative possibilities. *Navigating The Coming Chaos* ends then, not in gloom and dire finger pointing, nor in stoic resignation but in an unabashed celebration of the kind of world it is still in our power to imagine and will and create if we have the courage to face where we are and to plunge into the inner and outer work that we are challenged to. All of my work in sacred activism is dedicated to this celebration of what could be possible, and I recognize in Carolyn someone who has dared to see both the face of our communal crucifixion and that of our potential beauty and glory in and under the divine.

All I can do in closing is thank my dear friend for having lived, worked, suffered, and rejoiced enough to write such a book, and urge everyone who wants to be useful in our time to read it.

Andrew Harvey

What a pleasure it is to endorse a book of this quality and genius. But more to the point, a book of great urgency. I not only recommend this book, I urge you to it.

Caroline Myss, author of *Defy Gravity:*
Healing Beyond The Bounds of Reason

INTRODUCTION

We are here…to love as broadly and as deeply as we possibly can—knowing that we cannot do this without the support of the entire community of Life. Our purpose is to consciously further evolution in ways that serve everyone and everything, not just ourselves. This is our calling. This is our Great Work. Indeed, this is our destiny!

~Miriam MacGillis, Director of Genesis Farm, Blairstown, New Jersey~

In the closing months of the first decade of the twenty-first century, what does the world need most? Does it need another book on Peak Oil—another confirmation of the disappearance of cheap and abundant fossil fuel energy? Will the world benefit from yet another among tens of thousands of books on climate change as global warming, now operating with a life of its own, ravages the planet with natural disasters of epic proportions? Is the world crying out for another book on economic theory that will champion a particular system of resource acquisition and distribution? While an analysis of these three factors—energy, environment, and economics is pivotal in making sense of the predicament in which we find ourselves, is yet another and deeper analysis what the human species is demanding?

I have been researching the state of the world since approximately the year 2000. Few books or movies on the topic of the unprecedented changes facing our species have escaped my attention. My intention in writing *this* book is to offer something more in alignment with what the human heart and the community of beings inhabiting this planet are crying out for because I understand viscerally that one more piece of analysis will only bore the mind and completely bypass the heart.

My deep conviction regarding this issue was underscored by the words of Clive Hamilton in his brilliant 2010 book *Requiem For A Species: Why We Resist The Truth About Climate Change:*

> Climate disruption's assault on all we believed—endless progress, a stable future, our capacity to control the natural world with science and technology—will corrode the pillars that hold up the psyche of modern humanity. It will be psychologically destabilizing in a way exceeded in human history perhaps only by the shift to agriculture and the rise of industrial society.[1]

While Hamilton's assertion was written in relation to climate change, it is applicable to the impact of energy depletion and global economic meltdown on humans and their responses to those, especially as these three crises converge in our lifetime in an unprecedented fashion.

In 2006 the Transition movement was born in Totnes, England and since then has virally spread throughout the world until there are now over 300 Transition initiatives on the planet. Some people reading this book are familiar with Transition and the efforts it continues to make to create sustainable communities everywhere on earth. Its model offers a brilliant map for transforming the conditions of the external world, or in situations where that may not be possible, responding to them resiliently. However, even though the *Transition Handbook* contains a section on the psychology of change, the focus of the movement remains on external Transition. Because I feel passionately that external Transition cannot succeed without a transformation of consciousness among the human species, *Navigating The Coming Chaos* has been written to address the void created by a predominant emphasis on outer Transition and offer specific tools to facilitate inner Transition. My hope is that this book will become an intimate companion of the *Transition Handbook* as well as a map of inner transition for individuals who are completely unfamiliar with the Transition movement.

But before proceeding, I want to tell the reader what this book is *not*. It is not a book for gleaning information; *it is a study*. If you crave more facts and do not wish to explore the myriad aspects of the human soul which may offer an antidote to the lethal cocktail of horrors which our species has created, this is not the book for you. If you have picked up this book in order to get more for yourself but have little interest in giving anything momentous to yourself or the world, it is likely that you will soon lose interest in what is written here.

Perhaps you have been preparing logistically for the collapse of industrial civilization for some time. You may have attended to food and water storage, energy supply, herbal medicines, organic gardens, and sustainable shelter. Perhaps you are exquisitely prepared for what James Howard Kunstler calls *The Long Emergency*[2], and you have every base of logistical preparation covered, but some part of you feels queasy when you contemplate living in a chaotic world during or following the collapse of most or all of the systems of civilization which at this moment in history we take for granted, and have all of our lives.

Perhaps you have envisioned possible scenarios of that world or read books or seen movies suggesting similar or worse scenarios. As you sit with them you notice an eddy of emotions that churn and spin like whirlpools of molten lava throughout your body. One moment you feel fear, the next sorrow, and in another, disorientation as you imagine events, landscapes, situations, and behavior that in present time are scarcely fathomable.

Many options for responding to those feelings present themselves to you. You may choose to reach for a stiff drink, a comforting dessert, a hug from a loved one, the furry snuggle of a household pet, a mindless TV series—or you may just choose to go to sleep and forget about what you're feeling. Yet some part of you knows that sooner or later, you are likely to be faced not only with one of the disturbing scenarios you imagine or one like it, but even more poignantly, the *feelings* that such an event will activate in you.

Still another part of you hopes that everything you've read or imagined about the future is false. Perhaps all the prognosticators are wrong, and the diehard champions of "technology will eventually save us" are right. Perhaps the future isn't so bright that you "need to wear shades," as the eighties rock hit boasts, but perhaps it really won't be as bleak as the "doomers" say it will be.

In fact, even now as you read these words, you may fear or resent me for writing them. You may argue that I shouldn't be scaring people. Yet after a decade of studying the state of the planet in depth and after witnessing that the majority of the human species is still unwilling to acknowledge its plight, I cannot in good conscience report to you "good news" that does not exist. More recently, James Gustave Speth, environmental attorney and author of *The Bridge at the Edge of the World: Capitalism, the Environment, and Crossing from Crisis to Sustainability,* asserts that "We need to be reminded of the nightmare ahead...we will never do the things that are needed unless we know the full extent of our predicament."[3]

In his June 18, 2010 blog piece, "Waiting For the Millennium: The Limits of Magic"[4], John Michael Greer writes:

> ...the thing that most people in the industrial world are going to want most in the very near future is something that neither a revitalization movement nor anything else can do. We are passing from an age of unparalleled abundance to an age of scarcity, economic contraction, and environmental payback. As the reality of peak oil goes mainstream and the end of abundance becomes impossible to ignore, most people in the industrial world will begin to flail about with rising desperation for anything that will bring the age of abundance back. Even those who insist they despise that age and everything it stands for have in many cases already shown an eagerness to cling to as many of its benefits as they themselves find appealing.
>
> The difficulty, of course, is that the end of the age of abundance isn't happening because of changes in consciousness; it's happening because of the laws of physics. The abundance we've all grown up thinking as normal was there only because

a handful of nations burned their way through the Earth's store of fossil carbon at breakneck speed. Most of the fossil fuel reserves that can be gotten cheaply and quickly have already been extracted and burnt; the dregs that remain – high-sulfur oil, tar sands, brown coal, and the like – yield less energy after what's needed to extract them is taken into account, and impose steep ecological costs as well; renewables and other alternative energy resources have problems of their own, and have proved unable to take up more than a small fraction of the slack. These limitations are not subject to change, or even to negotiation; they define a predicament that we will all have to live with, one way or another, for a very long time to come.

…there is no bright future ahead.

It does not predict a future of unbroken misery, or claim that there will be no gains to measure against the immense losses most of us will suffer.

What it means is that the core faith of the age that is passing, the faith that the future will be better than the past or present, has become a delusion. In almost every sense, the future ahead of us will be worse than the present and the recent past. The vast majority of us will be much poorer than we have been; many of us will have to worry at least now and then about getting enough food to stay alive; most of us will have to do without adequate medical care; most of us will not have the opportunity to retire; most of us will die at least a little sooner than we otherwise would have done. The security most of us take for granted, with police and firefighters on call and the rule of law acknowledged even when it's not equally enforced, will in many places become a fading memory; many areas that have been at peace for a long time will have to cope with the ghastly realities of domestic insurgency or war. All these things will be part of everyday life for the vast majority of us for decades, and on the other side of it lies, not some imagined golden age, but a temporary respite of stabilization and partial recovery that might last for half a century at most before the next wave of crises hits.

This is the way civilizations decline and fall. It's our bad luck to be living at the dawn of the second great wave of decline to hit Western civilization – the first, for those who haven't

been keeping track of their history, began in 1914 and ended
in the early 1950s – and this wave will probably be a great
deal worse than the first, if only because it comes right after
the peak of conventional petroleum production and thus has
to face a decline in net energy per capita on top of everything
else. It's comforting, and will doubtless be common, to look
for scapegoats for the troubled times ahead, but it seems more
useful to recognize that this is simply what happens at this point
on the curve of history's wheel.

Nearly all of our ancestors lived in times when there was no
bright future on the horizon; nearly all of our descendants will
experience the same thing. The great majority of the former and,
no doubt, of the latter as well, found other reasons for living.
That's an equally viable option right now, given a willingness
to think the unthinkable, recognize that the age of abundance is
ending, and consider the possibility that doing the right thing in
a time of crisis, no matter how uncomfortable or challenging the
right thing might be, may be a more potent source of meaning
than waiting for magic to make a bright future arrive.

Nowhere in the literature of the Long Emergency have I read a more poignant description
of the future than this. But during this past decade, I have learned much more about
holding the tension of this overall bleakness with the profound inspiration the last sentence
of Greer's forecast offers, namely, that *doing the right thing in a time of crisis, no matter how
uncomfortable or challenging the right thing might be, may be a more potent source of meaning than
waiting for magic to make a bright future arrive.*

So here Greer nails it. When industrial civilization as we know it no longer exists, what
will matter—and perhaps all that will matter, is meaning.

Likewise, Clive Hamilton notes that:

As the climate crisis unfolds, and poses the question of the
future of humankind, the meaning of our lives will come
increasingly to the fore. After a long period of psychological
disruption stability will return only with the emergence of a new
understanding of the Earth, a story to replace the one in which
the globe is seen as a repository of resources to fuel endless
growth.[5]

But what is the fundamental definition of *meaning*, and isn't it different for everyone?

Before he left us in 2009, the brilliant and lovable Thomas Berry gave us in *The Great Work* the bigger picture of "meaning":

> History is governed by those overarching movements that give shape and meaning to life *by relating the human venture to the larger destinies of the universe* (italics mine). Creating such a movement might be called the Great Work of a people.[6]

Humans have accessed and perpetuated the Great Work many times in our history, but industrial civilization has been a project designed to facilitate our forgetting that work, yet the work seems to keep returning incessantly to humans, however, not without incalculable anguish whenever they forget its pivotal role in their story.

Berry also tells us that the universe knows itself through humans who have developed conscious self-awareness. And certainly history seems to reveal that when humans devalue conscious self-awareness, they behave destructively, but when they deem it sacred, they function more harmoniously with the community of life on earth.

Miriam MacGillis, student and promoter of Thomas Berry's work, adds that:

> The human is the being in whom the Earth has become spiritually aware, has awakened into consciousness, has become self-aware and self-reflecting. In the human, the Earth begins to reflect on itself, its meaning, who it is, where it came from, and where it's going. So in our deepest definition and its deepest subjectivity, humans are the Earth—conscious.

Mathematical cosmologist and physicist, Brian Swimme, in his lecture series "The Powers of The Universe" emphasizes that cataclysm, or the constant rising and falling of life, is contiguous and cannot be reversed because it is inherent in the Second Law of Thermodynamics, that is, "things fall apart and break down."[7] But for Swimme, the issue is not preventing or avoiding cataclysm but rather, attentively responding to it. "Cataclysm is happening," he says, but "the choice before us is whether we will participate consciously."

This was precisely the red thread which ran through my 2009 book *Sacred Demise: Walking The Spiritual Path of Industrial Civilization's Collapse.* Essentially, in that book I emphasized repeatedly: Stop trying to avoid or prevent collapse. Open to collapse, understand it, move with it, do not resist it, and discover what it is asking from you. Or as Brian Swimme states: "By allowing the destruction of the earth to be the ground out of which we think, we enable cataclysm to proceed in a more conscious way."

Yet some would argue that the earth may be saved by alien beings in the universe who are more intelligent or more highly evolved. Others would argue that humans need to vacate the planet they have nearly destroyed and colonize other worlds, simply relocating their venue of pillage after having learned nothing. While I do not wish to argue these theories here, I hold unequivocally that just as a "savior" politician or President cannot provide solutions that address the needs of local communities, alien beings or geographic relocations in our galaxy cannot enable humans to cross the evolutionary threshold to which I believe we are being inexorably called by our own conscious self-awareness.

Recently, John Peterson of the Arlington Institute spoke to a group here in Boulder, Colorado and asked the question: What's happening to us? What are we becoming? He called our predicament "a punctuation in the human species," an evolutionary threshold, and asserted that a "new kind of human being" is necessary.

Peterson then asked: Do you really want to become a new kind of human being? If we do, he suggested that we ask the question: What is my purpose?

When someone asked Peterson, "But how do I find out my purpose?" he replied, "Just ask, because when you do, magic starts to happen."

In fact, it may be that without deep reflection on our life purpose, we lack the capacity to create meaningful change in our own lives and in the functioning of our communities. The great Czech playwright and politician, Vaclav Havel, asks:

> What could change the direction of today's civilization? It is my
> deep conviction that the only option is a change in the sphere
> of the spirit, in the sphere of human conscience. It's not enough
> to invent new machines, new regulations, new institutions. We
> must develop a new understanding of the true purpose of our
> existence on this Earth. Only by making such a fundamental shift
> will we be able to create new models of behavior and a new set
> of values for the planet. [8]

Much of this book is designed to assist the reader in asking and receiving the answers that serious reflection on one's purpose and calling may arouse. However, in order to ask the question and respond consciously, the wounds of industrial civilization in the form of so-called "dark emotions" must be explored. An entire section of the book is devoted to understanding and working with those.

Without adequate emotional and spiritual preparation for the collapse of industrial civilization, the human psyche is very likely to be overwhelmed to the point of madness or death. Collapse is humanity's next rite of passage, our imminent initiation into adulthood as a species. And as is sometimes the case, those undergoing initiation do not survive. In an August, 2010 interview I conducted with Transition Colorado's Co-Director, Michael Brownlee, he stated, "Primarily because of our use of fossil fuels and our profligate burning of fossil fuels, we've unleashed profound changes in our climate that are probably going to give us the equivalent of a species near-death experience. The near-death experiences for many individuals will be a profound wake up call and will produce a shift from an aimless, dissipated, wasted life to a focus on purpose and service. Climate change is likely to be affording us as a species, that kind of opportunity."

The "good" news, you see, is that we *have* such an opportunity because without it, we will have precious little to motivate us in persevering. Clive Hamilton reminds us that "The foundational beliefs of modernity—the unlimited scope of human achievements, our capacity to control the world around us, our belief in the power of knowledge to solve whatever discomforts us—will collapse."[9]

One of the qualities desperately needed in navigating the coming chaos is resilience. All resources for preparing for the Long Emergency emphasize resilience, but few offer a detailed explanation of what it is and how to cultivate it. Within the following pages lie several explanations along with many opportunities to practice greater resilience.

This book is a hands-on, practical toolkit. Because it is a study, it offers a cache of personal reflection exercises to which a great deal of deep thought and contemplation have been given. These provide the essential implements of inner transition. If you are reading this book only for information and do not work through all of the exercises, you will have missed a treasure-trove of guidance, inspiration, and untapped inner resources. Again, this is about giving—to yourself and to the people and experiences you may encounter in the collapse process, as well as to the earth community. You will give and receive the most if you treasure and work the exercises that are provided at the end of every chapter.

The first section of this book "Building Your Internal Bunker" focuses on cultivating an inner life and utilizing internal resources to confront the shadow self in order to savor our inherent connectedness with the earth community. Without the fortification and nurturance of a rich inner life, it may be exceedingly difficult, if not impossible, to engage in the work of subsequent sections of the book. Moreover, without a robust internal bunker, it will be virtually impossible to navigate the coming chaos.

The second section "Allies In The Great Turning—Who's Turning With You?" explores the issue of relationship and relatedness—with nature, with other human beings, and even with our own bodies. A broader definition of relationship is offered than we typically encounter in modern culture with the intention of also expanding our sense of support as we prepare to navigate a daunting future.

Section three "Emotions: Becoming A Warrior of Vulnerability" provides extensive support for consciously befriending all of our human emotions, with particular attention to the so-called "dark" emotions. In this section we draw upon the extraordinary wisdom of psychologist Miriam Greenspan whose life and work offer tangible tools for enhancing our emotional health and deepening our capacity to experience joy as well as the emotions we may prefer to avoid but which will be invariably stirred in the Long Emergency.

In the fourth and final section, "Elderhood At Any Age: The Skillful Use of Inner Transition Tools" we examine the concept of elderhood and its relevance to our community and our own lives, no matter how old or young we are. Here we discover the seeds of wisdom and the capacity to create beauty which enable us to prepare for the many unknowns of the future as well as imagine and create a new culture.

I give special thanks to Andrew Harvey, Miriam Greenspan, Miriam MacGillis, Seanna Ashburn, Andre Angelantoni, Sarah Edwards, Mike Ruppert, Janaia Donaldson and Robyn Mallgren, Keith Farnish, the members of Transition Colorado's heart and soul group in Boulder, Kathleen Bradley, and Janis Dolnick.

I am deeply grateful for the financial support of William Nelson, Patrick Ford, Jon Davis, Gary McGrath, and Mike Mintz.

Thank you David and Elise for your proofreading skills. Thank you, Sammy, my best canine friend, for lying under my chair and dreaming as the words came forth onto the screen.

I give thanks to my soul mentors, among whom are Carl Gustav Jung, Malidoma and Sobonfu Somé, Michael Meade, John O'Donohue, Pema Chodron, Eckhart Tolle, Thomas Berry, Marshall Vian Summers, Rumi, Hafiz, Kabir, Mary Oliver, Theodore Roethke, Rainer Maria Rilke, and David Whyte.

10 Things You Can Do Right Now

1. Utilize the tools in Chapter 1 of this book to cultivate or deepen your inner life. Logistical preparation alone is inadequate for navigating a world that will present unprecedented emotional and spiritual challenges.

2. Ally with a local group that has awareness of the *3 E's* of energy, environment, and economics. Contribute your time and skills to helping this group create a more sustainable community and bring food security, energy independence, and local currency to your place.

3. Create or ally with a group of trusted individuals with whom you can discuss emotional and spiritual preparation in the face of a chaotic and uncertain future.

4. Commit to simplicity. Carefully inventory your possessions and evaluate which ones you need for navigating the future and which ones may burden or impede your preparation.

5. Commit to establishing relationships that support your preparation. Carefully inventory all the relationships you have and evaluate which ones support your preparation and which ones may jeopardize it.

6. Commit to exploring your emotions and deepening communication skills particularly with respect to your emotions. Even if you have done many years of psychological work, you and your world are functioning at a different level today. A chaotic world will be more emotionally taxing than any of us can imagine.

7. One of your most important relationships is the one you have with your body. Commit to some form of exercise or movement for a specific period of time daily.

8. Practice gratitude in every situation, even the ones that challenge you or feel unfair or bothersome.

9. Practice kindness on every occasion, especially in situations where you are least inclined to it.

10. Create something beautiful every single day. Creating and appreciating art, music, poetry, or storytelling are exquisite antidotes to destruction and will nourish the soul in what may become a fundamentally soul-less world.

Section I

Building Your Internal Bunker: Cultivating An Inner Life

Chapter 1: Cultivating An Inner Life

I am not I
I am this one
Walking beside me whom I do not see,
Whom at times I manage to visit,
And at other times forget.
The one who remains silent when I talk,
The one who forgives, sweet, when I hate,
The one who takes a walk when I am indoors,
The one who will remain standing when I die.

~Juan Ramon Jimenez~

The first humans were fundamentally concerned with survival. Brain and body had not evolved beyond unambiguous pre-occupation with acquiring food, water, and shelter in cooperation with other friendly beings. These were hunter-gatherers whose survival needs dictated constant mobility and a division of labor based on gender. Population was limited by incessant relocation, and life spans were comparatively short.

We do not know with certainty why our nomadic ancestors chose to pause and become sedentary. Anthropologists and historians posit a variety of theories, but we should not underestimate the fundamental desire of our species for creature comforts. It is simply easier, less taxing, and less stressful to settle in one place. Hunting and gathering is daunting and sometimes frightening. The nervous system must remain on alert, any lassitude being potentially life-threatening.

And so it was that Western civilization ultimately spawned along the shores of the great rivers of the Middle East, proliferating into numerous villages and tribes whose sustenance and societal structure emerged from an agricultural lifestyle. Whatever sense of connection with nature hunter-gatherers had was now profoundly altered by their direct connection with the land. Sedentary living engendered a dramatic growth in population and a different mode of relating to the earth and to the community.

In arid climates where food production depended entirely on sufficient rainfall, our ancestors imagined forces of nature which they assumed were intimately concerned with their day-to-day well being, and most importantly, their sustenance. Thus, at this time in history, we see a proliferation of earth-based religions which emphasized the necessity of living in harmony with the gods and goddesses of the natural world. Their perspective became increasingly natural and also native—two words inextricably connected having to do with origins, that is to say, origins from physical birth and origins from the natural world.

From this point forth, we notice two values characteristic of thought systems before the proliferation of industrial civilization, namely a greater emphasis on connection with the inner world and with the community and the natural world. In fact, from the earliest agricultural civilizations until modernity, humans have generally revered these two principles, seeking to cultivate an inner life alongside vital participation in the community.

According to the psychology of Carl Jung, the introverted personality draws its inspiration and energy from the inner world, while the extroverted person draws those from the external world. It is clear that modern industrial society is extroverted, whereas the societies of the ancients were far more introverted. Even as the latter accomplished impressive cultural, artistic, political, and economic feats, they were societies that valued the inner world as much as, if not more than, the external.

Today, voices of sustainability and transformation such as David Korten and Joanna Macy speak of "The Great Turning." The turning to which they are referring might also be called the "Second Great Turning" because the first great turning was a turning away from the inner world. Korten and Macy are essentially inviting us to turn back to the inner world of indigenous wisdom which modernity turned *away from*. In fact, I would argue that industrial civilization is not only focused on the external world, but appallingly possessed by it. Much of this book will examine ways of permanently extricating ourselves from that possession.

Some may contend that the first turning to the external world was not necessarily unfortunate. Because of it we have penicillin, humans walk on the moon, and you are reading this book as a result of technological achievements actualized in an extroverted civilization. While I heartily agree, I must raise the question of what price we have paid for our extroversion and what has been lost, as well as what monsters have been created by our disconnection from the inner world. As James Gustave Speth notes in *The Bridge at The End of The World*, "For all the material blessings economic progress has provided, for all the disease and destitution avoided, for all the glories that shine in the best of our civilization, the costs to the natural world, the costs to the glories of nature, have been huge and must be counted in the balance as tragic loss."[10]

Disconnection from the inner world estranges us from that which in the outer world matters most—other members of the earth community and the earth itself. Attending to the inner world does not produce stunted navel-gazers, but rather informs and enlivens our connection with the external. It enables our ability to discern that which holds intrinsic value and that which has the capacity to annihilate. The inner world potentially offers a kind of innate "global positioning system" (GPS) that if consulted and honored, re-evaluates the external world in terms of what is life-supporting, sustainable, and authentic. Just as we require interaction with the external world in order to experience the value of earth/community connection, we require regular immersion in the inner world in order to function congruently and compassionately in the outer world.

Not surprisingly, most citizens of civilization are not only unfamiliar with the inner world but profoundly uncomfortable in it or perhaps even terrified of it. Ours is a world addicted to noise, meaningless activity, and superficial interactions with our fellow humans. Many humans cannot imagine sitting quietly alone with no distractions and being only with themselves. For some, this would be synonymous with being waterboarded or walking barefoot on broken glass.

Yet as industrial civilization increasingly disintegrates, as fewer and fewer people are employed securing their livelihoods as wage-earners—as there is less noise and more silence, as there is less light and more darkness, be it the darkness caused by the depletion of fossil fuels or the darkness of chronic loss, we will all be confronted with the inner world on an unprecedented scale. Just since the financial collapse of 2008, suicide rates in the United States have increased.[11] Undoubtedly, the long-term collapse process will take a brutal emotional toll. Humans will feel feelings they have successfully kept at bay for a very long time or perhaps have never felt. Night time for many will bring episodes of insomnia alternating with nightmares, and daytime will shine its light on realities we would all prefer not to see.

Later in this book we will consider in depth a number of possible emotions that are likely to surface in collapse, but at this point, it is important to simply validate the need to explore and become familiar with the inner world and the treasures it may hold for us at a time when the outer world as we have known it is crumbling. Then, we must consider several avenues for accessing the treasure. In other words, how do we make friends with the inner world and allow it to assist us in navigating the outer world, in whatever condition the outer world may be?

No matter how foreign the inner world may feel to us, we experience it on a regular basis. When we sleep, we frequently dream. Most citizens of civilization are aware of the unconscious mind. We all occasionally have our "Freudian slips" or say or do things that baffle us or about which we may feel embarrassed because they seem so contradictory to our perception of ourselves, and we are left wondering, where did that come from?

Cultivating an inner life is about being willing to explore this unconscious psychic territory and not only explore it but utilize its untapped resources in preparation for navigating our uncertain future. Yet even beyond this, by making friends with the inner world, we have the capacity to integrate it with our external experience which not only empowers but transforms us.

The Greek word *psyche* means *soul*, and psychology is fundamentally the study of the soul. As the concept of soul diminished during the rise of civilization, psychology became increasingly defined as the study of behavior, but the earliest thinkers who endeavored to understand human beings did so by contemplating the meaning and function of the soul. For the Greeks, the soul represented the part of us that is in touch with something greater—something numinous, intangible, and transcendental. Today we would probably use the word *spiritual* to describe that aspect of the psyche, but as we will notice in a subsequent chapter on the distinction between soul and spirit, other words such as *the sacred*, may be more appropriate.

While there are myriad forms of psychology, depth psychology, which has its roots in the work of Jung, is specifically focused on the study of the psyche, as opposed to merely the study of behavior. Both depth psychology and Eastern philosophy posit the psyche as multi-faceted, consisting of at least four components: soul, Self (the transcendent within), personality, and ego. Not infrequently, the voices of Eastern philosophy have proclaimed that the ego is our enemy, an obstruction to the discovery of the Self which must be diminished so that we may more fully experience and express the Self.

Paradoxically, however, a strong ego is required for engaging in the process of intentional ego diminishment and welcoming fuller expressions of the Self. In a later chapter addressing the dark emotions and the dark night of the soul, we will explore the reasons this is so. Nevertheless, at this point we must understand the role of the ego as gatekeeper between the conscious and unconscious minds. The familiar analogy of the ego as the conductor of an orchestra may be useful. The maestro signals for more volume from the string section and less from the brass. She waves the baton toward the percussion section inviting a heavier beat, then beckons the entire orchestra to decrease volume as the solo pianist is spotlighted. In this way, a strong ego conducts the psychic orchestra. The resultant melodies may range from exquisite harmony to a cacophony of *dis*harmony, but at least a conductor is on the podium.

Yet even as we acknowledge the ego's strategic and crucial role, the reality that industrial civilization has been the ego's most monumental accomplishment must not be overlooked. From start to finish, it has been an ego-based phenomenon. And just as the individual human who is driven and dominated by the ego must ultimately confront its limits, civilization is now entering a protracted ego-shattering breakdown which I believe is forcing confrontation with the deeper aspects of the individual and collective psyche such as the soul and Self.

Paradoxically, with strong egos we must open to this break-*down* of the ego which contains within it the promise of break-*through*. Somehow, something is inviting us to step across an evolutionary threshold into a new kind of humanity—a humanity in which soul and Self orchestrate our individual lives and our relationship with the community "in concert" with the entire earth community, in service of the glorious symphony of life on this planet.

But in order for this to happen, who we think we are must give way to who we really are, as the poem of Juan Ramon Jimenez above so beautifully articulates. "I am not I, I am this one," he says—this one walking beside me that I don't see and don't think about often, in fact forget, most of the time. This energy—this something greater that I don't see or ponder and only visit once in awhile—this presence is always with me. It's always doing the opposite of what "I" am doing or perhaps the opposite of what I want to do, but it never goes away. In fact, it will remain standing when I die.

Jimenez is referring to that something greater that lives within the psyche that has nothing to do with religion, ideology, or piety. For the past 300 years of industrial civilization, we have not needed to pay attention to it. The ego served and served well. But the ego alone can no longer serve us in a collapsing world. The "I that is not I" must be accessed and its resources utilized if we are to persevere and remain intact when people and institutions around us have turned to dust.

How then to we begin accessing the "I that is not I"? How do we cultivate an inner life? And if we have already begun the process, what will assist us in deepening it?

Journaling

One useful tool with which you may or may not be familiar is *journaling*. Journaling done on a daily basis is an opportunity to have a conversation with oneself. The "I and not I" have a place to converse or at least have permission to do so. Journaling is not a log of daily events or a diary, i.e., "Woke up, took a shower, took the kids to school, went to work, ate lunch with Joe…" It is a place to record and appreciate feelings that surface around daily experiences or to record moments of inspiration, insight, turbulence, uncertainty, or any other feelings. It is a place to become transparent with oneself and in some cases, brutally honest. Getting the words out of one's head and on paper is a courageous act of crossing a psychic line, a point of no return. Once I've put the words on paper, there's no denying, no taking them back, no minimizing. I can choose to modify or question them, but now they are no longer just swimming around in my head. They are real, tangible, external evidence of my inner experience.

Journals may be written on computers, but for me, it is important to write in my journal in longhand. The physiology of writing which involves fingers, hand, arm, all of the senses and the nervous system in the process, is part of writing from the heart and from the entire body. In a world of text messaging and computer writing, few people write letters or journals in longhand. The soulful art of writing emotions and experiences by hand is nearly lost. For this reason, I find going back and reading journals I've written in longhand profoundly moving. In doing so, I feel more compassion for the part of my psyche from which the words were written. I recognize the effort required to record my words and feelings on paper, and as a result, I honor the content more fully.

On a more practical note, journaling allows us to hash out problems and improves our cognitive functioning. Studies with people who journal indicate that it is a useful stress management tool and may even be useful in strengthening the immune system.[12]

A journal is also an excellent place to record dreams. Keeping one beside the bed and writing down a dream upon awakening can be very useful in making sense of one's dreams. A former therapist once reminded me that when a place is made for dreams to be written, it is as if one sends a message to the unconscious to bring forth more dreams because one is ready to receive them, and they are deeply appreciated.

Psychologist Bill Plotkin, in his marvelous book *Soulcraft*, offers two notable suggestions for journaling. The first could be utilized when one is confronting a major life passage, whether one has begun it, ended it, or is in the middle of it. He suggests that we be as specific as possible about what is actually dying rather than what we would hope is dying. According to Plotkin:

> A true life passage is not an opportunity to happily and
> easily rid yourself of unwanted or unpleasant traits, roles or
> relationships. A recognition of what is really dying should evoke
> some grief whether or not it also evokes relief. What transition(s)
> are you going through? How do you feel about these shifts?
> What in you is getting ready to be born? Make your best guess.
> Don't worry, it will be different from what you imagine. Project
> it nonetheless. Imagining what's next will help you cast off from
> the shore of your past.[13]

Another suggestion from Plotkin which provides rich contemplation for journaling is in the following questions: What do I most deeply seek? In what specific ways am I prepared to surrender to the deepest strivings of my soul, to my unique gifts or powers? Who are my people (some may be members of non-human species)? For what do I pray?

Dreams

I am grateful to have experienced a number of years of depth psychotherapy and to have done considerable work during that time with dreams. While numerous approaches to dreams have proliferated throughout human history, my personal experiences have confirmed the value of interpreting my dreams as comments from myriad aspects of the psyche rather than as information directly relevant to the external world. Yet at the same time, I have noticed that my dreams consistently inform me about the state of the psyche and what it might be needing, requesting, warning about, or validating in my outer life.

Many people state that they do not remember their dreams, which is quite common. However, through writing down dreams that we do remember, carefully pondering them, and asking the psyche for additional dreams, we may be able to develop and maintain a conscious relationship with the unconscious mind. In most cases, making this effort yields more dreams and more success in remembering them. Working diligently with one's dreams is an exquisite practice for creating an intimate connection with deeper layers of the psyche and cultivating a rich, flourishing inner life. As a result, the distance between the conscious and unconscious mind grows progressively shorter as the two former strangers embark on a journey of reconciliation and integration.

We may choose to keep some dreams to ourselves, whereas other dreams, we may want to write in a journal or discuss with others who appreciate them and may also be engaged in dream work. Frequently, this kind of sharing can illuminate one's own dreams, but one must be cautious about accepting others' interpretations of one's own dreams. Just as we should not assume that a friend can correctly interpret a conversation between ourselves and another human being which we have related to him or her, we should not assume that a friend can sufficiently analyze a communication from our unconscious to our conscious mind. While sharing dreams with another may shed some light, the authentic meaning of the dream must ultimately come from within oneself.

It is also true that it may take days, weeks, months, or even years before we can fully understand or appreciate the significance of our dreams. In some cases, a great deal more of life will have to be lived before we can make sense of some dreams. Making sense from hindsight is often our only option, but in doing so, we may become increasingly familiar with the psyche's way of communicating with us so that we can apprehend the meaning of our dreams more readily.

Poetry

My friend Keith Farnish at The Earth Blog recently wrote an article entitled "Taking Back Our Words." This is not as one might think, an article about apologizing for something we have said, but rather, reclaiming the meaning of words which have been distorted by civilization—or what Farnish calls the "predefinition".

Unquestionably, industrial civilization has distorted our language, but even more fundamentally, our thinking about language. Clearly, our literate ancestors spoke and wrote much more poetically than we do in the twenty-first century because they were much more in tune with the right brain and the language of poetry. The project of civilization is inherently linear and left-brain; its language is prose and goal-oriented message delivery.

Just read and feel the words of the poet Hafiz: "A poet is someone who can pour light into a cup, then raise it to nourish your beautiful parched holy mouth." The thought of even attempting to text message such an exquisite, heart-melting, sensuous utterance is beyond absurd. It is a thoroughly right-brain statement which when contemplated, repeated, and opened to, affects our physiology down to the bone. Civilization has no place for such "extravagances," no patience for the swirls of sensuality and literary moistness, nor their attendant images. It uses the language of the mind—rational and linear because it has a mission to accomplish, a message to deliver.

Poetry, however, has nothing to deliver, no goal, no mission to accomplish. It is quite simply the language of the heart, breath, blood, genitals. It is marinated in emotion and embarrassingly irrational. Poetry, like art, music, dance, and drama, articulates the language of the soul. For this reason, it is an ideal conduit for the flow of energy between the inner and outer worlds, and in turbulent times, it is the most reparative and appropriate language for holding deeply disturbing emotions and thoughts. It facilitates the containment of psychic material which is potentially overwhelming.

In a 2009 article "Memorizing Poetry" in *Literature and Literacy*, Matthew Koslowski lauds the value of learning poems "by heart" and *with* the heart and refers to memorized poems as "pillars of the temple of thought." He concludes with the caveat: "By committing poetry to memory, you are controlling what ideals and images constitute the pillars in the temple of your thought. If you don't decide what you want to think, the marketers are going to do it for you."[14]

Not only does memorizing poetry build strong pillars of the temple of thought, but in a post-industrial world where few people will have access to books and probably no access to the internet, memorized poems may provide a kind of glue that holds the psyches of traumatized individuals together. It could be a healing salve not only for oneself but for many around us. Contained within poetic language is an ancient memory—a memory of earlier times and earlier ordeals when the psyches of individuals and cultures were pushed to the brink of extinction. In those times, poems and proverbs sustained people when nothing else could.

Over the past two decades I have collected many books of poetry but memorized many fewer actual poems. Yet I utilize poetry incessantly in my writing and in public speaking and workshop events. I've also written a few of my own poems and committed them to my personal journals and once or twice incorporated them in my public writing.

I believe that in preparing emotionally and spiritually for collapse, it is crucial to read and appreciate poetry. Memorize it, write your own poems, but however you ultimately engage with it, linger beside and luxuriate in the deep, sensuous, heartfelt pools of passionate poetry. For after all, as Rumi says, "Poems are rough notations for the music we *are*."

The Irish poet, William Butler Yeats, experienced many inner collapses and wrote passionately about the deteriorating world around him at the time of World War I. He clearly saw where industrial civilization was headed yet was able to discover and create treasures amid the debris of his troubled era. These lines from Yeats' "The Circus Animals' Desertion" are profoundly instructive for our time:

> *Those masterful images because complete*
> *Grew in pure mind, but out of what began?*
> *A mound of refuse or the sweeping of a street,*
> *Old kettles, old bottles, and a broken can,*
> *Old iron, old bones, old rags, that raving slut*
> *Who keeps the till. Now my ladder's gone,*
> *I must lie down where all the ladders start,*
> *In the foul rag-and-bone shop of the heart.*

In subsequent chapters we will explore the value of descent alluded to here by Yeats and the treasures to be found in "the foul rag-and-bone shop of the heart."

In earlier times, poets were considered the prophets and wise women and men of their communities. When the tribe was battered, bewildered, and in despair, the poets were consulted for inspiration and even for direction. Today, the poet is marginalized to the edge of society as if her/his vocation is irrelevant or somehow a luxury in which only a few among us can afford to indulge. Thus, we must individually take poems and their authors to our breasts, holding their treasures close to our hearts to draw upon in moments of personal and collective suffering. So many poets know so much about suffering. As with music in the mind of the tormented composer Beethoven, the lyric art of poetry provides a container that allows it to endure in the face of loss, depression, and madness.

Storyteller Michael Meade, notes that poets are always ahead of their time because creating art of any kind is a prophetic act. Prophecy, he says, is not telling people what *will* happen but what is *about* to happen. Here one is reminded of Bob Dylan's popular ballad of the 1960s, "The Times They Are A Changin' ":

> *Come writers and critics*
> *Who prophesize with your pen*
> *And keep your eyes wide*
> *The chance won't come again*
> *And don't speak too soon*
> *For the wheel's still in spin*

And there's no tellin' who
That it's namin'.
For the loser now
Will be later to win
For the times they are a-changin'.

Meditation

Our ancient ancestors discovered and brought forth to subsequent generations myriad forms of meditation. If like me you are one of those individuals who sometimes erroneously confuses the words "mediation" and "meditation" when you write or type them, there may be a good reason for that. Both words are related to the ideas of measuring, bringing together, and healing. Meditation is perhaps the most conscious and intentional method of creating and sustaining a relationship with the inner world. In my opinion, the form does not matter; what does matter is the practice, and the word *practice* is key. No human being meditates "perfectly". Everyone who meditates, even if they have done so for decades, is practicing.

Meditation is a journey, both in the moments of sitting quietly and throughout years of thousands of meditations. Some would argue that the goal of meditation is enlightenment. Others would argue that the goal is stress-reduction or having a direct experience of the divine or calming and focusing the mind. There are as many reasons to meditate as there are techniques, but in a collapsing world, meditation is likely to be not only a useful tool, but an absolute necessity.

Some forms of meditation occur as one deeply contemplates an object, a landscape, or an idea with eyes open; other practitioners argue that meditating with eyes closed may be more conducive to connection with the inner world. After more than three decades of twice-daily mediation practice, I have come to believe that it serves at least two pivotal purposes for me: 1) Experiencing deep stillness and rest, and 2) Becoming intimately acquainted with the inner world. While the "practical" purpose of the latter is regarded as absurd by an inordinately extroverted, civilized culture, a long-term practitioner's experience almost always validates the utility of the practice. In ways sometimes ambiguous and at other times unequivocally obvious, practitioners notice tangible benefits in their external world experiences.

Volumes of research have been conducted on the benefits of meditation physically, mentally, and emotionally. After more than three decades of research on meditation, Dr. Herbert Benson states that meditation can actually turn off stress genes in the body. This from a 2008 *Washington Post* article on meditation and yoga: "It's not all in your head," said Dr. Herbert Benson, president emeritus of the Benson-Henry Institute for Mind/Body Medicine at Massachusetts General Hospital and an associate professor of medicine at Harvard Medical School. "What we have found is that when you evoke the relaxation response, the very genes that are turned on or off by stress are turned the other way. The mind can actively turn on and turn off genes. The mind is not separated from the body."[15]

For the purposes of this book, suffice it to say that in a turbulent, traumatic milieu such as the collapse of civilization, a regular meditation practice may become as necessary as food, water, shelter, and a group of trusted allies.

Two words bandied about during the last 50 years of personal growth and consciousness movements have been the words *grounded* and *centered*. Both are difficult to describe but once experienced are rarely forgotten. In any chaotic situation, being grounded or centered will be as critical psychologically as being fed will be critical physiologically. In the earlier stages of collapse trauma, most people will be overcome with panic; few will be grounded. Thus, being able to ground ourselves and assist others in doing so will be a quintessential skill.

In the Appendix section of this book the reader will find numerous resources for utilizing meditation and relaxation exercises to enhance access to the inner world.

Creating Beauty

The notion of meaninglessness will be mentioned many times in this book, and Michael Meade comments that the job of poets and artists is to keep creating events and objects of meaning because the call of cultural meaningfulness is the call to be creative. This is not the first time that nations and cultures have collapsed into meaninglessness, and in other times of collapse, people have turned to songs, stories, poems, and works of art for emotional and spiritual sustenance.

The decades of the 1950s and '60s were sometimes called "the age of anxiety". Today, we abide in the age of terror. Meade suggests that the antidote to terror is a sense of awe and that when that sense is lost, terror increases. Poetry and art evoke awe, offering a balm of healing in a world that is likely to become far more terrifying than it now is.

In a post-petroleum world, unlike our current techno-obsessed milieu, we will need to create beauty without electricity, digital dependency, or oil-intensive objects or supplies. Yet we have only to observe ancient petroglyphs, sculpture, pottery, and jewelry to be reminded that art can be made from the simplest, most natural materials. Without sophisticated technology at their disposal, our ancient ancestors created many works of beauty inspired by nature and using objects of stone, wood, sand, plants, seeds, bone, and hide.

While a post-industrial world may contain much less pollution, we do not know what calamities may occur in the collapse process. A post-industrial world is likely to be gray and largely colorless. Nor do we know to what drastic extent climate chaos will have progressed, and therefore, we cannot predict how much sunshine or blue sky will be visible. In that world, it is very likely that we will hunger for objects of beauty, sweet sounds and soothing melodies, and that our bodies will want to dance and move in liberating natural rhythms away from the robotic machinations of industrial civilization. In spite of, but also because of the suffering within and around us, creating beauty will become necessary and salutary for our species.

The late Irish poet and philosopher, John O'Donohue's extraordinary book *Beauty: The Invisible Embrace*, is a must-read for anyone endeavoring to prepare emotionally and spiritually for collapse. In it, he asserts that "In a sense, all the contemporary crises can be reduced to a crisis about the nature of beauty." Therefore, it is crucial to awaken a sense of beauty in our lives. How do we do this? According to Donohue:

> We may awaken to Beauty through a renewed perception of the world 'as it is', beyond stereotypes and collective views, in nature, the arts and in ordinary everyday moments. It may evoke a taste of the eternal, breed a generous desire to share with others or stimulate its shadow, which is possessiveness. Beauty has a central place in the Kabbalistic Tree of Life, and integrates the opposite forces of kindness and power. We will explore our own relationship with beauty in our lives, and experientially find our personal ways to awaken its mysterious force in times of a global crisis.[16]

Delighting In Nature

Teaching college-level psychology allowed me the opportunity to incorporate a segment of ecopsychology in my courses. For those unfamiliar with the discipline, Ecopsychology Professor, John Davis, of Naropa University defines it as follows:

> Ecopsychology integrates ecology and psychology. Among its contributions are bringing psychological principles and practices to environmental education and action, bringing the contributions of ecological thinking and the values of the natural world to psychotherapy and personal growth, and fostering lifestyles that are both ecologically and psychologically healthy.[17]

In recent decades a distinct discipline of ecopsychology has evolved and has become increasingly popular amid the daunting challenges now faced by the ecosystems. Yet we need not enroll in an ecopsychology course to practice its principles or experience its personal benefits.

Again from Bill Plotkin in *Soulcraft* we are given nuggets of wisdom regarding the willingness to commune with nature as a powerful tool for cultivating an inner life. As we explore this option, we discover that our entire being–mind, body, and senses are engaged.

Communing with nature involves more than just putting on some comfortable clothes and shoes and heading for the forest. For maximum benefit, it should be undertaken with as much intention as one would implement when engaging in any other method of cultivating the inner life.

In *Soulcraft*, Plotkin provides simple, succinct guidelines for this endeavor:

> Nature has much to teach us in her vast classroom. You can acquire an entire education merely by observing carefully. But you must be patient and offer your attention, like a lizard stalking a fly. This takes skill, and practice. What you find in nature is what works. It wouldn't be there if it didn't. Boundless wisdom awaits.
>
> Skillful nature observation requires your willingness to sit motionless for long periods and focus on what is in front and around and inside of you, bringing your attention always back to the present moment. Look with care. Look into things, not just at them. Listen to the texture of a sound as well as its origin and volume. Track scent as well as color and shifting shade. Become acquainted with the feel of surfaces as well as the touch of wind and stillness, the dance of warmth and chill. Be truly curious. Observe with innocence and delight. In addition to the behavior of animals and insects and the movement of vegetation, there is the lively life of the air and sky, the flow of water and light. Some things you will learn by sitting still. Some by tracking slowly. Some by returning to the same spot time and time again over different seasons and many years, getting to know not just the species there but individual animals and plants as well.[18]

As you read these words, you may be asking what the value of expending this kind of energy communing with nature might be. Plotkin offers a lovely explanation:

> In spending an hour or more tracking an animal or flower, your consciousness gradually shifts. While focused on an outer, elusive presence, changes happen on the inside. You quiet down. Life becomes simpler. You come to belong more fully to the place you wander, following a track or scent or sound. Eventually, you notice, "being on track" is its own reward, just as life is about

the journey, not the destination. You may or may not catch up to
the one leaving the prints or other signs. No matter. You begin
to notice the one who is tracking now is not the same as the one
who began tracking a few hours or days earlier. You wonder,
"Who is it that tracks?" And you wonder in new ways. Maybe
the question becomes "What is the quality in me that allows me
to track in my unique way?" You need not name that quality, but
rather just learn to feel it, imagine it, act it, be it.[19]

More recently, Professor Raymond De Young of the University of Michigan's School of
Natural Resources and Environment writes in his remarkable article "Some Attentional
Benefits of Walking In Natural Settings," that coping with the environmental challenges we
face demands a number of distinct mental and behavioral abilities and that these abilities
each draw upon a mental resource defined as the capacity to direct attention. De Young
argues that these attentional skills may be extremely valuable in coping with societal
collapse and transition to a new paradigm. In summary:

> The general prescription presented here is to spend more time
> in natural settings regardless of what other activities we are
> pursuing during our day. However, theory and research allow
> us to be somewhat more specific. Because at this time most of
> us would benefit from doing more walking, we can use it as
> a prototype behavior. Soon we may need to walk not just for
> contemplation and restoration, but for basic locomotion.[20]

Clearly, De Young's research suggests that the inner and outer worlds are not only connected
but need each other. Thus it makes sense that the mind is sharpened by the experience of
walking in nature, and likewise Plotkin's work emphasizes the many ways in which the
psyche is nourished by intentionally communing with nature.

In summary, if we are serious about confronting collapse, we must attend to our relationship
with the inner world. While it is true that the inner and outer worlds are connected, it is
equally true that we are less functional when we are only or even predominantly familiar
with the external world. We need only consult the world's most notable artists, philosophers,
musicians, and poets to realize the magnitude of the inner world and its impact on the earth
community. All of our species' great wisdom traditions agree, whether it be the Christian
tradition which invites us to seek the kingdom within, or the 16th century female Hindu
poet Mirabai who writes:

> *In my travels I spent time with a great yogi.*
> *Once he said to me,*

"Become so still you hear the blood flowing
Through your veins."

One night as I sat in quiet,
I seemed on the verge of entering a world inside so vast
I know it is the source of all of us.

CONFRONTING AND CONTEMPLATING
(Writing answers to these questions or drawing images in relation to them in a journal is highly recommended.)

1. How does your body react to the previous chapter? What do you feel as you read these words?

2. What does it mean to you to have an inner life? If you feel that you are cultivating an inner life, what does that look like? Please write about that. If you feel devoid of an inner life, write about that. Do you notice any longing for one? If so, explain.

3. Which one(s) of the tools recommended in the previous chapter such as journaling, mediation, etc. are you currently utilizing? Write about your experience with using these tools. What more might you need to do in order to refine and more skillfully use these tools?

4. What forms of beauty do you appreciate in your world? Write about that and explain the impact of your appreciation of beauty in your life. If you are inclined to draw your response instead of write it, do so.

5. Structure a time in nature when you can apply Plotkin's suggestions for skillful observation. Make this a sacred time set aside for nothing but communing with the non-human world. Later, record your experiences in your journal.

6. In what ways are you creating beauty in your world? What is the impact in your life and in the lives of others? Are there other ways of creating beauty that you would like to explore and why?

7. To what extent is your creation of beauty dependent on technology? Do you engage in forms of creativity that are not technology-dependent? Contemplate the notion of the simplicity of beauty and write more about this.

Chapter 2: The Momentous Distinction Between Spirit and Soul

You know the value of every article of merchandise,
but if you don't know the value of your own soul,
it's all foolishness.

You've come to know the fortunate and the inauspicious stars;
but you don't know whether you yourself are fortunate or unclean.

~Rumi~

Indigenous wisdom is knowledge grounded in the soul. As we have already seen, it is inextricably connected with nature and community. But we cannot appreciate the significance of the soul without first attempting to define it.

The first thing we must notice about the soul is that it is not a "thing". The Greek word for soul is *psyche*. Jungian psychologist, Robert Sardello, says that, "Jung considered the activity of the soul to be the ceaseless flow of images that move through dreams, daydreams, fantasy, and myth."[21] The soul is the part of us that frames our experiences with meaning. While it is impossible to define specifically what the soul is, we know with certainty that it is not the part of us that thinks or reasons, but rather the part that feels, intuits, and seeks meaning. It craves love, connection, community, sensuality, and nature, as well as solitude and reflection. From the soul, beauty is created, and art is dreamed, expressed, and appreciated.

Our ancient ancestors were immersed in the soul as they hunted, gathered, grew food, and attended to their families and communities. Their earth-centered, mystery religions filled their lives with meaning and nurtured intimate knowledge of everyone and everything around them.

In the first great turning away from the earth as civilization burgeoned around the world and as progress, economic growth, conquest, colonization, and empire became the measure of humankind, the soul was increasingly eclipsed by a fascination with spirit. Nowhere is this more evident than in the proliferation of the Christian religion.

Spirit and soul are not synonymous. Unlike soul, spirit is the transcendent within. Jung frequently referred to the Self, the center of the psyche, as spirit within. It is that "something greater" that is at the core of our essence. Soul, however, may function somewhat as a bridge between spirit and the physical world.

17

It was not modernity in and of itself which fostered the rejection by Christianity of soul in favor of spirit because after the demise of the Roman Empire, the so-called civilized world entered an era which we now call the Dark Ages—a period of history which was anathema to the engineers of modern civilization and which they vowed to eradicate and never replicate. Yet even in the midst of this darkness, modernity's nemesis, spirit prevailed as soul was increasingly identified with all things pagan. And while we see astonishing manifestations of soul in the creation of Gothic cathedrals, manuscript illuminations, and mosaic facades, the preponderance of artistic expression was intended to draw the eye and the mind away from the body and the earth toward the celestial realm which from the Medieval Christian perspective was the domain of spirit.

The flight from soul to spirit in the early Christian era was a repudiation of pagan, earth-based mystery religions and the feminine archetypes in which they were embedded. Paganism and femaleness were deemed dirty, messy, irrational, savage, and unsophisticated. One Christian sect for which orthodox church fathers held particular contempt was Gnosticism. From the Gnostic perspective, women and men were equals, and Gnostic women held positions of authority and traveled alongside men throughout the ancient world as teachers of the Christian gospel. Ultimately, Gnosticism was declared heresy by adherents of Christian orthodoxy who prevailed in their attempt to rid the church of both paganism and female leadership.

The history of the Christian church is the saga of the triumph of spirit over soul. As we shall see below in considering specific distinctions between the two, the perspective of embracing spirit and disavowing soul is astonishingly congruent with the project of industrial civilization. In fact, industrial civilization is the stellar and enduring legacy of a religion obsessed with spirit.

Michael Meade, inspired by Jungian psychologist, James Hillman has succinctly characterized the distinction between soul and spirit which I am paraphrasing as follows:

- Spirit seeks to ascend, reach the heights, and have peak experiences. It wants to be world-class and at the top. When people get "high," it's because they can't experience spirit any other way. On one level, substance abuse happens because people can't find their spiritual substance. Soul finds value in a downturn. It favors descent and diversity and finds ways to grow in a depression.

- Spirit would try to unite by way of an overriding principle (i.e., "united we stand"), but Soul finds unity in authentic community and is usually on the margins of an overriding principle.

- Spirit is dualistic and favors only one idea. Soul is diverse and holds many ideas at the same time. Spirit would seek a global, one-world government or system while Soul would seek small-scale, local connections—the village and uniqueness of place.

- Spirit polarizes whereas Soul holds the opposites. Jung said that maturity is the increasing capacity to hold the opposites together. Out of the tension, if it is held long enough, comes tremendous creativity—a third element born from holding the tension of the opposites. When it gets rough, the answers aren't on one side or the other but in holding the opposites together. If you consider the idea that we're in an end/beginning, then our job is to hold those two ideas as the whole world goes through collapse. We are transitioning from an age of Spirit to an age of Soul, and this is a fabulous opportunity to make more Soul in the world and in ourselves.

- Spirit is pre-occupied with information while Soul's greatest asset is wisdom. The modern world contains a great deal of information, some knowledge, and very little wisdom. The Soul is the source of wisdom, and an old definition of wisdom is "dark knowledge." The Soul knows what it wants to do in the world, and very often, traditional education gets in the way.

- Spirit venerates youth, speed, and innovation. Soul venerates ancient origins, moves us toward slowness, elder consciousness, and understands that nothing is ever new but rather, a remaking of the old. Soul has its own timing which is organic and womblike, and it knows that "it takes as long as it takes."

- Spirit values linear movement—simplification, getting from Point A to Point B, the end product. Soul moves in spirals and weaves webs. It values the process rather than the destination and knows that wherever we are is where we are meant to be and that everything is interconnected.

- Spirit is hierarchical and creates pecking orders. Soul is inclusive and embraces the gifts of each person and his/her inner authority.[22]

I encourage the reader to return to these distinctions while journeying through this book. They are rich and replete with significance for all that is written here and beyond.

Not Either/Or But Both/And

I also want to emphasize that in no way am I attacking spirituality or the call to walk a spiritual path. The calling, in my opinion, issues from the soul, and the path is usually a means of providing structure for responding to the call. To perceive either spirit or soul as "more correct" than the other would simply be a replication of spirit-dominated thinking. Both are necessary aspects of our relationship with the sacred. Soul and spirit need each other. Spirit without soul is dry, rigid, judgmental, and in the worst case scenario, heartless. Soul without spirit can become an irrational, emotion-drenched ego fest in which we become so absorbed in our personal pain or ecstasy that we lose sight of the divine within and in the world.

A soulful analogy from the culinary arts may be helpful. In allowing the sacred to "cook" in our lives, we need many ingredients of spirit, but we also need the spice of soul. An ideal "recipe" for communing with the sacred is the mixing of many spiritual truths and practices with the savory elements of poetry, story, visual arts, and music. This combination serves not only to enhance the flavor of our relationship with the sacred, but also to maintain a necessary equilibrium between spirit and soul within it.

Patrick Harpur, author of *A Complete Guide to The Soul,* emphasizes in an article on Soul and Spirit[23] that it is important not to polarize the two. Doing so, Harpur says, "is the result of the preponderantly 'spirit' perspective of our culture, founded on a monotheism which tends to polarize…. Such oppositions have been carried over into modern society where subject is at odds with object, mind with matter, fact with fiction and so forth." From this perspective, "A wholesome life, it seems, is made out of holding spirit and soul together, in tandem and in tension."

Harpur's article is a brilliant explanation of the meaning and purpose of soul and spirit in the universe and the extent to which they are not at odds, but very much in need of each other:

> Thus soul and spirit can only be grasped in relation to each
> other. I have been opposing them in order to bring out their
> differences; but opposition is only one way in which they relate,
> albeit the way favored by modernity. Really, they are forever
> intertwined, mutually mirroring.

The Triumph of Spirit Over Soul In Western Civilization

The Medieval era gave way to the European Renaissance—a period of some of humanity's most astonishing manifestations of soul in visual artistic expression. Concurrently, the Christian church began fragmenting, eventually mutating into a plethora of denominations and sects. In reaction to the Copernican revolution[24] and the humanistic perspective of the Renaissance which revered the human body as the crowning achievement of God's creation, and with its hierarchy jeopardized by a menacing Protestant reformation, the church instituted massive, spirit-driven repression. Ghastly torture and execution which constituted nothing less than ecclesiastical terrorism, gave birth to the Enlightenment which, in opposition to religious dogma, touted reason as the ultimate criterion of human thought and action. And while the appeal to reason was a breath of fresh air subsequent to serial inquisitions, the Enlightenment's fatal flaw was its unequivocal repudiation of soul and its spirit-tinged obsession with limitless human progress.

Thomas Berry wrote in *The Great Work*, that this aversion to soul was strongly influenced by the Black Death that swept Europe from 1347-1349—an event which traumatized the Western world. Had the masses been educated in scientific principles and not enslaved by superstition and unsanitary practices, the Great Plague may have been averted. Much of the Enlightenment's "religious" denunciation of religion was a reaction to the conditions that led to this catastrophe.

French philosopher and mathematician, Rene Descartes, is perhaps most famous for his dichotomization of mind from the natural world and his maxim "I think, therefore I am." With this, according to Berry, Descartes "desouled" the earth, and since Descartes, the Western world has perceived the natural world as a mechanism that "could be, and even must be, exploited for human benefit."[25]

Mankind could now only ascend toward the light, and any suggestion to the contrary was anathema and had to be repudiated. A cultural annihilation of the soul was unconsciously institutionalized and deceptively reinforced as humanity proceeded to discover the magic elixir of modernity, petroleum—a resource that some 300 years after its discovery would leave humankind and the earth community ensconsed in a quality of affluence never before experienced by our species, yet eviscerated by unimaginable consequences.

At the close of the first decade of the 21st century, the earth community is confronted with the dire results of the repudiation of soul in favor of a frantic pursuit of the spirit-motivated enterprise of industrial civilization. As Jung has revealed, rejecting any part of the individual or collective psyche does not cause it to vanish, but rather ultimately return to consciousness to make itself visible again, refusing to be permanently banished. This assertion is fully congruent with Einstein's discovery that energy can be transformed, but cannot be made to disappear.

The collapse of industrial civilization, which is well underway, is a natural consequence of spirit possession and soul repudiation. As Meade comments, spirit seeks to ascend and reach the heights, while soul prefers descent and flourishes in the downturn. The Enlightenment paradigm has served, among other things, as a protracted flight away from the earth and rewarded us for not being fully present here. As emphasized in my book, *Sacred Demise*, collapse is the soul's gift to us at this moment in human history as it pulls our species back down to and *into* the earth. It as if the earth itself were screaming its rage at humanity in the form of natural disasters and climate chaos, and soul were wailing its sorrow in the form of myriad economic catastrophes and unprecedented financial devastation. The earth and the human soul cry out to us to return at long last to the *humus* or soil from which comes the word *human* and be fully present here.

For this reason, we cannot, we dare not, ignore collapse. It will continue to demand our attention, and we can choose to answer the cries of the earth and the soul consciously, asking ourselves with intention what they may be requesting from us, or we can deny their ubiquitous upheavals, delusionally pretending that a return to normal is preferable, or even possible.

Soul is calling us now into its favorite territory—darkness. The Enlightenment and its legacy are fading into the archives of human history. We have entered the *Age of Endarkenment*, a term introduced some years ago by the poet, Robert Bly. Confronting collapse consciously is an intentional response, an agreement to make the descent into the darkness, not because of a masochistic preference for suffering, but in order to mine the gold that cannot be discovered elsewhere.

CONFRONTING AND CONTEMPLATING
(Writing answers to these questions or drawing images in relation to them in a journal is highly recommended.)

1. Write about your response to Chapter 2. What intrigued you most? Did you encounter new ideas or new ways of approaching old ideas? Were any ideas in Chapter 2 disturbing? Explain.

2. Contemplate and write about differences between soul and spirit in your world and in your own life? How do they show up?

3. Organized religion is often the domain of spirit-mind dominance. How have you experienced this personally? How does your connection with soul differ from this? Be specific.

4. What are some of your favorite soul delights, i.e., poetry, art, music, story? Write at length about this, or draw images. You may want to write a poem, create an image, compose a song or story.

**I highly recommend reading *Care of The Soul* and *The Re-Enchantment of Everyday Life*, both by Thomas Moore, as delightful refreshers for living and experiencing life soulfully.

Chapter 3: The Mythopoetic Heart
vs. The Rational Mind

Your vision will become clear only when you look into your heart ... Who looks outside, dreams. Who looks inside, awakens.

~Carl Jung~

Evidently, the only way to find the path is to set fire to my own life.

~Rabindranath Tagore~

The *Age of Endarkenment* is the age of the soul, as opposed to the *Age of Enlightenment* which was the age of mind and spirit. The currency of the soul is the image or symbol, not the mental concepts so highly esteemed by rational thinkers. I hasten to add, however, that becoming intimately acquainted with the soul does not mean a disavowal of rational thinking. Rather, it means experiencing from our bodies and emotions that mind and spirit reveal only one segment of our totality. Rational, critical thinking is indispensible because it empowers the ego in ways that serve us, enabling us to solve problems and carry on the daily business of living in a linear world. A world beyond civilization will not allow us to reject the rational mind. In fact, we may need it more than ever for moment-to-moment problem solving. However, a post-collapse world will undoubtedly offer unprecedented opportunities, wanted or unwanted, for not only tempering rational mind dominance with deep immersion in the territory of the soul, but actually living from it.

The principal organ of the Enlightenment is the brain whereas Endarkenment fosters soul awareness and functioning from the heart. The rational mind's favorite mode of communication is prose—linear text, facts, charts, and graphs. The soul, however, prefers poetry, myth, and story. Civilization has made "myth" synonymous with "untrue" or "lie" so that in current time, when people speak of something fictitious, they often use the phrase "the myth of" in relation to whatever they assert is untrue. From the soul's perspective, a myth is *true*, not because it did or did not occur in real time, but because of its message, and more importantly, because of its meaning.

The Mythopoetic Human

Personally, I have endeavored in recent years to avoid using the word myth synonymously with untruth because for me, it is crucial to understand the power and significance of myth. Since a real myth is larger than life, issuing in my opinion, from archetypal depths in the human psyche, I believe that I do a disservice by associating it with fiction. Thus, I have come to revere the mythical and the poetic—two words which some have joined in recent decades, creating the word *mythopoetic*. Myths are almost always poetic in some way, and the most powerful poetry transports us to mythical territory in the psyche. The soul is nothing if not mythopoetic.

The demise of civilization will very likely facilitate soul exploration and may proliferate soul language as the rational and linear become increasingly ineffectual in holding the momentous reality of collapse and transition. In the first stages of collapse which we currently witness around us, the notion of demise, collapse, or anything less than the triumph of civilization is anathema to the rational mind. The Enlightenment will not succumb gently to the dustbin of history. Too much is at stake for the shadow-phobic human ego. However, when it becomes unarguable that the Enlightenment paradigm is wholly inadequate to cope with the unraveling, humankind is likely to be driven to its soul depths and there discover the deeper meaning of the demise.

As Michael Meade notes, from the soul's perspective, things can be both dark and comfortable at the same time because the soul is, in fact, more comfortable with darkness than with the centuries-old insults to it of "white, bright, and light." It knows how to expand in the darkness and assimilate tragic loss because it has lived through tragic losses throughout human history.

Therefore, according to Meade, individuals who are genuinely conscious of the soul's value in our world—people such as poets, musicians, artists, and storytellers must "drag in the darkness," especially in a culture obsessed with light. Not only must they introduce darkness, but they must also keep creating beauty and objects of great meaning.

For nearly a decade, I have been one of those dreaded individuals who drags in the darkness. As a result, I've often been labeled a "doomer" because I refuse to capitulate to the demands of a culture that insists on remaining in the light and disowning the darkness. Through my writing, storytelling, and workshops, I have endeavored to demonstrate the urgency of opening to the darkness, working with it, and thereby receiving the gifts it offers when we are willing to explore it. For this insistence, I have paid a high price, as anyone does who is committed to persevering with the soul's journey. Yet I have no regrets, for the rewards have been inexplicably profound.

The Pivotal Question: Meaning

As promised, I return to the theme of meaning. Our overarching purpose in navigating collapse spiritually and emotionally is to find what has real meaning for us in it. Thereby, one might discover that the meaning collapse offers may well be the place one's life was intended to go before industrial civilization got in the way. Civilization has brought forth an unprecedented crisis in meaninglessness. However, as there is less and less of civilization, there are likely to be more manifestations of soul, and therefore, more meaning within and around us than we are currently experiencing.

But what does it mean to live in the territory of soul and thereby to find meaning? First, it is necessary to notice that soul cannot be fully experienced in the light. Even as we delight in moments of joy, ecstasy, and creativity, we must remember that soul will invariably lure us into their opposites, and these opposites need each other if we are to live soulfully. Individuals who insist on remaining in the light, letting only the good times roll, are experiencing a kind of "soul deficit disorder" which profoundly limits who they are and who they have the capacity to become. They cannot experience the depth of their humanity or the exquisite gifts of soul until they are willing to enter the darkness where soul abides and thrives.

In times of darkness and loss, the soul is not at a loss because it knows what to do. This is the value of people gathering together during collective loss. For example, we have witnessed profound eruptions of soul in the midst of public mourning events such as the days following September 11, 2001, the death of Princess Diana, and the Oklahoma City bombing. The soul is there, waiting and hoping for opportunities to reveal itself and to make suffering souls and their world larger as a result of being acknowledged.

In his public workshops, Michael Meade notes that dark times deepen people and that deepening is far more difficult when people are holding on to "things" and using them to remain in a spirit-mind trance. Clearly, we have seen since the financial collapse of 2008 an avalanche of economic loss and the discovery on the part of many human beings that there is something greater and more rewarding than simply owning a home, having a full-time job, having money in the bank or a bulging 401K retirement account. While these losses are grinding ordeals for millions, some are attesting to the fact that long-term unemployment has provided an opportunity to explore their deeper purpose. Others speak of drastically trimming their budgets, living on far less than they imagined they could, but at the same time, enjoying more simplicity and peace of mind.

Soul wants to take us deeper, but deeper into what? I cannot answer this definitively but only from my personal experience. For me, loss has taken me deeper into my humanity, deeper into my essence, and into that which connects me with the earth community. And in fact, Michael Meade suggests that as the culture falls apart and civilization collapses, the most appropriate way to respond is to go deeper. The Enlightenment mindset has insisted on ascendance and "getting to the top." The Endarkenment, however, asks us to go down and to go deep because this is the way the soul progresses. This is not to say that the collapse of civilization is not or will not be painful, but rather, since it is happening in spite of human reason, we have the opportunity to move with it and discover more fully what the soul is asking from us through the experience.

The unraveling of Enlightenment and the advent of Endarkenment will offer us myriad opportunities to "see with the heart" as Meade describes it in his book *The World Behind The World*.

> Our vision, like our speech, is meant to be metaphorical, able to see and communicate things beyond any measure. The eye of the heart is shaped for seeing the mysteries of life and love and for sighting new ways for making both.….Trying to see that way again requires that the heart crack wider open and that brings back the original pain of separation from the divine. Many try to avoid that heart-breaking pain; yet, the eye of the heart can only see through cracks in this world. It used to be better known that the only heart worth having is a broken heart. Only then can others find a way in, only then do people develop insight into their own wound and its healing….
>
> Refusing to see with the inner eyes makes a person blind to the way that life and death pass back and forth in each moment. Each moment we die and come back to life, in the blink of an eye, in the exchanges of blood in the inner chambers of the heart. The heart knows this passage back and forth and the knowledge found between. Seen with that eye, death becomes the way we grow, continually dying to one way of seeing in order to find a greater vision.[26]

The Community of Soul

In dark times, soul has the capacity not only to center us as individuals, but to produce eruptions of community which connect us deeply with everything else. In indigenous cultures, the community is periodically bonded by the glue of mourning a loss, celebrating a blessing, the singing of songs, the telling of stories, and moments, hours, or even days of sacred ritual. As the darkness intensifies and people need to become increasingly interdependent, many of the mind-spirit-based inhibitors of authentic community fade, and people can connect at a deeper soul level.

I very frequently interact with people who have attempted to create or join intentional living communities. While at this writing, some of these communities are flourishing, by far, the majority of reports I've heard about people's experiences with community are negative. When attempting to create a living community, they soon discover that civilization has so programmed us to live individualistic, isolated, self-absorbed lives, that living harmoniously in community with others requires unimaginable amounts of time and energy for addressing all of the internal inhibitors to it. From my perspective, it is one thing to *need* interdependence and quite another to just simply *want* it. At this moment in history, we may have a deep longing for interdependent community, but we don't yet require it for survival. In that sense, community is still somewhat of a luxury, and because it is a luxury, our style of living with other human beings is a manifestation of our civilized programming. When our lives become thoroughly contingent on interdependence, we are likely to find ourselves taken to the next level of experiencing community—a level which most people cannot now access even with the best of intention and effort.

One of myriad reasons that industrial civilization's inhabitants have such a difficult time living in community is that they are so unfamiliar with the internal community that comprises the psyche. Generally, there is a repudiation of the unwanted parts of the psyche and a championing of those parts by which the human ego is fed. In subsequent chapters the issue of owning and working with the shadow will be addressed, but suffice it to say at this juncture that external community is either enhanced or impeded by the degree to which we have integrated multitudinous aspects of the psyche. If this sounds like a task so monumental that it can never be completed in one lifetime, you are hearing correctly: It is.

Two ways of preparing for living in community when it is no longer a choice or a luxury is to build a substantial internal bunker and to do as much inner work attending to healing emotional wounds as possible. The intention is not to attain perfection in either realm. Building an internal bunker is a practice which no one ever completes or accomplishes with finality. Likewise, healing emotional wounds and integrating aspects of a fragmented psyche are lifelong processes. Nevertheless, consciously attending to these tasks now will only augment one's capacity to function sufficiently in welcomed or unwelcomed engagements with communal living situations in the future.

Community does not happen as a result of process groups and dialog circles. While these tools may be valuable in many respects, they cannot take us where soul is calling us. Only soul can take us there, and it will do so by pulling us down into the darkness where we encounter loss and pain and where we can "commune" with other suffering souls through poetry, story, ritual, song, celebration, and creating beauty. In communing in this way and through these eruptions of community out of soul, we find an "unintentional" community that may be more solidifying than anything we could have tried to make happen. Whether this results in an actual living community is less important than the soul connectedness we experience with each other in the soup of suffering. And, if being part of a living community *is* the outcome, then how we live with others from day to day is likely to be remarkably different from how we might have lived with them as a result of elaborate planning.

This is not to say that we should disavow vision and forethought. I am well acquainted with numerous individuals working in the Transition movement, with permaculture design, and engaged in other in endeavors which mobilize neighborhoods and towns to prepare for the future. Their work is and will be crucial in navigating the unraveling. However, we must recognize yet another tension of opposites that cries out to be held, namely, the need for our far-sighted preparation alongside unpredictable eruptions of soul. We and the earth community desperately need both, and only a clear mind and a heart mythopoetically attuned can craft a viable lifeboat of community that can weather the approaching storm.

CONFRONTING AND CONTEMPLATING
(Writing answers to these questions or drawing images in relation to them in a journal is highly recommended.)

1. In what ways have you in the past or in present time been deceived by the paradigm of Enlightenment as it is described in this chapter?

2. What is your experience with the soul's deepening amid darkness? It may be helpful to choose a particular experience and write about it at length noticing the nature of the darkness and tracking how the soul was deepened through the experience.

3. What experiences have you had of soulful community erupting and bringing you closer to other people, the earth, and yourself? Describe the context, the experience, the feelings, and the aftermath.

4. What experiences have you had with collective mourning or grieving rituals? Describe those and their impact on you.

5. Have you encountered people who "drag in the darkness"? Perhaps you are one of those people yourself. What has it been like for you when other people do this? If you have done this yourself, how did you do it? What was it like for you? How did people respond to you?

6. In what ways are you "mythopoetic"? Do you have people in your life with whom you can express this aspect of yourself? If you do, describe what that is like. If you don't, describe how that is for you.

Chapter 4: Darkness, Shadow, and the Divine

I tell you that goodness—what we in our ordinary daylight selves call goodness: the ordinary, the decent—these are nothing without the hidden powers that pour forth continually from their shadow sides.

~Doris Lessing~

The great epochs of our lives are the points when we gain courage to rebaptize our badness as the best in us.

~Friedrich Nietzsche~

One thing that comes out in myths is that at the bottom of the abyss comes the voice of salvation.

~Joseph Campbell~

When we embrace all that we are, even the evil, the evil in us is transformed.

~Andrew Bard Schmookler~

Having weathered the vicissitudes of growing up in a fundamentalist Christian home in the Midwest in the 1950s, I heartily embraced New Age spirituality in the 1970s and 80s. The emphasis on love and acceptance in the absence of a judgmental, punishing deity was irresistible. Affirming the positive only and excluding the negative felt, quite simply, too good to pass up. However, it was not long before I experienced the full impact of living my life primarily from a desire to abide in my mind and disavow my body—a most comfortable venue for survivors of all manner of abuse. It would be another decade before I would come to understand the differences between soul and spirit, and the body as one of the most palpable constituents of the soul. Breast cancer and memories of abuse buried within my body would be my teachers.

No reader of this book needs to be reminded that the collapse of industrial civilization is the ultimate consequence of humanity's dark side—our current suicidal trajectory resulting from an inability to live within limits, our intractable insistence on dominating the natural world, our voracious consumption of resources, and our addiction to power and control. Human history is replete with poster children for all manner of darkness. Yet two fundamental realties continue to escape us, namely, the value of darkness itself as it manifests in our individual and collective spheres and the presence and power of the human shadow which also abides in the macro and micro environments of our existence.

As emphasized above, soul does not flourish in the light but only in the territory of grief, loss, anger, terror, depression, betrayal, and all other so-called negative facets of human experience. These offer the nutrients required by the soul for diminishing the human ego and cultivating the deeper self. Thus darkness, while frightening, repugnant, heartbreaking, or enraging, is precisely the venue where soul is made and deepened.

The Long Bag of The Shadow Self

Equally necessary for the soul's well being is familiarity with those parts of self that we disown as "not me." Robert Bly has written prolifically of the "long bag we drag behind us" which is the human shadow—the container of the "not me." It is unconscious which makes it even more perilous. Because it is unconscious, we are unaware not only of the contents of the long bag but that we invariably project the contents onto other human beings. This is particularly true in our relationships with people who "push our buttons" or "get under our skin." Something about them evokes the "not me," and they become exquisite objects onto which we hang our projections.

Our unawareness of the shadow is not only perilous but profoundly energy- depleting. As Bly notes, "When we have put a lot in our private bag, we often have as a result little energy. The bigger the bag, the less energy." [27] Thus it behooves every human being, and particularly those who wish to create a new paradigm in the collapse process, to attend to working consciously with the shadow. Numerous possibilities for doing this work abound, and some will be offered at the end of this chapter. One of those is simply to be aware of what isn't being spoken, thought, or felt in any particular situation. For example, in a setting where one is aware of feeling compassion, it is useful to open to the possibility that an opposite emotion such as envy, repulsion, or fear may also be present, even if not consciously experienced. Most of the time, it is less important to do anything about what is not being acknowledged and much more helpful to simply pay attention and be curious about it.

Attending to the shadow is particularly important in groups and communities where people endeavor to work or live together. Conscious intentions may be impeccable, yet when the shadow is not acknowledged, it will demand attention and may do so in ways that undermine or sabotage the group.

I hasten to add that the shadow is not always dark or undesirable. In fact, Jung believed that the shadow is only "negative" from the point of view of the ego and the conscious mind. In the totality of the human psyche, the shadow simply exists and is neither good nor bad. Moreover, hidden in "the bag" may be qualities of warmth, caring, compassion, softness or other characteristics that we may have disowned because they seemed too threatening to embrace or display as is often the case with children raised in homes where abuse or trauma overwhelmed them. In such circumstances it may seem prudent to disavow certain positive emotions in order to survive. Meanwhile, those qualities remain in "the bag," waiting to be owned and expressed.

Stanford University Psychiatry Professor, Irvin Yalom, astutely reminds us of the ultimate value of shadow work: "Being human," he says, "especially being a self-aware human, entails facing bitter truths about existence. The price one pays for self-awareness is to see the dark side—not so much to dwell there, but to penetrate, to somehow get through and actually affirm your destiny." And not only do we each individually cast a shadow, but so do cultures and nations.

Jeremiah Abrams' excellent 1994 book *The Shadow In America* names explicitly some of the characteristics of the American shadow. Those include the effects of Puritanism on our work ethic and sexual mores; the slave trade and modern day racism; the imperialist Manifest Destiny imperative that has driven and continues to drive U.S. foreign policy; the military industrial complex; the Vietnam War and its legacy (including the wars of Iraq and Afghanistan); and rampant consumerism resulting in environmental degradation.

When individuals, cultures, or nations do not address their shadow, they project it, act it out, and ultimately implode. Individuals who have in the past recoiled from dealing with darkness and shadow realities may find themselves overwhelmed in the throes of collapse, for collapse is nothing if not a descent into darkness. While it will also offer opportunities for joy, celebration, play, and profound transformation, it will test every human being to the fullest extent of his/her limits. Therefore, developing an intimate relationship with darkness and the shadow today will invariably serve us well in the future, whereas our soaring toward the light in avoidance of encountering the darkness will only be a liability in the throes of collapse.

Finding The Sacred in Darkness and Shadow

Rainer Maria Rilke in his poem "I Come Home From Soaring" writes:

> I come home from the soaring
> In which I lost myself.
> I was song, and the refrain which is God
> Is still roaring in my ears.
>
> Now I am still
> And plain:
> No more words.
>
> To the others I was like a wind:
> I made them shake.
> I'd gone very far, as far as the angels,
> And high, where light thins into nothing.
>
> But deep in the darkness is God.

The question facing all of us who are willing to be conscious is: How *do* I find God in the darkness of collapse? What moves me, humbles me, brings me to tears, breaks my heart, frightens me, compels me to think and live differently, challenges me, and tests me to the breaking point? Chances are, that is where soul abides, offering me more aliveness, more energy, more wholeness, more richness, more love.

One of the paradoxes of collapse is that the possibility of our own death and the ubiquitousness of death around us, may offer us unprecedented opportunity to feel and be more alive than we have ever been. It is easy to experience the fullness of life on a glorious, sun-filled, summer day under a cloudless sky, intoxicated with the songs of birds and the fragrances of flowers. Yet it is much more difficult, but perhaps even more rewarding, to savor our aliveness in the midst of the darkness. Aliveness results from a deep appreciation of our humanity and at the same time nurtures it. Soul seeks to lure us into the depths where our fully alive humanity can be tasted, smelled, heard, seen, and touched. Another poet, D.H. Lawrence, argues that there is no other reason to be here:

Being Alive

The only reason for living is being fully alive; And you can't be
fully alive if you are crushed by secret fear,
And bullied with the threat: Get money or eat dirt—
And forced to do a thousand mean things meaner than your
nature,
And forced to clutch onto possessions in hope they'll make you
feel safe,
And forced to watch everyone that comes near you, lest they've
come to let you down.

Without a bit of common trust in one another, we can't live.
In the end, we go insane.
It is the penalty of fear and meanness, being meaner than our
natures are.

To be alive, you've got to feel a generous flow,
And under a competitive system, that is impossible, really.
The world is waiting for a new great movement of generosity,
Or for a great wave of death.
We must change the system, and make living free to all men,
Or we must see men die, and then die ourselves.

Curiously, Lawrence wrote this in 1929, the year of the infamous American stock market crash. He incisively describes the madness that obsession with material wealth engenders and the extent to which it alienates us from our aliveness. Clearly, the collapse of industrial civilization will brutally extricate people from their possessions and compel them to confront their values, and most importantly, the meaning of their existence on earth. Lawrence unequivocally lays out the choice before the human race: We will create a great new movement of generosity, or a great wave of death. Living must not only be free, he implies, but the fullness of our aliveness must be savored.

Michael Meade is fond of quoting Malidoma Somé [28], a shaman from the Dagara Tribe of West Africa, who frequently speaks of "trouble" as the tool of soul to draw us into the darkness for the purpose of being re-made by it. Meade states that "when the times go dark, we have a chance to learn the world again. The soul wants us to be in the drama of life—in trouble which means turbulence because it causes us to go inward to the resources of the soul. And if we don't get into the 'right' trouble, the 'wrong' trouble will come and get us."

Also, in the domain of soul, the supreme connector, we find ourselves deeply connected with others. As stated above, authentic community erupts out of soul because soul is where people genuinely commune, and not infrequently, a breakdown in community is a result of a failure to deeply *commune* in the territory of soul.

With our willingness to open to trouble from a mythopoetic heart, we begin, as Michael Meade puts it, "swimming towards God". We need not fear that word "God" because it merely means:

> "accepting the waters of one's life and learning to trust the
> vague shape on the horizon of one's present knowledge. In this
> emotional, spiritual swimming, accuracy counts less than a
> willingness to brave the waters of uncertainty….God is who or
> what we implore when all seems lost and there's nowhere else
> to turn….We are made of the stuff of dreams and of nightmares,
> tossed back and forth on the breath of the gods. We live in two
> worlds, subjects of both visions. Awakening means knowing
> something of each, learning the song we carry within and facing
> the traumas handed to us as well. Awakening involves learning
> to swim in the waters of life." [29]

CONFRONTING AND CONTEMPLATING
(Writing answers to these questions or drawing images in relation to them in a journal is highly recommended.)

1. Choose a time, an event, an experience when you were pulled into the darkness. Describe what happened and the accompanying feelings. What did you learn from this experience? How was your soul fed, nurtured, sustained, or enlarged as a result of the experience?

2. Think about a time when your shadow projected itself on someone or something else. What happened as a result? Were you able to own your part of the projections? If not, what happened? If you *were* able to own your part, what happened?

3. Think about a quality of yourself in which you take great pride. What would be the shadow side of that characteristic? Does that shadow side reveal itself anywhere in your life?

4. Take some time to list all the things that you consider "not me" and then look at where aspects of those characteristics have surfaced in your life or where they possibly could surface.

5. Are you aware of any specific instances of your energy being drained by working hard to suppress your shadow?

6. Choose one of the poems in this chapter—the one by Rilke or the one by Lawrence, and ponder it deeply. Journal or draw your reactions to it. Describe how it speaks to your soul and how your soul resonates with it.

Chapter 5: The Eros of Collapse and Transition

We're supposed to be in an erotic exchange with this world. The soul loves to love.
~Michael Meade~

My work is loving the world.
~Mary Oliver~

Eros is a divine force. It infuses all the earth. Yet too often, in our culture, Eros is equated with lust and sexual greed. But it is a more profound and sacred force than this. Eros is the light of wisdom that awakens and guides the sensuous. It is the energy that illuminates the earth. Without it, earth would be a bare, cold planet for Eros is the soul of the earth.

John O'Donohue from *Beauty: The Invisible Embrace*

Industrial civilization has eviscerated the essence of eros and relegated the "erotic" exclusively to the domain of sexuality and lust. Our ancient ancestors, however, held a very different perception of eros. While the Greek god Eros was the god of love, sometimes called Cupid, the ancient definition of eros was much broader than mere romantic love. Eros for the ancients implied affection, longing, kinship, compassion, empathy, sensuality, and relatedness.

Eros is the soul's core, for the soul does not call us into the depths in order to give us "growth experiences" or to make us smart, or even wise. It woos us into the depths—or occasionally drags us there, in order to cultivate relationship. Since soul functions as a bridge of sorts between our inner essence and the outer world, it serves to orchestrate connection between ourselves and the earth community and among all parts of the psyche internally.

The soul is not watered and fertilized by moving to a mountaintop and living a hermitically sealed life. While connection with nature is extremely nourishing for the soul, without relationships with other human beings, the soul is stunted, for in those relationships, soul flourishes. It is also in those relationships where we are most likely to encounter "trouble": conflict, disappointment, abandonment, rejection, betrayal, and loss. Conversely, human relationships offer unique opportunities for intimacy, support, validation, affection, respect, companionship, and healing.

Eros is also the soul's passion. When we feel passionate about something, eros is at work. As with all emotions, passion has its light and dark sides. A dictator can be passionate about ethnic cleansing, and a mystic can be passionate about her intimate relationship with a flower.

Perhaps the greatest gift eros offers is an open heart. When we live from the rational mind rather than from the heart, eros is marginalized and must work harder to get our attention. On the other hand, when we are open-hearted and when our hearts are soft, accessible, attentive, and capable of being touched, we are more present to the earth community for responding from compassion, for healing, and for making a difference in the lives of all other beings including our human community.

The trauma and loss of collapse will challenge our affinity with eros. When we feel safe, secure, have plenty to eat, have a warm bed to sleep in, have sufficient income and support, it's much easier to maintain an open heart. However, when basic creature comforts are not available and if we are surrounded with troubled people whose behavior may be volatile or chaotic, we may feel quite vulnerable, and opening our hearts may feel unsafe or even foolhardy. Having an open heart, however, does not mean throwing caution to the wind. Yet if we have been cultivating a connection with eros, it may be easier to maintain an attitude of openheartedness alongside caution.

In more secure, less turbulent times, we may feel eros pulsating through our bodies as we linger in a meadow fragrant with flowers, as we share a delicious meal with friends, as we luxuriate in a warm bath, or as we snuggle with a soft, furry pet. Beauty is an exquisite catalyst for eros, but when a formerly beautiful landscape becomes an ugly casualty of climate change, toxic waste, or some form of environmental devastation, the natural world may no longer activate eros. Under such circumstances, eros is more likely to be encountered predominantly in human relationships.

In the context of civilization, relationships are frequently shallow and superficial. Surrounded by relative peace and affluence, we have the luxury of choosing our friends and social contacts. We keep our emotional boundaries up and our doors locked and exclude from our lives those we consider "undesirable." We frequently do not know our neighbors and prefer to keep it that way. Even if we go camping, we have our tent or our recreational vehicle, and the walls remain intact between ourselves and the rest of the world.

Interacting with other human beings in a world unraveling will be dramatically different and replete with challenges. Homelessness is likely to be the rule rather than the exception, and families and friends who do have shelter will probably be forced to live close together in smaller spaces. Sharing not only space but food and other necessities is likely to be unavoidable, and it's fair to assume that everyone will have many fewer choices about physical and emotional space and who they do or do not relate with. Undoubtedly, we will be interacting with strangers as much or more than with close friends.

As collapse radically alters our values and priorities, it may be easier for some people to live in close proximity with others than it is in the present moment—or not. Moreover, as survival from day to day becomes the predominant motivator, the idiosyncratic preferences we currently cherish in our relationships are likely to diminish or vanish entirely. Those who can adapt to this reality will probably fare much better than those who cannot. Maintaining a mentality of "we're all in this together" will benefit everyone and make interactions more amicable.

In an unraveling society, especially one replete with traumatized individuals, there is likely to be much abuse and distortion of eros. People who are used to sexualizing their emotional needs instead of getting them met directly and consciously may indulge in frequent, casual sexual relationships for comfort in an uncertain, volatile, dangerous world. In Chapter 6, which addresses relationships and women and sexuality in a chaotic world, this topic will be addressed in more depth. While the subject of eros could have been included in that chapter, I believe that focusing specifically on eros and on understanding and appreciating the principle of eros, as well as its myriad nuances, is fundamental.

The Eros of Collapse Redefines Pleasure

Eros is synonymous in mythology with pleasure—pleasure both within and beyond romantic love. Whenever we experience pleasure, we commune with eros. It may seem difficult to imagine the possibility of experiencing pleasure in a collapsing world, yet I have no doubt that such moments will occur. With diminishing conveniences of modernity which we take shamelessly for granted, our pleasure may come in forms so simple that as we contemplate them today, they may not even feel like pleasure simply because pleasure is more pleasurable when that which gives pleasure is less frequently experienced. A gourmet, five-course meal ingested every day of the week soon loses its ability to delight the senses whereas on the palate of a famished human being, a slice of bread with peanut butter could feel like a feast.

Therefore, in a world of dramatically reduced resources and conveniences, pleasure will be redefined by its frequency and its meaningfulness in the moment. The daily warm shower we now take for granted or somehow assume is a human right, may become an inexplicable source of pleasure in a world where both water and the energy for heating it may be extremely scarce. Listening to the MP3 player one keeps plugged into the ears throughout the day could at some point in the future happen only when enough very precious and rare electricity is available for charging it.

And in the process of the unraveling itself, there may be much that we can take pleasure in. Communities bonded socially and economically around local food, local currencies, community healthcare and educational endeavors, and just simply living and navigating gargantuan changes together—yes *communing*, could offer a quality of pleasure that we may have never experienced in the context of industrial civilization.

The next era will be one in which we will be compelled to revere the fullest significance of supposedly small things and seemingly mundane experiences in order to emotionally and spiritually navigate what may be daunting conditions around us. We will be better equipped to do this if we have become accustomed to savoring that which is momentous, concealed within bare bones simplicity.

For many years, the poetry of Mary Oliver has assisted me in my own practice of this process. Her gift is an uncanny capacity for treasuring every moment and nuance of human existence. Her stunning poem "The Sun" is but one example:

> Have you ever seen
> Anything
> In your life
> More wonderful
>
> Than the way the sun,
> Every evening,
> Relaxed and easy,
> Floats toward the horizon
>
> And into the clouds or the hills,
> Or the rumpled sea
> And is gone—
> And how it slides again
>
> Out of the blackness
> Every morning,
> On the other side of the world,
> Like a red flower
>
> Streaming upward on its heavenly oils,
> Say, on a morning in early summer,
> At its perfect imperial distance—
> And have you ever felt for anything
>
> Such wild love—
> Do you think there is anywhere, in any language,
> A word billowing enough
> For the pleasure
>
> That fills you,
> As the sun
> Reaches out,
> As it warms you

As you stand there,
Empty-handed—
Or have you too
Turned from this world—

Or have you too
Gone crazy
For power,
For things?

CONFRONTING AND CONTEMPLATING
(Writing answers to these questions or drawing images in relation to them in a journal is highly recommended.)

1. Where do you currently experience eros non-sexually in your life? Write or draw in detail about this.

2. Recall an experience in your life that caused your heart to open. Write about the experience. What were the circumstances? Who was there? What happened? What was it like to feel your heart opening? What happened in the aftermath of the experience? How do you feel today as you revisit the experience?

3. Have you ever experienced a situation of crisis or high stress where you were sharing space and possibly food and other necessities with other people on a sudden or emergency basis? Describe how this felt. How did you respond? How did others in the situation respond? Was there any sense of "we're all in this together" and if so, did you have any awareness of putting your own immediate concerns on the back burner for the sake of the well being of the group?

4. What simple pleasures do you savor? How do you do this? If you rarely savor simple pleasures, you may want to practice doing so. For example, practice savoring simple sensations that give pleasure such as lying down on flannel sheets on a cold night; savoring a hot shower or bath; savoring a juicy, ripe, fresh tomato; asking a friend to massage your shoulders and savoring the sensations.

5. Read again the Mary Oliver poem, "The Sun," at the end of this chapter. Now take yourself to a quiet space either at home or in nature, and contemplate a particular simple pleasure. Write a poem that you need not share with anyone that verbally savors what is momentous for you in this very simple pleasure.

Allies In The Great Turning: Who's Turning With You?

Chapter 6: Most Immoderately Married–Relationships in A Chaotic World

I thirst by day. I watch by night
I receive! I have been received!
I hear the flowers drinking in their light,
I have taken counsel of the crab and the sea urchin,
I recall the falling of small waters,
The stream slipping beneath the mossy logs,
Winding down to the stretch of irregular sand,
The great logs piled like matchsticks.

I am most immoderately married.
The Lord God has taken my heaviness away.
I have merged, like the bird, with the bright air,
And my thought flies to the place by the bo-tree.

Being, not doing, is my first job.

~Theodore Roethke~

When the topic of relationships emerges, many individuals assume that it can only apply to romantic relationships of partnership or marriage. The topic chosen for this chapter is intentional but may feel confusing when I reveal that from my perspective, the subject of relationship is so enormous and so inclusive that literal marriage between two human beings is only one aspect of it. That is to say that I want to clarify at the outset that given all that I have asserted in the preceding chapters, our inherent connection with all life in the universe, by definition, dictates that we are married to everyone and everything. Eros, the part of us that longs for connection, is present in all relationships, and it does not assign labels to them; only the human mind can do that.

The above poem by Roethke exquisitely weaves the notion of marriage, relatedness, and intimate connection with the earth community and the universe into a tapestry of celebration of an identity grounded in "something greater"—the "I" that "is not I" introduced by the Juan Ramon Jimenez poem at the beginning of Chapter One. Not only is Roethke celebrating relatedness with all life, but the reality that because of that intimate connection, his and our identity is fundamentally dictated by it. Therefore, "being" or who we essentially are, is at the core of all relationship. It is through that common essence that we relate to every other life form in the universe, regardless of how uniquely divergent we appear externally. Something greater in you relates to something greater in me, even if we are not consciously aware of that relationship.

In a chaotic world of endings, unraveling, catastrophe, or protracted demise, relationship will be a pivotal issue. For this reason, the survivalist mentality which purports to "go it alone" with an "every man for himself" attitude, not only will not serve those who embrace it, but will profoundly put their physical survival at risk. For our well being, we will absolutely require connection with other human beings in times of chaos and crisis. Therefore, cultivating a broader perspective of relationship in advance of the coming chaos may be exceedingly useful in learning how to navigate relationship challenges in the future—challenges on which our survival may depend.

Violence

A world in which resource depletion, economic collapse, out of control climate change, massive unemployment, loss of healthcare, the evaporation of retirement savings, natural disaster, a crumbling infrastructure, the demise of public education, and possibly failed governments reverting to military repression will be a violent world. As much as those of us working for a slow and gentle transition may hope that it will occur peacefully, the likelihood of violence is enormous.

At this writing, we are witnessing the escalation of a powerful grassroots Tea Party movement in the United States. This noisy flock appears devoid of any sophisticated political analysis and ignorant of the fundamental underpinnings of American history. They seem unable to grasp the difference between socialists and corporatists and rather than formulating a coherent, succinct political platform, are spewing rage and vitriol in reaction to a moderate, politically Democratic administration which they appear to be targeting as the origin of all of the nation's woes. While most have assembled peacefully, some have called for the assassination of President Obama.

Simultaneously, the militia movement in the United States seems to be making a comeback, with some groups planning acts of terror and assassination against the government and other groups, brandishing weapons in public demonstrations as a way of virtually daring the government to challenge their Second Amendment rights. What is most frightening about these groups is their lack of information and their misguided interpretations of American history, combined with white hot rage. However much one may fear this mob mentality, one need only consider a world of dramatically depleted resources and economic conditions far more dire than those of the present moment to imagine a level of violence previously unknown in the United States.

We now know that much of the economic collapse in America was triggered by rampant corporate fraud and what is now being labeled "casino capitalism." The consequences of the ghoulish greed motivating the ruling elite to perpetrate previously unimagined fiscal crimes against the middle and working classes of the nation are now playing out in the form of record unemployment, loss of retirement savings, the inability of states and cities to provide essential services, loss of health insurance benefits, and an unprecedented number of bankruptcies and foreclosures. The American Dream has been demolished and permanently disabled, and only the most tenacious, clinging to the most delusional morsels of denial, currently maintain their faith in it.

At this writing, the terror of total collapse pervades the psyches of most inhabitants of civilization—whether they are fully conscious of it or not, and regardless of how much they may protest being confronted with the facts, something in them knows that we are rapidly sliding down the slope of every peak humanity has become aware of in the past decade—peak oil, peak water, peak soil—and yes as Richard Heinberg tells us, *Peak Everything*.[30] Perhaps more than any other earthlings, Americans recoil from the emotion of fear and believe themselves "entitled" to escape feeling it. Yet it is now epidemic among us, and invariably, unequivocally, the moment is rapidly approaching when we will be required to deal with it.

In addition, the masses in denial, who at this point constitute the majority of the population of the United States, have overall become so identified with their possessions, investments, jobs, houses, and roles that losing them will feel catastrophic and perhaps psychologically unbearable. Because their identity has become synonymous with those, emotional breakdowns may well become commonplace, suicides much more frequent, and explosive eruptions of personal exasperation the norm.

A 2010 Pew Research study reveals that with declining living standards in the United States, anger has escalated.[31] Commenting on the study, the World Socialist Web states:

> Taken as a whole, the Pew studies from March and April offer additional insight into the growing social misery under conditions of the worst economic crisis since the Great Depression, and the outrage it is generating.
>
> Wide layers of the population, who have seen trillions of dollars funneled from the public treasury into the coffers of Wall Street executives while their own living standards have been assaulted, their jobs slashed, their children's schools closed, and vital social programs such as Medicare cut by billions of dollars, have no faith in the US government to secure their most basic social needs.

Raucous militia and Tea Party pontificators in present time indiscriminately discharge their rage verbally, beneath which their own terror percolates. Whether or not they have been personally dispossessed, they understand on some level that the American dream lies beneath their feet in ashes—the sacrosanct delusion of American success and exceptionalism to which they have committed their souls. We have not yet begun to witness the consequences of their sense of betrayal because they have not yet experienced the depths of that reality, and when they do, we will all discover that current Tea Party tantruming is but the tip of the iceberg.

We can safely assume that our future holds a significant degree of violence as those who have unequivocally relied on their government and the conventional values of working hard and playing by the rules to redeem them, discover the extent to which they have been deceived. Add to deception, dispossession, and you have a powder keg of rage which if turned upon oneself becomes suicidal and if turned upon others, becomes socially volatile or even homicidal.

I am frequently asked about the likelihood of violence in a collapsing world and whether or not I advocate arming oneself. My response is consistently one of caution in which I support people in protecting themselves and their loved ones but with several caveats. First, if one owns firearms, one has an obligation to be properly trained in how to use them, to protect innocent people in one's life from being harmed by them, and to take responsibility for skillfully using them in safe and controlled situations such as on supervised target ranges.

Secondly, it is absurd to assume that one must have a vast cache of firearms to protect oneself in a chaotic world. No amount of weapons will guarantee safety. Building relationships in current time with neighbors and the surrounding community is as much or more effective than arming to the teeth. The paradigm of civilization, based as it is on individualism, assumes that our safety is in weapons and elaborate, isolated logistical preparation. The new paradigm of cooperation understands the extent to which we are "married" to all life and must function interdependently in order to survive. While it may be wise to invest in a small collection of firearms, it is infinitely wiser to cultivate relationships with people in our local place, even if they do not presently understand what is unfolding or what the future is likely to manifest.

No one articulates this more exquisitely than Bill McKibben in a 2010 article entitled "The Surprising Reason Why Americans Are So Lonely, and Why Future Prosperity Means Socializing With Your Neighbors":

> *Community* may suffer from overuse more sorely than any word in the dictionary. Politicians left and right sprinkle it through their remarks the way a bad Chinese restaurant uses MSG, to mask the lack of wholesome ingredients. But we need to rescue it; we need to make sure that community will become, on this tougher planet, one of the most prosaic terms in the lexicon, like *hoe* or *bicycle* or *computer*. Access to endless amounts of cheap energy made us rich, and wrecked our climate, and it *also made us the first people on earth who had no practical need of our neighbors.*

In the halcyon days of the final economic booms, everyone on your *cul de sac* could have died overnight from some mysterious plague, and while you might have been sad, you wouldn't have been inconvenienced. Our economy, unlike any that came before it, is designed to work without the input of your neighbors. Borne on cheap oil, our food arrives as if by magic from a great distance (typically, two thousand miles). If you have a credit card and an Internet connection, you can order most of what you need and have it left anonymously at your door. We've evolved a neighborless lifestyle; on average an American eats half as many meals with family and friends as she did fifty years ago. On average, we have half as many close friends.

I've written extensively, in a book called *Deep Economy*, about the psychological implications of our hyperindividualism. In short, we're less happy than we used to be, and no wonder – we are, after all, highly evolved social animals. There aren't enough iPods on earth to compensate for those missing friendships. But I'm determined to be relentlessly practical – to talk about surviving, not thriving. And so it heartens me that around the world people are starting to purposefully rebuild communities as functioning economic entities, in the hope that they'll be able to buffer some of the effects of peak oil and climate change.[32]

In 2010 I taught an online course related to the material in *Sacred Demise*. One student in the class had grown up in Germany after World War II and shared with the class how dire the economic conditions were at that time. Because of shortages and post-war infrastructure disruptions, food was in short supply—so much so that everyone's safety depended on keeping one's neighbors fed.

In a chaotic, collapsing world, neighborlessness may well become lethal. For this reason, we should be cultivating connections with neighbors and others in our communities sooner, rather than later. Whether or not our neighbors understand the collapse of industrial civilization is far less important than whether or not we have formed cordial relationships with them. One act of cordiality we can perform as we get to know our neighbors is to seize opportunities to share food with them, to share in neighborhood safety and beautification projects, plant community gardens, organize block parties or celebrations, or create other opportunities for working together to mutually support each other and the immediate vicinity around us.

Women and Sexuality

In 2007 I read James Howard Kunstler's *World Made By Hand*, a futuristic novel describing a small, post-collapse community in upstate New York. The novel's main characters were men, with women playing auxiliary roles or sexually servicing them. Many of my friends were appalled at the roles ascribed to women by Kunstler, yet I sensed that in fact, he was onto something. Since then, I have viewed the movies "The Road" and "The Book of Eli" in which women in these post-apocalyptic stories are routinely victimized sexually and physically in a world where males dominate people and resources for their own purposes. We have no way of knowing how accurate these projections will be, but there is little doubt that in a collapsing and post-collapse world, women will be objectified, owned, traded, and kept in subservient roles in exchange for getting their survival needs met. I hasten to add that in a collapsing world men will also be victims of violence, but they are not as likely to be brutalized in the same way or for the same reasons as women.

the war against women

I personally believe that ultimately, should the human species survive, women and men will forge a new level of respect and parity with each other and that women may, in fact, become spiritual leaders in a new paradigm grounded in the interconnectedness of all life. However, it seems likely that in the interim, women will be grossly exploited and abused.

In today's affluent milieu of social networking, fitness and body obsession, tanning salons, fine dining and dance clubbing, the roles that civilization has prescribed for men and women are maintained and nurtured impeccably. In navigating the dating scene in an effort to secure a partner, men generally prefer to present themselves as well-groomed, sensitive gentlemen, and women typically project intelligence and self-sufficiency alongside beauty and sexual prowess. The protocol for relationships between the genders is civil and respectful.

But imagine a world in chaos where projecting the current popular persona of one's gender is rendered irrelevant, absurd, or even dangerous. Stereotypes and the roles we consent to play will no longer serve us because in that world, survival will be paramount. Yet no matter how daunting the challenges facing humans, eros will not evaporate, and just as many individuals will become dependent on alcohol and drugs to sustain them in the midst of terror and trauma, many will also turn to casual sexual relationships to help them medicate themselves with internal chemical baths of comfort and a sense of belonging.

For this reason, it behooves anyone consciously preparing emotionally and spiritually for a chaotic future to forge strong relationships with friends, neighbors, and family members. In fact, I believe it is wise to consider all of the relationships we have in our lives as sacred in that they are venues for learning about and cultivating our inner world. Even more importantly, they are opportunities for serving the earth community with whom we are inextricably connected. In this way we begin to understand the relationships in our lives as part of our preparation for the future because they are as essential for our inevitable well being as food, water, shelter, or weapons. In fact, they may constitute the ultimate advantage.

As we allow ourselves to be schooled by our relationships, we recognize places where we have fallen short of how we prefer to relate to another, places where we have transgressed boundaries, failed to be present, subtly or blatantly abandoned others, failed to speak our truth, or perhaps, spoken our truth so forcefully and insensitively that we have inadvertently hurt the very ones we care about deeply. From our errors we can learn how we need to be in relationship and increasingly glimpse the momentousness of our connection with every person in our world. Quite naturally we may entertain the notion that people are in our lives and we are in theirs for specific purposes, and though we may never know the totality of the purpose, from hindsight we gradually understand that some purpose was served.

Yet as the first paragraph of this chapter articulates, the topic of relationships is immense. Not only must we, in my opinion, contemplate relationships between ourselves and other humans, but between ourselves and everything in our lives, for the truth is that we have a relationship with our homes, our possessions, our pets, our careers, our roles, our communities, our neighbors, our past, our present, and our future.

In his 2009 book *Great Waves of Change*[33], author and spiritual teacher, Marshall Vian Summers provides a manual of emotional and spiritual preparation for collapse which parallels much of what I wrote in *Sacred Demise*. An essential chapter in the book invites the reader to deeply evaluate all of his/her relationships with all people, things, roles, and tasks, in one's life. I heartily recommend the book and completing the evaluation the author suggests.

If we are willing to consciously and deeply evaluate our relationships, we clarify their place in our lives. As a result, we counteract a tendency to wed our identity to people, places, and things while paradoxically making it possible to cherish them more because we are more keenly aware of their purpose in our lives. Likewise, this deep evaluation may precipitate a natural letting go of those things in our lives which drain our energy or finances or which make our lives more complicated and less resilient at a time in human history when survival depends on simplicity.

Relationships with Purpose

The purpose served by all of our relationships is inextricably connected with our individual life purpose. Life purpose is not deeply mysterious or esoteric. It can most easily be discovered by answering the question: What is it that I came here to do? What is my calling? Anyone who chooses to read this book is likely to have found an answer or answers to those questions or be in the process of formulating them. And now we have returned to the "I who is not I," or the one Jimenez says "will remain standing when I die." With these questions we enter the domain of the sacred, the territory of something greater, and most importantly, the venue of one's relationship with oneself.

Yet attending to the relationship we have with ourselves must be balanced by a sense of service in the world. In a chaotic world, sitting in isolation and meditating all day or focusing only on our personal spiritual path may not only be physically impossible and dangerous, but dishonors our interdependence with all life. Our work in the world in current time and in the future must include some aspect of service to the community, And it must not be motivated merely by a desire to awaken others from their denial. Service, melded with life purpose and calling, must be employed for its own sake out of compassion for all beings. Paradoxically, as we serve for the sake of service, we plant seeds which may well come to fruition in the form of raising awareness and motivating others to prepare for the future.

Stripped of that to which we have wedded our identity, we will be compelled by the coming chaos to confront questions of purpose on a regular basis, perhaps hourly—perhaps moment to moment. We are likely to find ourselves contemplating every meaningful relationship in our lives, and many that seem devoid of meaning. Relating to diverse human beings and their idiosyncrasies, even depending for survival on individuals one may never have encountered in a less chaotic world, could become our new normal.

In myriad situations of interdependence in a chaotic world, we will find our own egos in relationship with other egos, and this may be daunting—unless we focus on the "I that is not I" in every other individual. That "something greater" in each of us is wiser and more ancient than our emotions, preferences, or even our survival needs. This is why Roethke can write, "Being, not doing is my first job." His poem is an eruption of celebrating connection with all life and the resonance of the sacred within and between all beings.

It may be tempting to dismiss Roethke's elation, assuming that he knew little of adversity. Yet in reality, he struggled throughout his adult life with a bipolar psyche and experienced many of the emotions a collapsing world is likely to evoke. As with numerous artists and musicians throughout human history, not a few poets have endured unfathomable anguish, producing a descent of the psyche into personal horrors resembling what a world in chaos could look like.

Most instructive in this particular Roethke poem is not only the celebration of being "most immoderately married" with all life, but a reminder that that marriage, in the case of human connection, consists of relationship between two personal minds and two "I's that are not I." Therefore, I suspect that one of the most formidable challenges in relationships in a chaotic world will be the capacity to hold in our awareness that we are relating not only with the ego of another person but also with the sacred in that individual. And while our egos may find it difficult to relate harmoniously, the sacred within and between us is inextricably, intimately connected. This is not to diminish the need to protect oneself physically and emotionally or to encourage trusting untrustworthy individuals. Rather I wish to remind us all that every moment, every encounter, every relationship holds sacred possibilities for healing, transformation, and comprehending our profound soul-relatedness and the extent to which we are "most immoderately married" to one another. As John O'Donohue reminds us, "Everything that happens to you has the potential to deepen you." Nowhere is this more evident than in relationships of every kind with every person, place, or thing in our lives.

Utilizing Invisible Webs of Connection

Author David Spangler's 2010 essay "Creating Support Systems in 'Interesting Times' " reminds us of the web of relationships among and between all life and offers a specific tool for strengthening those connections as our world becomes more chaotic. It is, I believe, an apt conclusion for this chapter:

> We have a large maple tree in our backyard. Its branches overhang our back porch so that in the summer, it can seem as if we are living in a treehouse. In fact, when our children were small, we actually built a treehouse amongst its branches where the kids would go to lie and read or just dream; we even on occasion would have family picnics there. As you can tell, this tree has been an important part of our family.
>
> As the years went by, I began to notice that some of the higher branches of the tree were dying. We can get strong winds blowing through our valley out of the Cascade Mountains, and I worried that some of these large branches, or even the top of the tree itself, might snap off and come crashing through our roof. So I had a tree expert come out and look the situation over. He gave me various options, and the one we chose was to build a webbing that would enable the branches to support each other. "If you ever see that webbing go tight," he told me, "call me right away because it will mean something has snapped and the top of the tree will have to be cut down." So far all is well.
>
> I thought about this webbing as the events of the past month have unfolded. There's been the eruption of Iceland's Eyjafjallajökull volcano which shut down air travel throughout Europe for five days causing economic havoc around the globe. There were unusual storms in the Southeast of America that

created unprecedented flooding in the State of Tennessee. There is the debt crisis in Greece which threatens the stability of the Euro and could tip other countries such as Spain and Ireland into bankruptcy, damaging the tentative economic recovery occurring in the United States after the crash of two years ago. And there is the oil spill taking place in the Gulf of Mexico, threatening to destroy the fragile ecosystems of the wetlands and marshes of coastal Louisiana and bidding to become the worst ecological disaster in America's history with enormous economic repercussions of its own.

Winds of change are blowing through our world system, and like the branches of my maple tree, there are lots of places it could break.

We need to build some webbing. We need to build our support system so that in times of crisis and disaster, we have something to hold us up and keep us from crashing through the roof.

Here's the good news. Such webbing isn't another layer of bureaucracy in an already overly complex governmental system; it's not a new organization we need to join. It's not an insurance plan we need to buy into. It's something much simpler than that. It's an attitude of love, compassion, generosity, and mutual caring. With it we can create safety for each other. Without it, we are left to stand alone and at a disadvantage in the face of possible disasters.

Imagine that you and your family have flown to Europe for a vacation. You've had a good time, and now you're headed home. Good thing, too, as you've about run out of cash and your credit card is near its limit. But as you wait to board your aircraft, an announcement tells you that your flight is delayed. Well, that's no fun, but you can wait. However, as an hour or so passes, you are next informed that your flight is cancelled. Indeed, all flights are cancelled as a volcanic ash cloud is grounding all jet planes.

Hmm, you think, this is more serious, but how long can a volcanic ash cloud last? Surely you'll be up in the air and on your way in a few hours. Except that it's not a few hours. It's a few days, and in the process you exhaust all your remaining money. But your family needs food and water and a place to rest.

Surely the airline will provide help. No, it won't. You're told it's not the airline's responsibility; you're on your own. The airport management isn't helping either. Well, perhaps you can squeeze a few more dollars out of your credit card. But wait, restaurants and hotels have just doubled and tripled all their prices for the duration of the crisis. Even that recourse is suddenly beyond your means. And now you have a nightmare vision of you and your family starving to death in the middle of a modern, European airport because no one cares to help and compassion has vanished.

For you, a branch has crashed.

This is exactly the nightmare that many foreign travelers, particularly poorer ones from Africa, were facing only a few days ago as the ash cloud from Iceland's Eyjafjallajökull volcano blanketed Europe and shut down all air travel. I learned about this through a number of radio reports. In interview after interview, passengers described running out of money and expressed their anger at the callousness of airline companies and airport personnel who denied any responsibility for providing aid. In some cases, even water was unavailable except for purchase. Restaurants and hotels were raising their prices in exorbitant ways to take advantage of those who had the money to buy food or lodging, and heaven help those who didn't.

Where this took place, it was a stunning demonstration of a lack of compassion and of placing commercial opportunities over human need.

By contrast, the Schiphol international airport in Amsterdam put up webbing. The airport administration hired musicians and clowns and brought in movies to entertain the stranded passengers. They installed portable showers and provided food and water, all at its own expense. They created such a festive, supportive atmosphere that passengers who had musical instruments brought them out and added to the entertainment. An international community came spontaneously into being. When some officials arrived from one of the embassies to offer passengers from their nation hotel accommodations, the passengers told them they'd rather stay at the airport. They were having too good a time!

The goodwill this simple act of compassion and generosity generated for the Schiphol airport and for the people of Amsterdam was enormous. Here no branches crashed. Should I ever be trapped in Europe by a disaster, I hope I'm in the Netherlands.

In the final analysis, if our civilization collapses, it won't be because of disasters and catastrophes; it will be because we failed in our compassion for each other. We failed in creating inner webs of support that can translate into outer acts of caring.

There are those who feel the disasters we've seen this past month, whether natural or human-caused, are just the start of what might become an Age of Disasters. This is certainly possible. I have no question, as I said, that winds of change and challenge are blowing through our world. There's also no question that human choices and activities, especially when motivated by fear and greed or by a sense of parochialism, can magnify the problems and turn challenges into catastrophes. We saw this graphically demonstrated when Hurricane Katrina hit New Orleans. The inept and at times self-serving responses of the Federal and State governments to the crisis added to the suffering and the death toll from that disaster. (To read some riveting accounts of how survivors of disasters come together to create compassionate communities to support each other—and how governmental officials more often than not end up hindering this process and even making matters worse—I recommend Rebecca Solnit's recent book, *A Paradise Built in Hell: The Extraordinary Communities that Arise in Disaster*, from Penguin Books.)

The value of being compassionate with each other and caring for each other's welfare sufficiently to be able to help each other—to help strangers—in times of emergency is important and probably one of those things most people would agree with. It's certainly not a new idea. But there's another wrinkle to this I'd like to suggest.

As regular readers know, I view the world as having a physical and a non-physical side. (If you want to know in more detail my thoughts in this area, I suggest my book, *Subtle Worlds: An Explorer's Field Notes* as a place to start.) Working with what I call the "subtle environment" offers additional possibilities for building a supportive web. In my experience, these intermeshing fields of consciousness and spirit, energy and probability surround and influence our world as much as does the planet's magnetic field. While nothing is a substitute for direct physical action and help to deal with physical emergencies, there are few events that do not have a non-physical component that could use help as well or that could be made a supportive environment for physical action.

For example, think of what the emotional and mental atmosphere might have been like in those European airports where people were stranded and had run out of money, food and water. I've been in airports where a flight was simply delayed for an hour or two and have felt the inner environment roiled with feelings of irritation, anger, anxiety and so on. I can only imagine what it might have been like if sheer survival had become an issue.

The nature of the subtle environment is that it affects everyone, though in different degrees and in different ways. It's a sea we all swim in, and when it becomes tainted with hurtful energies, we all have to deal with that contamination just as fish in the Gulf are now having to deal with oil and chemical dispersants in the water in which they live. Generally speaking, there's nothing like a powerful and intentional presence of love and calm radiating in such a subtle environment to transform that kind of psychic pollution and create a better and cleaner flow of subtle energies. The nice thing is that that kind of presence doesn't have to come only from a person on the scene, though it will be very powerful if it does; it can be projected by anyone from anywhere. That's the essence of subtle activism.

So one form of support when you hear of a disaster somewhere is to center yourself in a state of calmness and peace, fill your heart with love, and imagine yourself invisibly present where that disaster is going on, being a presence that contributes that peace and love to the subtle environment. In effect, you're providing another option for the subtle energies in that place or condition, an alternative to condensing around fear and anger or confusion, for instance and an opportunity to configure to the calm that you're providing. This calmness can provide a psychic space for those on the scene to avoid being caught up in emotional and mental turmoil and instead to have an opportunity to think and feel with clarity. This alone can lead to better and wiser decisions being made and compassionate actions being taken.

For example, those who are working to contain the oil spill in the Gulf are doing so under great pressure and are exposed to the anger being directed towards BP and those responsible for the oil spill. Holding those engineers and others in a calm, compassionate, loving presence can do much to support their ability to take wise and appropriate actions. Blaming them or focusing anxiety in their direction accomplishes nothing but to roil the subtle energies around them which can make their task harder.

But there's another form of webbing that subtle activism can provide; after all, subtle activism isn't just for disasters and emergencies. Here is where the analogy of my tree can help. The webbing we put up isn't fixing a specific problem but is a way in which weak branches can mutually support each other and be better supported by the main trunk.

This form of subtle activism is very simple. It consists of creating a line of supportive energy between yourself and another person and the sacredness that is the Ground of Being. Center yourself in sacredness, in the Sacred, whatever that means to you as a universal presence of compassion and love. Center yourself in your own capacity for compassion and love, and link these two together, connecting your branch with the trunk from which all branches come. Then imagine a line of Light extending from you to a neighbor in your community. This line of Light has as its sole intent communicating that that person is not alone but is connected to a source of support, which ultimately is the "trunk," the Sacred. Do this with another neighbor, then another. Build a web of inner support throughout your neighborhood. Remember, this web is not anchored in you but in the Sacred, but you are the one spinning it out into your world.

Once you get the sense of this, you can simply spin these webs of Light out into your world; it need not be limited to your neighborhood, nor to people you know. Do this with the intent that the subtle connections of energy that naturally exist between all of us be filled with Light and "tied to the trunk," so to speak, that is, attuned to the compassion and love within the Sacred. The idea is to support the arising of compassion organically and naturally within people's hearts. You can't make anyone be compassionate, and you wouldn't want to (that would be an act of coercion, not compassion), but you can intentionally add your energy and thought to strengthening the lines of loving support that can weave between us and that bring compassion into the subtle environments in which we live and act.

In time you may find yourself naturally and automatically radiating these supportive lines of Light throughout your environment, to animals, plants, and objects as well as people. It primes the subtle environment to be responsive to compassionate and loving actions should an emergency arise.

CONFRONTING AND CONTEMPLATING
(Writing answers to these questions or drawing images in relation to them in a journal is highly recommended.)

1. Understanding that we have a relationship with everyone and everything in our lives, a powerful exercise of preparation, mentioned in this chapter, for living in a chaotic world is to deeply evaluate those relationships. This exercise requires making time and space for such an evaluation. I recommend extensive journaling for completing the evaluation and doing so in a quiet place without distractions where you can focus full attention on the exercise. You may want to complete the exercise over the course of several journaling sessions. This exercise could take weeks or months to complete, and it is likely to evoke deep feelings. However, it is an extremely valuable exercise for establishing priorities and focusing your intention regarding preparation for the future.

   Think about your relationship with people in your life: family members, a significant other, children, grandchildren, employers, close friends, pets. Then think about relationships with your possessions—shelter, auto, furniture, clothing, and other possessions. As you contemplate these relationships, notice in each one what is energizing, uplifting, supportive, and meaningful. Also notice what is draining, unsupportive, debilitating, and lacking meaning.

   After you have done this, journal about how these relationships will serve you or not serve you in a chaotic world in which industrial civilization is collapsing, and life as you have known it is ending. Also journal about what changes you would like to make or are making in relationships that are not serving you well.

2. What economic losses have you experienced in the past two years? Loss of employment, pension, retirement savings, home equity? Have you experienced bankruptcy or foreclosure? What has been the impact of economic/professional/ career losses in your life? What feelings have they evoked? How have these losses impacted your priorities? How have you responded tangibly to the losses?

3. Take plenty of time to journal about what you consider to be your purpose in life. What did you come here to do? In what ways are you fulfilling your purpose in life? In what ways have you not yet fulfilled your purpose as you understand it, and what would you like to do about that?

4. Where are you engaged in service in your life? How do you feel about this? Are there other areas where you feel called to serve and how so? Do you find meaning in the service you offer? Journal about this in depth.

5. Do you fear for your physical safety in a chaotic world? Have you taken steps to learn methods of self-protection such as self-defense classes, weapons training, wilderness survival training, or other methods?

6. How well do you know your neighbors? If you do not know them yet, utilize some of the suggestions in this chapter to begin that process. If you do know your neighbors, consider sharing food with them if you have an abundance of it, creating a community garden, or if they are open to it, organizing an emergency response plan for the neighborhood. If they seem amenable, you may want to organize a documentary viewing event in your home where issues regarding collapse and transition can be discussed, paying specific attention to how the neighborhood can prepare for the future.

7. Take some time to journal about your personal mind or ego. What do you know about it? Your ego is the part of you that functions in the world, that presents a certain persona to the world, and that cares about how you show up in the world. Your ego prefers to be liked, needed, approved of, and appreciated. Where and how does your ego encounter conflict with other egos?

8. Take some time to journal about your deeper, sacred Self. What do you know about it? How do you connect with it? How does it serve you? Where and how does your deeper self connect with the deeper self of another? Have you ever experienced your deeper self being more powerful than your ego at a particular moment in time? What was that like?

9. Are you living in a community or region where you have the opportunity to meet regularly with other individuals who are aware of the coming chaos and discuss not only logistical preparation together, but also spiritual and emotional preparation? If not, consider organizing such a group. If you are isolated in an area where you cannot discuss these issues with anyone else, consider relocating, and deeply evaluate your relationship with your local place.

Chapter 7: Creating Livelihood
for Means and Meaning

Every person, in the course of his life, must build—starting with
the natural territory of his own self—a work, an opus, into which
something enters from all the elements of the earth. He makes his own
soul throughout all his earthly days; and at the same time he collaborates
in another work, in another opus, which infinitely transcends, while at
the same time it narrowly determines, the perspectives of his individual
achievement; the completing of the world.

Pierre Teilhard de Chardin, *The Divine Milieu*

A calling is the sense that you are on this earth for a reason, that you
have a destiny, no matter how great or small....A calling is a sensation or
intuition that life wants something from you....A calling is a deep sense
that your very being is implicated in what you do. You feel that you fit into
the scheme of things when you do this particular work. You have a sense
of purpose and completion in the work. It defines you and gives you an
essential tranquility.

Thomas Moore, *A Life at Work: The Joy of Discovering What You Were Born to Do*

The collapse of industrial civilization, by definition, means that livelihood and work as we have known it in the past will either no longer exist or will be altered in ways that we may not currently be able to imagine. A collapsing world is a world in transition in every aspect of life: economics, transportation, infrastructure, education, religion, health care, government, energy, environment, family, and individual functioning. In this milieu, unemployment may become so widespread that jobs as we know them today no longer exist.

A collapsing world is also a world in which alternative, underground, or informal economies are certain to proliferate. People must have income in order to trade some type of currency, services, or items of value in exchange for basic necessities. During the Great Depression in the United States, there were literally thousands of alternative currencies established in order to make purchases. However, in other venues throughout the world during dire economic times, such as in the Soviet Union during its collapse in 1989-1990, other forms of exchange were used such as alcohol, tobacco, medications, and recreational drugs. Likewise, myriad services were performed in exchange for meeting survival needs.

In this kind of scenario very few people are employed, and life for most people becomes all about living from moment to moment. People attempt to acquire necessities when and as they can, using whatever is marketable in order to do so. For example, a doctor may see a patient, but she realizes that the patient cannot pay money, so she accepts a chicken or a case of canned soup instead. Someone who has a stockpile of food may trade a box of powdered milk for soap or toothpaste.

Maslow's Hierarchy

This chapter began with quotes from two different individuals who have written of the deeper meaning of work—a meaning connected with *purpose* and *calling*. As we contemplate a world in chaos, such statements may feel ludicrous because in such a world, livelihood would be the foremost priority. As stated above, however, work as we know it may no longer be the standard form of livelihood. If we think of Maslow's hierarchy of needs, basic survival is foundational, and issues of meaning, purpose, and calling can be attended to only after people have met their needs for water, food, shelter, clothing, and sleep. In fact, in the hierarchy, meaning is located in the top self-actualization layer which cannot be addressed unless a host of other needs beyond survival, such as safety and security, love and belonging, and self-esteem have been met.

When contemplating a post-industrial milieu in which major institutions and infrastructure have collapsed and the world as we have known it has ended—a world in which many people may not know with absolute certainty when they will eat their next meal--are meaning, purpose, and calling in relation to livelihood germane? Will anyone be concerned with any other aspect of Maslow's hierarchy beyond the foundational layer?

I believe that while survival issues will consume an enormous amount of energy in a post-collapse world, meaning and purpose regarding livelihood will not become totally irrelevant. In fact, the work to which one currently feels called may prove congruent with future endeavors around livelihood. In other words, the foundational and uppermost layers of Maslow's hierarchy may not prove totally incompatible in a chaotic world. Therefore, it behooves us to attend to the meaning we derive from our current work in the world, paid or unpaid, at the same time that we contemplate how we will attend to livelihood in the future because the meaning we find in work now may be pertinent to our survival in a chaotic world.

Nevertheless, our calling should not limit us to pursue exclusively the work that resonates with it. As the decline of industrial civilization exacerbates, human survival will depend on resilience and flexibility. Intractable clinging to rationality and the desire to be in control may ultimately prove life-threatening. Therefore, it behooves us to learn a wide range of skills in present time so that we may apply them in the future. In the Hillman-Meade consideration of the differences between soul and spirit as outlined in Chapter 2, we notice that soul prefers not a choice between two opposite challenges but rather holding the tension of both. Thus, it may be important to cherish that to which we feel called and at the same time learn other skills to which we may not necessarily feel called but which might facilitate meeting our survival needs in the future.

Making a Living for You and Your Community

In my hometown of Boulder, Colorado, a group called Liberation Economics has formed this year using the motto "Making A Living Through Living Your Purpose."[34] According to one of the founders, Marco Lam, the group's focus is on "finding a way in which our gifts and talents…are the source of value from which we create abundance for ourselves and our community, a way in which our work is an expression of our highest values." A key mechanism of the group is the formation of *catalyst communities* which are small groups of individuals working toward this end who cooperate with each other to practice purposefully embodying their potential. The idea is that by practicing as a group, each person has the ability "to manifest an emerging potential that cannot be realized individually."

In his "Uncrash Course," Andre Angelantoni of Post Peak Living,[35] based in Marin County, California suggests that small groups of people who are preparing for collapse and share similar interests, goals, passions, and concerns about the future consider starting small businesses together which would offer goods and services needed in a post-industrial society. In this way they become a catalyst community as they launch their enterprise together. Naturally, they would need to remain resilient regarding their endeavor and be willing to adapt to fluctuating conditions in a chaotic world.

Sarah and Paul Edwards, also instructors at the Post Peak Living website teach a course on Sustainable Livelihoods. In their course description they explain something called the new Elm Street Economy "which we need to be creating in our local communities as the era of big business, Wall Street and the franchise-strip-malls of Main Street fade." They provide a snapshot of and a long list of possibilities for the kinds of livelihoods we can expect will flourish in place of the outdated jobs and careers we've been trained for and with which 90% of us support ourselves.

Alongside the concept of making a living through living our purpose is the concept of reskilling, an integral focus of the worldwide Transition movement. Reskilling emphasizes, as the name implies, learning skills which have been forgotten in the course of the development of industrial civilization but which may become necessary in order to navigate its demise. Transition groups throughout the world periodically offer workshops and trainings in such skills as permaculture design, organic gardening, food preservation and storage, foraging for wild edibles, herbal medicine, straw bale building, composting, emergency response training, and more.

The Transition Handbook, published in 2008, outlines three essential aspects of the Transition movement: Awareness raising, reskilling, and the psychology of change. Within the psychology of change is what the handbook calls "the heart and soul of transition" which refers to the emotional and spiritual aspects of transitioning from industrial civilization to a paradigm grounded in the earth community. Liberation Economics and making a living by living one's purpose is the heart and soul of our work in the world. Work without heart and soul quickly becomes drudgery while heart and soul without the means to meet our basic needs results in what may become a highly spiritualized impoverishment ungrounded in tangible reality.

Liberation Economics in tandem with reskilling may offer an ideal combination of elements conducive to forging a livelihood in a post-industrial world. Forming catalyst communities, that is to say *relationships* with others around creating livelihood, not only addresses financial security but cultivates heart and soul vibrancy and provides both a logistical as well as a psycho-spiritual hedge in the face of future uncertainties. In addition, the Liberation Economics model focuses not only on supporting members of one's catalyst community but the local economy in one's region by transacting business in ways that keep money circulating within that economy rather than outside it. Implicit in the model is the use of community currency and skill sharing as alternatives to indefinite engagement with the fiat money system. Both, in my opinion, prepare individuals and communities for making transactions in a post-industrial society in which money as we know it no longer exists.

Yet another model which will no doubt proliferate in a transitioning world is the notion of time banking. A number of cities throughout the United States have devised similar systems, including the one in my local community here in Boulder, Colorado. According to the Skillshare website: "Time Dollars constitute an alternative currency, one based on time, not cash. For every hour you spend doing something for someone in the SkillShare community, you earn one Time Dollar. Then you have one Time Dollar to spend on having someone do something for you. Simple, but powerful, both for you and your community."[36]

Charles Eisenstein's forthcoming book, *Sacred Economics*, endeavors to assist the reader in perceiving money and the human economy as sacred as everything else in the universe. An excerpt from the introduction to the book states:

> Obviously, if we are to make money into something sacred,
> nothing less than a wholesale revolution in money will suffice,
> a transformation of its essential nature. It is not merely our
> attitudes about money that must change, as some self-help gurus
> and "prosperity programming" teachers would have us believe;
> rather, we will create a new *kind* of money that embodies and
> reinforces our changed attitudes. *Sacred Economics* describes this

new money and the new economy that will coalesce around it. It also explores the metamorphosis in human identity that is both a cause and a result of the transformation of money. The changed attitudes of which I speak go all the way to the core of what it is to be human: they include our understanding of the purpose of life, humanity's role on the planet, the relationship of the individual to the human and natural community; even what it is to be an individual, a self. This should not be surprising, since we experience money (and property) as an extension of our selves; hence the possessive pronoun "mine" to describe it, the same pronoun we use to identify our arms and heads. My money, my car, my hand, my liver. Consider as well the sense of violation we feel when we are robbed or "ripped off," as if part of our very selves had been taken.[37]

In *Sacred Economics*, Eisenstein gives us a vision of a money system that is "no longer separate in fact or in perception from the natural matrix that underlies it," or in other words, the earth community in all of its "beauty, wholeness, and enchantment."

As industrial civilization's demise accelerates, it is crucial that we evaluate our talents, our skills, and which of those will be most marketable in a chaotic world, as well as which ones we derive the most meaning from. The two may be very different or not, but the sooner we can integrate means and meaning into our lives, the more resilient we are likely to be in meeting our needs and serving our community in the future.

I believe that in the words of John Peterson, stated in the Introduction of this book, when we ask to be shown our purpose, we will be. Furthermore, it is very likely that whatever we are shown will resonate with our most prized talents and skills. Focus on purpose is, in my opinion, one of the most important aspects of preparing to live in a chaotic world.

Typical of mythopoetic wisdom, Rumi says it best in this extraordinary poem entitled "The Real Work," edited by Andrew Harvey:

> There is one thing in this world that you must never forget to do. If you forget everything else and not this, there's nothing to worry about; but if you remember everything else and forget this, then you will have done nothing in your life.
>
> It's as if a king has sent you to some country to do a task, and you perform a hundred other services, but not the one he sent you to do. So human beings come to this world to do particular work. That work is the purpose, and each is specific to the

person. If you don't do it, it's as though a priceless Indian sword were used to slice rotten meat. It's a golden bowl being used to cook turnips, when one filing from the bowl could buy a hundred suitable pots. It's a knife of the finest tempering nailed into a wall to hang things on.

You say, "But look, I'm using the dagger. It's not lying idle." Do you hear how ludicrous that sounds? For a penny, an iron nail could be bought to serve the purpose. You say, "But I spend my energies on lofty enterprises. I study jurisprudence and philosophy and logic and astronomy and medicine and all the rest."

But consider why you do those things. They are all branches of yourself.

Remember the deep root of your being, the presence of your lord. Give your life to the one who already owns your breath and your moments. If you don't, you will be exactly like the man who takes a precious dagger and hammers it into his kitchen wall for a peg to hold his dipper gourd. You'll be wasting valuable keenness and foolishly ignoring your dignity and your purpose.

CONFRONTING AND CONTEMPLATING
(Writing answers to these questions or drawing images in relation to them in a journal is highly recommended.)

1. Currently, what is your work in the world? Is it what you feel called to do? If so, why? If not, what *are* you feeling called to do instead?

2. If you are not doing work that you feel called to, how might you change this situation? If you are forced to maintain work that feeds your body but does not feed your soul, how do you nourish your soul? If you are doing work to which you feel called, how could you improve, expand, or strengthen the impact of this work?

3. How are you preparing for a world in which employment as we currently know it may not exist? What skills do you have to offer in a post-industrial world?

4. Who are the people around you who are supporting your work? Are you getting from them what you need?

5. Which people in your community are you serving? How are you doing this? In what ways are you working to enhance, heal, beautify, or protect your community? What needs in your community call to you to become involved in meeting them?

6. Are you familiar with the foremost leaders of your community whether they are elected officials or not? Are you familiar with how your community works in terms of services, outreach, and public safety? In what ways can you support your community leaders? In what ways can you feasibly educate them around issues like energy descent, food security, water security, community currency, and local responses to climate change?

7. Take as much time as you need to contemplate and be with the Rumi poem at the end of this chapter. How does it speak to you? What most captivates you in the poem? How might you apply it to your life?

Chapter 8: Finding Home in a Volatile, Uncertain World

It may be that the satisfaction I need depends on my going away, so that when I've gone and come back, I'll find it at home.

~Rumi~

This being human is a guest house.
Every morning a new arrival.

A joy, a depression, a meanness,
some momentary awareness comes
as an unexpected visitor.

Welcome and entertain them all!
Even if they are a crowd of sorrows,
who violently sweep your house
empty of its furniture,
still, treat each guest honorably.
He may be clearing you out
for some new delight.

The dark thought, the shame, the malice.
Meet them at the door laughing and invite them in.

Be grateful for whatever comes.
Because each has been sent
as a guide from beyond.

~Rumi~

After a chapter focusing on relationships followed by a chapter exploring livelihood and one's relationship with the community, it is natural to wonder how the vicissitudes of collapse and transition might affect our living arrangements and our sense of home. Presently, in the early stages of collapse, we are witnessing unprecedented homelessness in the United States alone and record numbers of families and extended families living under one roof. Not since the Great Depression have we seen this, and by all indications, the trend is likely to continue and accelerate.

Since the end of World War II Americans have become used to living in massive structures, or at least dwelling in homes where large areas of space, even if used unwisely, are available.

Children of middle class families generally feel deprived if they cannot have their own rooms and are forced to share with siblings. Parents have their own room and sometimes a home office where they spend time while children isolate in their rooms; overall, the family spends little time together in a common area. At the end of the work and school day, it is not unusual for a fast food meal such as pizza or a bucket of fried chicken to be set on the kitchen table where family members grab portions of food then steal away to their segregated outposts to eat while watching TV, playing video games, or working on the computer.

For many middle class families, home is not unlike a hotel in which inhabitants depart from their individual rooms in the morning and return to them at the end of the day, making little or no contact with other family members. Occasionally, children may invite friends for a visit to the home, but time spent together often takes place in the child's own room or in the back yard. Myriad activities outside the home for both parents and children result in less time spent at home than ever before in modern history. Moreover, time at home is usually not quality time spent with other family members but more often, a period of isolation from the rest of the family, relating to the world outside the home through telephones, computers, or television. In fact, if a family member suggests that the family spend time together engaged in activities such as eating, shopping, or having a family meeting, other family members may feel resentful, as if their time and space have been infringed upon. In the stereotypical middle class home, there is plenty of space, privacy, and outside activity to serve as a buffer between family members. Sadly, under the guise of being part of a family, many children and parents inhabit space under the same roof, but in the milieu I've just described, that is a far cry from *living* together.

In post-industrial society, "home" as most middle class families know it today, will not exist. Increasingly, home will be about actual shelter and safety. The technological toys which permit us to isolate and distract our attention from other residents of our shelter will not be available. More people will be forced to live under one roof, share responsibilities, and have almost constant contact with each other. The notion of "needing one's space" may become ludicrous, and privacy may become almost non-existent. If one is fortunate enough to have shelter in a home, sharing time, possessions, food, water, conversation, comforts, and space will probably not be optional.

Currently in the early stages of collapse, it may be difficult to imagine the living arrangements that collapse may compel us to accept. As hungry as we may feel for community and support for navigating a post-industrial world, I believe that it will be very difficult to share time and space with other people until we are forced to do so. While it is true that some people are already practicing shared living as inhabitants of an intentional community or ecovillage, it is also true that for the most part, phenomenal amounts of time in those situations are devoted to group dialog and the processing of conflict. However, as stated above, it is likely that when we are forced to "commune," we will experience authentic community.

Communing will redefine our sense of home. This is not to say that we will no longer need personal time and space, but those may not be synonymous with "home" which is more likely to be about shelter and the meeting of basic human needs. Underlying the new sense of home will probably be the fundamental reality of survival and the absolute necessity of cooperation so that residents of a particular shelter can acquire food, water, medicine, and other items required for their health and well being.

Ironically, the financial crisis in the United States was set off by a housing bubble—the hyperinflation of home prices, virulent corruption in the financial system involving subprime home loans, and a toxic derivatives market. Much of the impetus for global economic meltdown has been quite simply, debt, but underlying that reality has been, in my opinion, an unarticulated fantasy on the part of nations and individuals that debt would never really need to be repaid. Although no one would state this explicitly, over time, it became implicit in the financial industry's barrage of messages to consumers such as "no money down," "no payments until...", and "for everything else there's Mastercard."

A culture of uninitiated children was seduced by implications that it could accumulate debt *ad infinitum* and magically, miraculously, never really have to repay it. And not only were individuals seduced, but so were entire countries.

Individuals in the United States were told that buying a house was perhaps easier than falling off a log. The perpetrators of infamous NINJA (no income, no job, no assets) loans assured prospective home owners, who really had no means with which to buy a home, that having no income, no job, and no assets would not stand in the way of securing a home loan. For other home owners, their homes became ATM machines as they were offered the option of cashing in on their home equity sooner rather than later. In this way, "housing" and "home" became words laden with symbolism and larger than life significance.

Since the end of World War II, Americans had come to believe that a home was far more than a place to live and share their lives with family members. As noted above, home became not a place of communion or conviviality but provided accommodations in which to reside and make oneself more comfortable while attending to the business of keeping oneself engaged in the outside world. But even more importantly, a home became an investment, a source of equity, something to refinance for ready cash, and at the height of an inflated real estate market, something to "flip" in order to acquire even more worth and more ready cash.

Thus the financial collapse in the United States has forced millions of home owners and their families into foreclosure and out of the housing market entirely as they reluctantly rent because they cannot afford to buy a home or because their credit rating is in tatters. Some have discovered that they actually prefer renting, but others resent their plight and the reality that the American dream and its most dazzling feature, house flipping, are over. As a result, for many families, especially those in which adults are unemployed or underemployed, the definition of "home" is returning to its pre-World War II significance, namely, a dwelling place for one's family where time and space are shared under the same roof.

As industrial civilization continues to disintegrate, as global financial meltdown economically eviscerates one country after another and many individuals are forced to share housing with each other, humans may begin to experience an entirely different sense of home in the world. The home of the nuclear family of the 1950s with its stereotypical 2.6 children will most certainly not return anytime soon. What is more likely are households comprised of many extended family members and trusted friends who have nowhere else to go. They will probably be forced to provide services and perform household tasks in exchange for the privilege of not being homeless and having shelter and food.

Many opportunities for community and mutual support will arise from such arrangements. An example with which I am personally familiar is a country inn located in Hancock, Vermont where my friend Kathleen Byrne, a registered nurse and gourmet chef, runs the Gathering Inn[38]. She has forsaken tourism as the primary use of her property and turned it into a boarding house. Most residents are employed, and others who are unemployed barter their time and skills in exchange for room and board. While it is not an ecovillage or intentional community, the conviviality among residents creates informal community as residents work together in the garden, raise chickens, cook, clean, chop wood, and share in the upkeep of the property. I anticipate that the Gathering Inn will flourish in the days ahead and become one of thousands of similar living arrangements around the world.

In a chaotic world, myriad models for discovering a new sense of home may emerge. For many people it will be like coming home for the first time. For others it will be challenging to share space with many other people, perhaps total strangers. For anyone who is fortunate enough to have shelter in that world, the criteria for sharing space and living harmoniously are likely to be radically altered. While I do not wish to romanticize the loss and estrangement that countless numbers of people may experience, neither do I wish to minimize the possibilities in these scenarios for people to feel at home with themselves, perhaps for the first time, and experience an intimate sense of human connection, yes even family, amid the daunting challenges around them.

Location and Relocation

In a preceding paragraph I mentioned a rural country inn located in Central Vermont. I became familiar with the Gathering Inn during the year I spent in Vermont during my first experiment with relocation. I had lived in the very climatically untenable Southwestern United States for over a decade and realized that I needed to relocate. While I discovered many positives about living in Vermont, I also realized that it lacked two things that I desperately needed: 1) A viable collapse-aware community and 2) Plenty of sunshine.

The second complaint may seem inconsequential, but I had lived in the West for 36 years and had grown accustomed to wide open spaces and plenty of sun. Vermont's predominantly overcast skies and endless forests presented a geographical challenge which I could not navigate. I would have been willing to persevere in adjusting to these realities had I also felt more of a sense of community. One of the original features of Vermont that attracted me was its low population of some 630,000 people. Eventually, this proved unrealistic for me because I lived in a rural area near my place of employment but far from areas populated enough to be able to distribute resources in the event of a societal breakdown. My sense of isolation increased, as did my longing for the kind of climate with which I was familiar. In addition, my friends who were preparing for collapse lived far away, and joining them meant either driving some distance to meet up with them or moving further away from my place of employment in order to be closer to friends, thereby creating a daily commute to work.

Meanwhile, an opportunity to relocate back to the West and live in close proximity with friends opened up to me, and in late 2009, I left Vermont and moved to Boulder, Colorado where today, I feel remarkably at home. While some would argue that I made a bad choice in terms of water issues in the American West, living close to the Rocky Mountains and living in a more densely populated area, I feel comfortable with my choice, living now in a climate with which I am familiar and close to a host of collapse-aware allies.

Choosing one's location or relocation for a worsening collapse scenario cannot be done based exclusively on logic or by way of following suggestions made by someone else. Heart and soul, as well as intellect, must be engaged in making such momentous decisions.

Far and away the most important awareness with respect to finding one's home base in the throes of a chaotic world is the bone marrow awareness that the soul's core is one's true north, one's ultimate home on earth. Regardless of how dispossessed or homeless we may become, or how comfortably ensconsed we may be in a literal residence, our ultimate home abides within us. From that home we establish our grounding at the same time that we move about in the world. That home is one that we must become intimately acquainted with as our world becomes increasingly chaotic. The adversities of the coming turbulence are likely to test our soul home beyond anything we can imagine and catalyze numerous emotional and spiritual homecomings so that, in the words of T.S. Eliot, we may "arrive where we started and know the place for the first time."

In the second poem at the beginning of this chapter, Rumi tells us that being human is like living in a guest house. We never know who or what will show up. That may become even more evident both symbolically and literally as collapse unfolds. Mythically speaking, our journey through a world in chaos will bring into our lives countless new experiences—some awkward, bizarre, terrifying, nurturing, validating, inspiring, heart-warming, *and* heart-wrenching. We are likely to feel every emotion humans are capable of feeling, and life is certain to become more unpredictable. And as mentioned above, one of the most important qualities we can cultivate in preparation for that world is resilience.

Literally speaking, we are almost certainly going to encounter a wide spectrum of people with whom we may initially feel incompatible. Living situations, even with family members or trusted friends may become strained or contentious. Yet I suspect that much discord will be tempered by the need for cooperative survival, even as conflict arises.

Rumi asks us to open to the conflict as we would open the door to a guest in our home. The guest has been sent from beyond, he says, and our first task is to be grateful that he or she has shown up. Of course this applies to all manner of challenge or adversity in our lives, but at the moment, our focus is on our sense of home in a chaotic world.

One quality we must begin to cultivate now is that of discernment. We should not always open the door, literally or symbolically, just because someone is knocking. Discernment assists us in knowing when to open and when to keep the door closed. While emotional and spiritual preparation can enhance discernment, it is more accessible to us when we are fully present in our bodies, a state likely to be far more challenging in a collapsing and chaotic world. For this reason, the following chapter on maintaining embodiment in a disembodied world has been included.

CONFRONTING AND CONTEMPLATING
(Writing answers to these questions or drawing images in relation to them in a journal is highly recommended.)

1. A fundamental exercise related to this chapter is a deep evaluation of where you are living in terms of geographical location and access to resources and support. Answer the following questions:

   • Is this the location where I prefer to live as the collapse of industrial civilization accelerates? Why? Why not?

   • Do I live close enough to sizeable population areas in order to get food and other resources?

   • Does this location have arable land and sufficient water?

   • Do I have a support system in this location?

   • Does this location resonate with my body and emotions, as well as my mind, as a viable place to live and prepare for the future?

   • Whether I choose to remain or relocate, what more do I need to do to prepare my home, the surrounding area, and my lifestyle for the unprecedented changes ahead?

2. Who are the people in my support system whom I can count on as life becomes more uncertain? List them individually and evaluate why you feel you can count on them. What makes them reliable? What skills do they offer you? What skills do you offer them? If you do not have a strong support system, what do you need to do to create one?

3. Describe your current living arrangement. Who lives with you? Are you living with extended family or friends? If so, describe how that works or doesn't work for your household. If you are living with extended family or friends, what are the advantages? What are the pitfalls? When conflicts arise, how do you resolve them?

4. If you live alone, how do you imagine you will navigate a situation in the future where you may be compelled to live with others? What tools will you use to make that workable? How will you resolve conflict?

5. Have you learned any conflict resolution skills or taken any formal training in conflict resolution? Bearing in mind that learning to resolve conflict effectively

is mastered through experience, are you willing to begin learning these skills within the next year?

6. What do you know about your inner home? Write extensively about this or create images if you prefer. How do you imagine you will be tested in the future? What resources reside in your soul home to meet those tests? What other resources in your soul home need to be cultivated? *Repeat this exercise once a week for one month.* It will be extremely helpful to begin the exercise with a period of silence, meditation, or deep inner listening.

Chapter 9: Embodied In a Disembodied World

On Resurrection Day

On Resurrection Day your body testifies against you.
Your hand says, "I stole money."
Your lips, "I said meanness."
Your feet, "I went where I shouldn't."
Your genitals, "Me too."

They will make your praying sound hypocritical.
Let the body's doings speak openly now,
Without your saying a word,
As a student's walking behind a teacher
Says, "This one knows more clearly than I the way."

~Rumi~

In an earlier chapter we considered Western civilization's disownment of soul in favor of a heroic, spirit-driven obsession with progress. Inherent in this repudiation of soul was disconnection from the human body, virtually institutionalized during the Middle Ages, followed by the reclamation of the body during the Renaissance. Later, the Enlightenment, in spite of its scientific breakthroughs and its negation of religion, ironically succeeded in accomplishing a feat similar to the Christian church's disavowal of pagan spirituality, namely widening the dichotomy between mind and body. Granted, the Enlightenment enhanced the scientific sophistication of such disciplines as anatomy and physiology, but from the perspective of the body as a machine. Subsequently throughout the nineteenth century, the natural healing arts became increasingly viewed as superstitious and pseudo-scientific. Ultimately, allopathic and technology-driven medicine prevailed within the paradigm of industrial civilization.

Philosophically speaking, the hallmark of this paradigm is dualistic separation. Thus the body becomes the mind's adversary—a distraction from mental acumen, now deemed the supreme human attribute. In the past 300 years, humans have become progressively estranged from their bodies, and hence their emotions, a reality confirmed by scientific research of the past century which validates the inextricable connection of the two. As a result, the human being of modernity is disembodied in the sense that we are profoundly disconnected from our bodies as compared with traditional peoples who have been less influenced by the values of industrial civilization.

During the 1970s and '80s a plethora of research revealed intimate connections between mind and body, giving birth to a new discipline known as holistic or integrative medicine.

Both early and subsequent research strongly suggests that emotions are indeed physiological responses to external stimuli. Moreover, suppression of them, we now know, is related to myriad physical ailments. Our language itself is replete with expressions related to the mind-body correlation. We speak of having a broken heart, having a gut feeling, putting our best foot forward, or we may describe an experience as nauseating, breathtaking, or causing our heart to skip a beat.

For the first time in the history of industrial civilization we are beginning to understand the extent to which we have a relationship with our bodies. This relationship may well be the most fundamental of all of our relationships during the coming chaos. If we are disembodied, that is, disconnected from our bodies at any point in our lives, we are at risk of not knowing what we feel or being able to respond to it. It is precisely at those times when the shadow can more easily erupt, leaving us perplexed about our communication or behavior. When we are disembodied, we are not fully present, and one of the most important qualities for relating to people, events, and experiences in our lives in a chaotic world is the ability to be present to them. Therefore, it behooves us to cultivate a conscious relationship with our bodies as part of our emotional and spiritual preparation for a turbulent future.

In *Sacred Demise* I emphasized repeatedly that in a chaotic world, we are likely to have little or no access to healthcare as we know it today. This means that our options for navigating that world will be enhanced if we are caring for our bodies now and seriously compromised if we aren't. While we may have fewer choices about the kind of food we eat in a collapsing world, it behooves us now to eat fresh, organic, preferably local food. It is also crucial that we incorporate regular physical exercise into our lives. This is not about becoming a marathon runner or a champion weightlifter. It is about moving the body, preferably in nature, increasing the heart rate, breathing fresh air, and balancing the sedentary lifestyle of industrial civilization with regular exercise. In Chapter One, De Young's research clarifies the variety of benefits gained from walking in nature daily. Exercise, a healthy diet, and frequent periods of play, in addition to a regular mindfulness practice are the optimum ingredients for creating and maintaining sustainable bodies and being present in the world.

Being Present—The Greatest Challenge During Chaos

Being present means that one is paying attention to what is happening in the moment. This does not mean forgetting about the past or future, but rather in the moment, fully attending to what is taking place right now. Being present also means being observant, listening carefully, not judging the situation or people in it, and being less occupied with thinking and more engaged in consciously being with whatever is occurring. It also means being embodied which does not mean that one must be aware of every body sensation at the time, but simply conscious of inhabiting one's body. What is most useful in supporting that awareness is the breath. Breathing deeply assists us in centering ourselves in the physical body and staying in the moment as opposed to becoming lost in the mind, thereby disconnecting from our physicality. Author and spiritual teacher, Eckhart Tolle provides an abundance of techniques for becoming and remaining present in his two extraordinary books *The Power of Now* and *A New Earth*. (In addition, the Appendix of this book contains access to a variety of exercises for grounding and being present.)

In navigating a world in chaos, it is likely to be even more challenging to become and remain present than it is in this stage of the unraveling. Some would argue that in fact it may be easier to be present then because there will be fewer distractions in that world. While that may very well be true, a collapsing world will almost certainly present us with more unavoidable crises, more frequently. Life may well become more unpredictable with fewer established routines.

An especially helpful tool that can be utilized in present time while still available is body work. Body work can range from everything from martial arts, to yoga, to Rolfing, to Reiki, to bioenergetics, and more. Simple daily exercise, although extremely beneficial for the body, is not the same as therapeutic body work focused on fine tuning the body-mind connection.

Yet another reason for cultivating a relationship with the body is the absolute necessity of maintaining optimum fitness and physical health in a world where healthcare as we know it today may not exist or where it may be rationed or become only sporadically accessible. Body awareness does not guarantee physical well being, but disembodiment opens the door to illness and behaviors that do not serve us in times of drastic, distressing change.

Disconnection from our bodies also compromises our ability to cope with emotions that will be evoked amid chaos. Conversely, grounding ourselves in the body is an extremely useful, even necessary skill when dealing with the upheavals of a world in crisis. When we are grounded in the body, we more likely to be present to our own emotions and to those of others around us.

I hasten to add, however, that a treasure trove of emotional preparation in the here and now is available to us so that we may become increasingly embodied and familiar with our emotions. This means that well in advance of crises that have become ubiquitous, we begin now to cultivate emotional resilience and develop the skills necessary for navigating a vast social landscape that may be filled with internal and external psychological minefields.

People prepare for the Long Emergency logistically and talk at length about resilience but often do not have a clear sense of what it actually is and what emotional and spiritual qualities are necessary factors in resilience.

George Bonanno, a long-time researcher on the subject of bereavement and author of *The Other Side of Sadness: What the New Science of Bereavement Tells Us About Life After a Loss* has much to say about resilient people. He writes:

> We know that there is almost certainly a genetic component in resilience. However, the science on this issue is not yet fully worked out. We also know that psychological factors are involved. One such factor is optimism. Another, revealed in my research, is coping flexibility. Earlier, I described resilient people as having more tools in their toolbox than people who are not resilient. One of those tools is being able to switch back and forth from sadness to positive emotions. Another is being more flexible in the way they use emotions.[39]

Why is emotion so crucial in the collapse of industrial civilization and the rebuilding of its replacement? Author Michael Dowd states in his book *Thank God For Evolution* that "Emotions are the means by which the parts of our brain that are unconscious communicate with the parts of our brain that 'we' can readily access. Emotions are the way that our paleo-mammalian brain, with its powerful drives for bonding and status, communicates its wishes and its fears to our conscious awareness."[40]

We hear a great deal about "emergency response" training in our communities, and of course, these efforts focus primarily on lifesaving and the prevention and treatment of injuries and assisting communities in maximizing physical survival. It is equally important, in my opinion, to cultivate our own emotional emergency response training by willingly accepting the challenge of working with our own so-called dark emotions.

The Art of Emotional Alchemy

In 2003, Miriam Greenspan, a psychotherapist and a child of holocaust survivors, published a remarkable book *Healing Through The Dark Emotions: The Wisdom of Grief, Fear and Despair*[41]. It is replete not only with abundant cognitive information regarding the dark emotions, but a wide variety of experiential exercises for working with them. She argues that we came equipped with these emotions because they serve us if we allow them to do so and do not insist on controlling them. They are, in fact, part of our life force energy which in some Eastern cultures is known as *chi* or *prana*. Quite simply, says Greenspan, "This energy is sacred." Yes, emotions can be overwhelming if we don't know how to tolerate them and work with them, but emotional energy itself enlivens us.

From my former experience as a psychotherapist and as a client in long-term therapy, I could not agree more. I spent decades being unaware of or attempting to control certain emotions, only to discover that when I allowed them in the container of therapy, they accelerated the healing process exponentially. Increasingly, I learned the skill of appropriately expressing emotion in my life outside of therapy and as a result, watched my world and my internal landscape transform.

Greenspan speaks extensively of "emotional alchemy," drawing upon the ancient mystical practice of transforming baser metals into gold. By this she means that when we allow emotions to flow, which is not the same as merely "letting it all hang out," and when we allow grief, fear, despair, or other "negative" emotions in the body, we allow their wisdom to unfold. "Emotional flow," she says, "is a state in which one is connected to the energy of emotions yet able to witness it mindfully. We ride the wave of emotion on the surfboard of awareness. When we do this skillfully, emotional energy in a state of flow naturally moves toward healing, harmony, and transformation. You don't have to force the alchemy of the dark emotions. It happens when the conditions are right."

The adversities we may encounter in a chaotic world are likely to evoke a panoply of dark emotions. However, Greenspan reminds us that the root word of *adversity* is a Latin word which means "to turn and pay heed or attention." That is to say that "In the midst of adversity, the dark emotions ask us to turn our attention to what's going on emotionally." From this perspective, adversity presents an opportunity to become conscious, to be present to ourselves and others, and thereby serve both.

Moreover, emotional alchemy is more than a tool for enhancing our psychological well being. It is in fact, a sacred practice. In other words, our emotions are inextricably connected with our soulful humanity. They facilitate the descent to which soul is always calling us in order to remake us and enhance our sense of meaning and purpose. The way of soul is the way of emotion as opposed to spirit's cerebral orientation. Emotion may well be the most exquisite conduit to our core, and when we are willing to swim in those waters, we are more likely to access "the I that is not I."

Grow Up or Die, But How?

In *Sacred Demise* I spoke of the collapse of industrial civilization as a rite of passage—an evolutionary process that presents an ordeal which if consciously navigated is capable of taking us to deeper layers of the soul so that transformation may occur. In tribal cultures a formal initiation is provided for every young person, and without that experience, members of the tribe are seen as children, not adults. In such cultures, one does not become an adult until one has completed the initiatory process.

Jung believed that something in humans longs for and requires the initiatory experience, and that when we do not have the opportunity to participate in it through a cultural ritual, life presents us with many initiatory passages in the external world. The citizens of modern culture do not have formal initiations, but ordeals such as divorce, loss of loved ones in death, loss of employment, a bankruptcy, a foreclosure, the loss of a lifelong dream, a terminal illness, or any other painful experience may serve as an initiation.

Many people who have been researching and writing about the collapse of industrial civilization have noted that modern, consumeristic, corporate capitalist culture has infantilized its citizens to the degree that they do not sufficiently think or behave as adults. The stellar example of this is modern humanity's refusal to live within the limits prescribed by the planet's carrying capacity, as well as the refusal to consciously consider the consequences of humanity's transgression of earth's limits.

For example writers such as myself and Daniel Quinn, Derrick Jensen, Richard Heinberg, Michael Meade, Malidoma Somé, Joanna Macy, and others have written extensively about the infantalization of the citizens of empire and have suggested that rites of passage or an initiatory process is needed in order for us to become responsible adults who accept and live within the limits of our planet. Clinton Callahan, director of the Callahan Institute in Munich, Germany and author of *Directing The Power of Conscious Feelings* states that:

> *Modern culture is a child level responsibility culture, far below adult level. Modern society does not require that a person grow up prior to being given (or allowed to take) positions of responsibility…Our society makes messes without having consciousness of, or taking responsibility for, the consequences of those messes.*

The example Callahan gives is the corporate practice of "externalizing costs," but a more timely and poignant example is quite simply, the worst manmade environmental disaster in the history of the United States, created by the BP Corporation, which may ultimately result in the Gulf of Mexico becoming a giant dead zone and which over time may have unfathomable ramifications globally. In a child's world, there are no worries about cleaning up messes. Caretakers (governments and taxpayers) exist in order to provide the child everything it wants and needs, and if messes are made in the process, then it is the caretaker's job to clean them up.

Yet few who have addressed infantalization have offered a specific path for the journey to adulthood. While Callhan has no formula for this, he asserts that the principal rite of passage from emotional immaturity to maturity is the capacity to consciously, constructively work with one's feelings, directing the power of feelings in service of the entire earth community. In *Directing The Power of Conscious Feelings*, he validates what most of us have felt all of our lives regarding our feelings in relation to modern culture, namely that *none* of them are acceptable.

Many of us have experienced that feeling sadness, fear, or anger in this culture is threatening to others, so we keep those feelings in check, preferring to share them only with trusted others. Yet even joy in the culture of empire is unacceptable.

While writing this book, I was speaking with a friend who had just returned from a visit with her son who is in his late-twenties and works as an executive with a major transnational corporation. My friend has done a great deal of work on feelings and appropriately expressing them. In a conversation with her son, she verbally expressed her sadness about something in her life, and he responded with, "Could we not have any drama today?" The next day she mentioned feeling angry about something that had nothing to do with her son, at which point, he said, "You know, I'm really tired of your drama."

I share this story because as Callahan clearly demonstrates, the ideal in the culture of empire is a state of numbness. No feelings---sorrow, fear, anger, and even joy, are acceptable. People are esteemed for abiding in a state of numbness which is defined as sane, stable, and even-tempered. In the early stages of the 2010 oil disaster in the Gulf of Mexico, there was a public outcry for President Obama to become outraged regarding the devastation BP had created, but the ideal perpetuated by political pundits and advisors was for Obama to remain "cool-headed." They and the President knew that a passionate display of any emotion would result in a decrease in popularity and a perception of him as "irrational." The desired and only acceptable state in the culture of empire is numbness, and any variation from it is frequently perceived as "drama."

In the following section, we will explore some of the dark emotions, as well as a few lighter ones. As we re-skill in preparation for a chaotic future, persistent practice in working with all emotions is essential. We may not yet be skillful in working with them, but if we are willing and allow ourselves to be schooled by them, seeking assistance from trusted others who have the capacity to teach and support us, we may experience the transformation of the baser metals of our being into gold. Cultivating an inner life and mindfulness practices in relation to the body will greatly assist us in maintaining our embodiment, the quintessential tool for experiencing the alchemy of emotion.

Our friend, the poet Theodore Roethke, offers wise counsel by reminding us that we do not need to have mapped out our journey with the dark emotions in advance. We need only follow where they lead and learn by going where we have to go.

> *I wake to sleep, and take my waking slow.*
> *I feel my fate in what I cannot fear.*
> *I learn by going where I have to go.*

> *We think by feeling. What is there to know?*
> *I hear my being dance from ear to ear.*
> *I wake to sleep, and take my waking slow.*

Of those so close beside me, which are you?
God bless the Ground! I shall walk softly there,
And learn by going where I have to go.

Light takes the Tree; but who can tell us how?
The lowly worm climbs up a winding stair;
I wake to sleep, and take my waking slow.

Great Nature has another thing to do
To you and me, so take the lively air,
And, lovely, learn by going where to go.

This shaking keeps me steady. I should know.
What falls away is always. And is near.
I wake to sleep, and take my waking slow.
I learn by going where I have to go.

CONFRONTING AND CONTEMPLATING
(Writing answers to these questions or drawing images in relation to them in a journal is highly recommended.)

1. Before proceeding with these reflections, take a moment to sit with both feet on the floor, sit comfortably, close your eyes, and take several deep breaths—as deep as you can possibly take them, feeling your belly and chest expand. After you have done this, notice the sensations in your body. Do not begin writing anything. Just *feel* the sensations. If your mind wanders, take another deep breath and bring the attention back to the body. Take several moments for this. Sit with the feeling of being present in your body. Such an experience is, in part, embodiment.

2. What have you been told at various times in your life about feelings? What messages have you received about not thinking negative thoughts or feeling negative emotions? Journal or draw this.

3. What challenging experiences have you had with feeling your emotions? What healing experiences with feeling your emotions have you had? Again, journal or draw.

4. What emotion are you most afraid of feeling? Explain why this is so.

5. Have you ever had an experience of feeling an emotion that was liberating and which may have resulted in an instance of emotional alchemy? Journal or draw that experience.

6. In what ways do you soothe yourself without using food or substances of any kind? Do these ways of soothing work for you and if so, how? If they do not work, what might be missing? If you have never consciously soothed yourself, how might you do so without using food, substances, or shopping?

7. Journal about how you see your personal dark emotions in the context of the culture or the macrocosm. How do you connect your grief, fear, anger or despair with the external world? You may also wish to draw this relationship.

8. Have you had the experience of channeling emotion into social or community action? If so, explain. If not, journal about options for doing so.

Emotions:
Becoming A Warrior of Vulnerability

Chapter 10: Befriending Grief and Depression in The Coming Chaos

In the face of the evidence of climate disruption, clinging to hopefulness becomes a means of forestalling the truth. Sooner or later we must respond and that means allowing ourselves to enter a phase of desolation and hopelessness, in short, to grieve.

~Joanna Macy as quoted by Clive Hamilton
in *Requiem For A Species*~

There is no coming to consciousness without pain.

~C.G. Jung~

Between grief and nothing, I will take grief.

William Faulkner

In my book *Sacred Demise: Walking The Spiritual Path of Industrial Civilization's Collapse*, I made frequent mention of the stages of grief as outlined by the late Elisabeth Kubler-Ross. More recently, Clive Hamilton, in *Requiem For A Species*, focusing specifically on the ultimate consequences of climate change, asserts that its repercussions will be equivalent to a planetary near-death experience. In Chapter 3, of *Sacred Demise*, "What Does Collapse Require Us to Face?" I stated that a conscious response to the unraveling of industrial civilization would no doubt include the emotions of Kubler-Ross's grief cycle: denial, anger, bargaining, grief, and acceptance. At the end of that chapter, I asked the reader to journal about his/her grief cycle and notice where he or she was in it. Although I did not state it explicitly, I believe that with a loss as herculean as the collapse of industrial civilization, the cycle of grief pertaining to that process may never cease in our lifetimes.

While the latter statement may feel daunting or even overwhelming, it could well be that grieving will become as much a part of our lives in a chaotic world as any other so-called "negative emotions" that may become our constant companions. This does not mean, however, that we will never have respite from grief or that we will never be able to experience gratitude, joy, celebration, or humor as I make very clear in *Sacred Demise* in a specific chapter entitled "Mirth-Making Amid Crumbling and Chaos."

Grief and Culture

In Malidoma Somé's Dagara village in West Africa, grief is like an old friend of the village.

Grief rituals are conducted on a regular basis because the Dagara feel there is so much loss in the human condition that the opportunity for grieving must regularly be utilized. Many years ago I participated in several Dagara grief rituals conducted by Malidoma here in the United States. One of the most profound aspects of the ritual was that it was structured to include not only the ideal conditions for deep mourning, but a venue where humor and joke-telling was occurring as part of the ritual, separate from but alongside the grieving. As is so often the case, indigenous cultures recognize that humor and sorrow are not opposites but travel together and need each other in order for all aspects of human experience to be present and revered. I suspect that in a world unraveling, civilization's splitting of emotions into "desirable" and "undesirable" will gradually become less relevant as humans are increasingly forced by circumstances to experience and appreciate a full repertoire of emotion.

Another aspect of indigenous awareness is relevant to our consideration of the topic of darkness. The Dagara, like many indigenous communities, have not become citizens of empire where much of one's identity and purpose is shaped by consuming material items. Societies based on mindless consumption are by definition averse to any conscious consideration of darkness. Consumption inherently depends on fantasy for its existence and sustenance. It cannot endure without a so-called "positive outlook" which seduces consumers into consuming ever more goods and services by way of the delusion that doing so will guarantee "the good life" or "the American dream" or "having it all." If we buy more stuff, according to this delusion, we'll feel happier, and if we feel happier, of course, we'll want to buy more stuff.

In her 2010 book *Bright-Sided: How The Relentless Promotion of Positive Thinking Has Undermined America*, Barbara Ehrenreich argues that positive thinking in American culture is believing that the world is shaped by our wants and desires and that by focusing on the good, the bad ceases to exist. Ehrenreich believes this notion has permeated our society and that the refusal to acknowledge that bad things could happen is in some way responsible for the current financial crisis. She, of course, attributes that crisis to many other causative factors as well but notes that positive thinking has become an integral aspect of corporate culture.[42] You can't sell things to people or convince them that they can't live without a certain product absent a positive attitude and the subtle message that they "need" a certain lifestyle in order to remain positive about life.

Moreover, I believe that since the end of World War II, positive thinking has become the quasi-religion of industrial civilization, and the failure to maintain it has become almost tantamount to treason. To be anything but positive is to question the fundamental underpinnings of consumerist, corporate culture. In fact, the Western world for nearly a century has touted the "we can" attitude as the deciding factor in its ascendancy to economic and military supremacy following the Great Depression and the Second World

War. More recently, a successful presidential candidate, Barack Obama, essentially based his campaign on it.

Indigenous people, who remain aloof from consumerism, generally feel less compulsion to maintain a positive attitude. They seem to have more capacity for being present with what is. If crops fail, and there is no food in the community, they may draw on their particular cosmology to explain the situation, but they are not likely to deny or sugar-coat it. On one occasion I heard Malidoma Somé state that the Dagara actually believe that life is more often cruel than kind, that it is filled with unjust suffering, and that moments of celebration, ritual, and grieving in the context of community are the fundamental elements that temper the preponderance of adversity in the human condition. Thus, the Dagara, like other indigenous peoples, rely on sharing their suffering with the community not only to make it bearable, but to deepen their sense of community itself.

John O'Donohue comments in *Eternal Echoes*, in a section of the book entitled "The Suffering of Self-Exile" that "Post-modern culture is deeply lonely. This loneliness derives in large part from the intense drive to avoid suffering and pain and the repudiation of commitment." The second time I read these words, I was struck with the insight that when we refuse to acknowledge and share suffering, we also refuse to experience community. Many of us in living in the United States and other industrial nations lament our isolation and pontificate about our longing for community, yet we still cherish fantasies of community as synonymous with an idyllic, bucolic existence in some conflict-free ecovillage where at last, we have "found our tribe."

While I do not disparage the longing, nor would I contest the fact that a number of ecovillages in the United States have survived all manner of adversity over the course of decades, I am aware that shared suffering is generally not the first image that leaps to the minds of those longing for community. This is not to say that communities in a collapsing world will never frolic together in euphoric merriment; it is rather to notice that a culture addicted to positive thinking may have spent decades, if not centuries, missing exquisite opportunities to heal its individualistic isolation by refusing to open to suffering as an extraordinary facilitator of community building.

When I contemplate a collapsing world in chaos, I am not as troubled by the possibility that many people will be experiencing grief, or that they already are as they prepare for the future, as I am that so many more people are not feeling and will not be feeling that emotion. Rather, what I notice in the current milieu is rampant, epidemic depression and rage in the psyches of the inhabitants of civilization. Although grief and depression are related in the psyche and are attended by similar symptoms, they are also very different emotions.

Grief is a response to an event or series of events that we are consciously aware of, even if we have not allowed ourselves to feel the full impact the event(s). Grief involves loss, perhaps sudden, perhaps protracted. When we are grieving, we usually have some sense of why we are grieving, and even if we cannot connect all of the emotional dots, we notice that a loss or ending has evoked our grief.

The Long-Term Consequences of Denying Grief

Depression, on the other hand, is a more amorphous emotion. Symptoms include feelings of sadness, low energy, difficulty in thinking or concentrating, a sense of hopelessness, and suicidal thoughts or actions. While it may be associated with loss, myriad other events can trigger a depressive syndrome. A 2005 MSNBC story entitled "Beyond Depression: When Grief Doesn't Go Away"[43] reports that recent studies indicate that grief and depression are very different emotional responses which may sometimes appear indistinguishable. Furthermore, left untreated, grief can *lead to* depression, suicide, drug and alcohol abuse, and even heart disease.

It is common knowledge that rates of depression are higher in industrialized countries, and almost everyone in the United States is either taking or knows someone who is taking antidepressants. We also know that rates of depression have increased in the United States since the financial collapse of 2008, as have suicide rates and the use of drugs and alcohol.

Denial is a factor, not only in the stages of grief, but in a host of emotional illnesses. It is one of the principal defense mechanisms of the human psyche and is not always pathological. Defense mechanisms are just that: psychological protective devices built-in to the human organism. However, at some point, denial no longer serves to protect us but begins to delude us, at which point we become incapable of facing what is so.

For example, in the face of the sudden loss of a loved one, we may at first deny that the loved one is dead, but to continue to deny that person's death after all evidence to the contrary has been presented to us exceeds the definition of denial. We have now entered the domain of delusion. However, at the moment that we can acknowledge the loved one's death, even if we cannot yet accept it, we have put ourselves on the pathway through the stages of grief. There are no guarantees that we will complete the journey, but at least now, the journey is possible.

In the case of the collapse of industrial civilization, the majority of civilization's inhabitants are not only in denial but delusional. Because they refuse to examine the overwhelming evidence of civilization's collapse, they have no access to the journey through the stages of grief. Perhaps they have lost homes, employment, credit ratings, financial solvency, insurance benefits, retirement savings—perhaps they have lost everything, yet they cannot, and in many cases will not, grasp that the challenges they are facing, along with climate change, energy depletion, and global economic catastrophe, are unprecedented in human history. While in many cases, some of these individuals may have been depressed before the first stages of collapse became evident, the unfolding of current events could only exacerbate their depression and also evoke depression in others who have never suffered from the illness in the past.

The collapse of industrial civilization and life as we have known it is an enormous loss, both materially and psychologically. If we can consciously open to the loss, we may encounter not only grief but a host of other emotions. However, I believe that if we cannot come to terms with the ubiquitous reality of collapse, and if we persist in our denial, then our risk of becoming depressed is dramatically increased.

Cataclysm embraced

Repeatedly in the past decade as I have presented evidence of the collapse of industrial civilization, I have heard hundreds of people report that when they were able to begin exploring the evidence and opening to the reality of the unraveling, they began experiencing a sense of relief, even as they allowed themselves to walk *through* the stages of grief. Many have told me that coming to terms with reality freed them up to pursue a different career path, to leave a troubled relationship, to choose not to have children, to launch a new enterprise more in alignment with serving the earth community and helping others prepare for the future. While these choices did not alleviate their grief, they somehow made these individuals larger than their grief; they became empowered by abandoning denial and confronting reality. As a result, new options for livelihood, relocation, relationships, and community involvement opened for them, all because they were willing to abandon their denial.

Miriam Greenspan reminds us of two essential truths regarding grief. First, it is a universal response to death and loss, built into our neurological systems, and it is a psycho-spiritual process. It is an opportunity, not for "resolution" or "closure" as we so often hear, but rather transformation. As we consider grief in this book, however, I will consistently address it in the context of the loss of a way of life grounded in the paradigm of industrial civilization. And as that paradigm dissolves, as institutions collapse, as climate change ravages the ecosystem, as cheap and abundant fossil fuels evaporate, as all resources become increasingly scarce, as incalculable numbers of species become extinct, as the likelihood of our planet becoming steadily more unrecognizable escalates, we may be confronted with staggering successions of loss.

In the late spring of 2010, the Gulf of Mexico was inundated with a toxic oil spill resulting from the explosion of the BP's Deep Water Horizon oil rig on April 20. Calculations of the quantity of oil gushing into Gulf waters varied from 5,000 barrels to over 100,000 barrels per day. For months, all attempts to stop the volcano of petroleum over a mile beneath the surface of the Gulf were futile. Toxic dispersants were dumped onto innumerable plumes of oil on the surface, all of which further polluted the water, land, and air onto or near which the oil continued to gather---endangering humans and myriad plant and animal species. Moreover, as the dispersants broke up the oil, they could not remove it. Rather, smaller chunks of oil are now ubiquitous in the Gulf, both on the surface and in very deep waters. In addition, parts of the spill entered the loop current of the Atlantic Ocean and according to many scientists, also entered the food chain.

Few human beings can grasp the magnitude of this cataclysm which unlike the blatant devastation of Hurricane Katrina which occurred almost five years ago in the same region, will linger for decades, if not centuries, creating dead zones in the Gulf of Mexico and neighboring oceans. How extensive and how catastrophic the spill will become over the years is anyone's guess, but at this moment, it is the worst man-made disaster in American history.

As thousands of fisherman on the Gulf Coast lost their livelihoods overnight and some faced financial ruin, as dead oil-soaked birds and sea creatures washed up on the shore, as the economies of the region were decimated by the ramifications of the spill, and as it became increasingly evident that the explosion was caused by the omission of numerous safety precautions in a frantic effort to drill faster and deeper as world demand for oil accelerates, the only sane response to this mindboggling tragedy is deep grief.

How do we grieve consciously and deeply as our species commits suicide? The vastness of what needs to be grieved is nothing if not overwhelming. Where do we begin?

I believe that we begin wherever the heart draws us. It may be drawn to the extinction of species, to climate chaos, to the destruction of oceans, to the clear-cutting of trees, to the pollution of rivers and streams. One way to begin is simply to watch what occurs around us. It may be in a region near us; it may be images or written accounts in the media; it may be something in the immediate landscape. Here where I live in Colorado, what used to be vast expanses of green forests are now punctuated with reddish-brown clusters of dead trees devastated by the pine beetle—a catastrophe directly linked to climate change.

We can then journal about our grief or draw it, paint it, or compose music or poems about it. In our journaling we can recount how we feel, and we can also address our departed or departing loved ones—those elements of nature that have been devastated by humans. And of course, humans themselves are casualties of catastrophes perpetrated by our own species. We must grieve what we have done to each other—physically, emotionally, and spiritually.

But no matter how much we express our grief privately, it is imperative that we verbalize it with others. Just as we might join a support group for grieving the loss of a human loved one, we need to mourn in the company of trusted others who comprehend the significance of our collective losses.

The Transition movement, mentioned above, is a worldwide network for promoting awareness regarding the state of our planet, for assisting people in preparing for life in a chaotic world, and for articulating the psychology of change and its reverberations in the soul. One unique feature of the Transition model is the creation of heart and soul groups in connection with one's local Transition initiative. In these groups, people have a safe space for sharing all emotions related to collapse and transition and for supporting each other in honoring what is truly sacred about this unprecedented demise.

But even if we do not have access to a Transition heart and soul group, we can create safe spaces where people can share with each other their grief about the state of the planet. I hear consistently from people who have read *Sacred Demise*, who perhaps have taken an online course with me based on the book, who subscribe to the Daily News Digest published by my website, or who attend my workshops and speaking events, that they are desperately lonely as they carry the knowledge of civilization's collapse but generally have to carry it without support. Without exception, they report their hunger to be able to share their grief with relatives, friends, neighbors, or almost anyone else who comprehends the gravity of collapse.

Anyone who has consciously grieved the loss of a loved one, a pet, a relationship, a career, or any other life-altering loss, understands that the journey of grief is a turbulent descent into the soul's depths. Both the intention and the result brought forth by the soul are generally an expansion of itself and the diminishing of the ego. This is the fundamental definition of transformation, articulated beautifully in the words of Miriam Greenspan: "Descending, the heart breaks open, and the ego loses its moorings."

When we consider that the fundamental underpinning of industrial civilization is the human ego, and when we ponder the ramifications of the collapse of civilization, we begin to glimpse the extent to which egos will be shattered, and unprepared individuals and communities will be emotionally shaken to their core. In a chaotic world people will need strong egos in order to solve problems and care for themselves in the moment, but living *from* the ego as if one is the center of the universe and entitled to revel in the unsustainable luxuries of a lifestyle based on the destruction of the earth community, will prove increasingly untenable except for the very wealthy.

If ego existence is the only option, if soul descent is so foreign and so abhorrent that people cannot open to it, then we are likely to see unimaginable madness and mayhem as collapse unfolds. Thus, the more familiar we can become with the soul's journey, and the more we are willing to open to it based upon previous experiences of surviving and being remade by it, the more equipped we may be to weather the tempest. Additionally, according to Miriam Greenspan, "If we can hang in and maintain our openness to grief, we find that the ego reestablishes itself with an expanded vista: less isolated and bound up in its narcissistic shell, more open, compassionate, and free of compulsive maneuvers to avoid pain, more connected to spirit." In other words, the journey of conscious grieving enables us to move from an ego-centered to a soul-centered life.

As we walk the road of conscious grieving, tears lubricate our footsteps. They bear witness to the surrender of the ego to its own death, and paradoxically, that surrender is profoundly enlivening. When we refuse to grieve, we choose to be less alive; we choose soul death and disavow our humanity, and of course, the ego always prefers heroic, beyond-human posturing. To embrace one's humanity opens one to feeling vulnerable, not in control, and longing for connection. While this feels like weakness to the ego, the soul is revitalized and empowered whenever we revere our authentic humanity.

In current time, grief in this ego-intoxicated milieu is perceived as the enemy, not only by the culture at large, but by the custodians of the mental health profession who argue that we should not grieve anything for too long, and that if we do, our grief may mushroom into a depressive syndrome. In this way, grief is pathologized, and society is "spared" from any interruption of its delusional "be happy" persona. Rather, we must listen to the soul's longing to descend and be reborn, and we must understand that this takes as long as it takes and that in fact, we are *less* likely to become depressed if we honor the journey of conscious grieving.

More Grieving, More Life

In my experience, individuals who have persevered in the grieving process report that as they have moved through it, they have ultimately felt more alive, more empowered, and that ironically, their ability to find humor in life has increased as a result of experiencing deep grief. Likewise, many report that their capacity for feeling gratitude has increased. Accordingly, Miriam Greenspan comments that "With this altered sight, the pre-occupation with what we've lost imperceptibly alchemizes into gratitude for what we've been given: for the gift of the beloved. For the gift of life itself. Gratitude comes from seeing through the eyes of grief."

With regard to depression, it is not a human emotion per se, but a syndrome comprised of numerous emotions including grief, anger, shame, anxiety, and despair. If you are reading these words and know that you are struggling with depression, it is very important to understand that in a chaotic world, you will almost certainly not have access to antidepressants. Therefore, it behooves anyone living with depression to begin now to work consciously with the emotions one recognizes to be part of the syndrome. I recommend exploring natural, herbal, or homeopathic remedies for addressing depression, but I also remind the reader that these too may become scarce or unavailable in the future.

More important may be journaling, creating art and music for expressing depressive moods, dancing, singing, exercising, chanting and consciously exploring, with the support of trusted others, one's grief, anger, despair, and anxiety. In addition, it is very important for people struggling with depression to become engaged with life by serving others. The stuck energy of the depressive syndrome is often loosened and allowed to flow outward when we have the opportunity to serve the earth community. In fact, service frequently tempers all of the dark emotions by shifting the focus from oneself to the needs of others. I hasten to add that service does not and should not cancel out one's own pain, but it may help put it in perspective.

While Greenspan's words are written in the context of grieving for a loved one, they may be applied to grieving any loss and certainly the sorrow we feel for the plethora of losses we witness around us in a world unraveling. We cannot and should not attempt to grieve alone; we need help because our grief is inextricably connected with all of life. In its infinite wisdom, the soul pulls us down from the heroic heights of spirit-obsessed industrial civilization and asks us to feel and taste our humanity on ever deeper levels. In this respect, the collapse of civilization and the disintegration of the assumptions out of which it emerged may be the most *sacred* demise in the history of our species—an exquisite opportunity to discover our deeper purpose and perhaps cross the evolutionary threshold before us, thereby becoming a new kind of human being inhabiting a radically altered planet. Perhaps this is what the poet Rilke glimpsed when he wrote:

> And it is possible a great presence is moving near me.

> I have faith in nights.

CONFRONTING AND CONTEMPLATING
(Writing answers to these questions or drawing images in relation to them in a journal is
highly recommended.)

1. What kind of messages did you receive in childhood about grieving? How have
those messages affected you in your adult life?

2. Take some time to journal about your past experiences with grieving. What
have they been like? What was the loss (or losses) you were grieving? What
kind of support did you have? What kinds of resistance did you or do you have
toward grieving? Describe in detail what has been healing about grieving. What
was frustrating or frightening?

3. Have you ever had the experience of humor being somehow connected with
grieving? Have you had other experiences of so-called "opposite" emotions
being present at approximately the same time?

4. Have you ever felt relief or a sense of liberation around accepting that the state
of industrial civilization and life as we have known it is unraveling? If so,
journal about that.

5. As you look around you, what losses in terms of the environment, economic
prosperity, and energy abundance do you see? Take time to journal in detail
your feelings about these.

6. What was your emotional response to the Gulf Oil Spill of 2010? Journal your
experience or create images of it.

7. Who in your life right now is available to support your grieving process? If you
have been supported in grieving, describe in detail what that has been like for
you.

8. Are you now or have you been available to support other people in grieving?
If so, how have you done this? What gifts do you possess that might be helpful
in helping others grieve?

9. Are you struggling with depression? If so, what tools have you found useful
in helping you cope with it? Are you using any of the tools mentioned in this
chapter? Are you engaged in service in the world? What kind of support do
you have in your life?

10. Many people have found that gratitude is a powerful antidote to depression. At
the end of each day, make a list of people, things, situations, and experiences
for which you are grateful. Carry the list with you into the next day and refer
to it many times throughout the day.

Chapter 11: Managing Fear, Anxiety, and Terror

In order to experience fearlessness, it is necessary to experience fear.

~Chogyam Trungpa~

You have the gift of a brilliant internal guardian that stands ready to warn you of hazards and guide you through risky situations.

~Gavin de Becker, author of *The Gift of Fear*~

Denial is a save now, pay later scheme.
~Gavin de Becker~

Since the September 11, 2001 attacks on the World Trade Center and the Pentagon, Americans have lived with a sense of terror, superbly manipulated and strategically exacerbated by the government of the United States for military and political purposes. At this writing the United States has been at war for over nine years. Domestically, we have become a surveillance society in which personal privacy is almost non-existent. While other nations are generally even more intrusive in the lives of their citizens, Americans are hardly less fearful of violence and terrorist attacks than the citizens of other nations are.

When asked if they are willing to forego some security in favor of freeing up funds spent for war and surveillance so that those funds might be spent on healthcare, environmental integrity, education, or other needs, Americans overwhelmingly state that safety is their most important priority. Whether or not the security measures which they so adamantly champion are providing them with the level of safety they demand is debatable. Nevertheless, they insist on maintaining at least the fantasy of living in a secure society.

As I have already noted, in a collapsing world, violence is certain to proliferate, in which case "the enemy" is less likely to be perceived as "those terrorists from the Middle East" and more likely to be perceived as "those immigrants in our town" or "those liberals in the media" or "those strange neighbors of ours." Increasingly, the level of fear will escalate, and anyone not in the inner circle of the terrified may become a scapegoat. This is yet another reason to know one's neighbors and to share time, food, and other resources with them in advance of societal collapse.

In 1999 Gavin de Becker published *The Gift of Fear* in which he tirelessly emphasizes that the emotion of fear is an evolutionary gift that has enabled our species to survive for millions of years and which, rather than attempting to deny or berate, we must honor and use wisely in service of our personal and community safety. Much of de Becker's book and his public seminars are devoted to teaching people how to skillfully utilize fear and the intuitive signals it generates in order to prevent physical assault and even charlatan scams which could constitute financial assault.

Whatever the fear level of Americans in 2010, it will be elevated, possibly off the scale, in a chaotic world. Panic and paranoia are likely to become epidemic. But even now, as we think about the collapse of industrial civilization and a world in catastrophic transition, our bodies become fearful, if not terrified. How do we, even in this moment, manage our anxiety about the future?

Throughout 2010 I have had the opportunity to teach online classes focused on my book, *Sacred Demise*. The classes have been part of the curriculum of Andre Angelantoni's Post Peak Living website[44] which offers a number of courses on logistical and emotional and spiritual preparation for collapse. In my first course of the year on navigating the coming chaos, New York Times reporter, John Leland, attended two of our four, three-hour sessions and subsequently published an article entitled "Imagining Life Without Oil and Being Ready." [45] While I disagree with some parts of the article, I found it fair overall and was delighted that it linked directly to information about my ongoing courses.

Even more rewarding was a response to the article from Jennifer Wilkerson, one of the students who attended my first 2010 class. She was pictured and quoted in the New York Times piece, and immediately after the article she published a response on her blog which related how her terror and panic about collapse has subsided, especially after taking our course. Her remarks may be instructive for anyone in the early stages of seriously grappling with the reality of collapse.[46] Essentially, Jennifer shared in the Times article and in her blog that upon initially understanding the consequences of Peak Oil, she became terrified, unable to sleep, and a difficult person to be around, but as she took my "Navigating The Coming Chaos" course, she found a place where she could discuss her fears with other people who had been doing the same research, and as a result, her fears subsided. She became no less concerned, but now she had the validation she needed, and her preparation became a spiritual practice, supported by trusted others she had bonded with in the course.

Being Afraid Is "Unspiritual"

In my public appearances I frequently encounter individuals who argue that I'm a fearmonger and that walking a spiritual path means focusing on love rather than fear. In response to their false dichotomizing between fear and love, I frequently share a story about fear as told by Malidoma Somé. He speaks of a distraction strategy used by African lions to lure their prey. An old, toothless male lion with an enormous roar is used as a decoy. Anyone or anything hearing his terrifying roar is bound to run in the opposite direction, but it is precisely in the opposite direction where younger lions, well endowed with murderous teeth and stupefying stamina lie in wait for the prey escaping from the roar. Thus in Malidoma's village, young people are told that when they hear the intimidating roar they should run toward it, and not away from it because being with the roar is infinitely preferable to the fate of anyone who runs away from it.

In no way do I concur with those who argue that being afraid is "unspiritual." Like de Becker I believe that fear can be one of our greatest teachers. He clarifies this notion by stating, "True fear is a gift; unwarranted fear is a curse, and we must learn how to tell the difference." Our work is to avoid becoming paralyzed by fear and instead, utilize it to assist us in becoming what Miriam Greenspan calls "warriors of vulnerability."

In the present moment, anxiety runs rampant in our culture. People feel terrified but are uncertain about what causes their panic. Although depression in our culture is pervasive, more people suffer from anxiety. Yet according to Greenspan, fear and anxiety are not synonymous. In *Healing Through The Dark Emotions*, she notes that "Fear is a discrete and powerful emotion with a particular referent, while anxiety is a state of unease." Fear has its reasons; anxiety does not.

Millions of people in the industrialized world are walking around feeling anxious about they know not what. Perhaps they are not informed about what is happening on our planet and may never read or watch the news, yet they remain on edge. I believe that much of their angst stems from a part of them that knows unconsciously that their way of life is crumbling. As Michael Meade says, when we talk about this unraveling, we are not "scaring people" because people are already scared. Something in them knows that normal is over, and that a return to it is impossible.

Perhaps the teeming masses of anxious individuals would be less anxious if like Jennifer Wilkerson, they were actually capable of staring down reality and understanding the *reasons* for their anxiety. If they could do this, then they would have a "discrete and powerful emotion with a particular referent" to work with. Perhaps like Jennifer they could "stay with the roar" instead of fleeing, and in the process of staying, find allies who are becoming warriors of vulnerability.

Greenspan and de Becker would agree that fear is a wake up call. It signals us to *pay attention*. Fear itself is not the problem, but the fear of fear. There is no way to be in a body on earth without experiencing fear from time to time. In fact, Greenspan reminds us that "the human condition is scary." She also notes that fear is probably the most shamed emotion in our culture, particularly for men who are taught to be the fear-conquerers while women are taught to be the fear-carriers. Perhaps one of the stellar reasons we feel disempowered is that we ignore or do not know what to do with our fear.

Like the collapse of industrial civilization itself, sometimes there is not much we can do *about* our fear, but there is much that we can do *with* it. In *Healing The Dark Emotions*, Greenspan discusses "The Way of Surrender" in relation to fear. She emphasizes that we can turn it into a kind of meditation, and I would add that we can work creatively with it---using drawing, journaling, or writing songs or poems about it. As we do this, the fear becomes less charged, less powerful.

In a chaotic world, fear may become ubiquitous. It may, in a sense, become part of the air we breathe, but that may not be the worst that could happen to us. Greenspan suggests that "mindful fear" can motivate us to act kindly and courageously in service to others and ourselves which may be useful in dispelling our fear. For example, if one is afraid of not having enough money, it may be helpful to work for the poor. If we can allow fear and allow it to move us to service, we can not only find our way through it, but we have the opportunity to alchemize it.[47]

I highly recommend Greenspan's *Healing Through The Dark Emotions* which provides a number of experiential exercises for working with and through one's fears.

The Heart and Hands of Love

One of the qualities often stimulated by fear is courage, a word which in French is synonymous with "heart." This is noteworthy because courage cannot come from our heads. It is a heartfelt, visceral response in the face of fear. Authentic courage is not foolhardy, but neither is it pre-occupied with its own survival. It compels us to take risks. Genuine courage, a quality of soul, is greater than the human ego, echoing the sacred within us and throughout human history has been the hallmark of individuals who have made a difference in the course of events. We recall Frederick Douglass, Joan of Arc, Thomas More, Martin Luther King, Jr., Mahatma Gandhi, Nelson Mandela, Rosa Parks, Harriett Tubman, and Erin Brockovich, to name only a few. Perhaps the antidote to fear is not merely the emotion of love but courage which springs from the heart and may be one of love's most compelling attributes.

Soul has the capacity to hold fear, to demonstrate courage, and thereby embody a quality of love far beyond our limited definitions of love which may be inadequate for the chaotic world toward which we are moving with increasing velocity. Paradoxically, we may become most loving when we are able to be present with and work consciously with our fear, allowing it to move us compassionately to service and courageous action.

Yet another response to fear, used alongside those already suggested, is ritual and prayer. The reader should not immediately assume that for me the word "prayer" connotes religion or even the existence of a deity. Rather I experience prayer as conversation with something greater than the human ego. There are myriad ways to pray—performing a ritual, giving thanks, surrendering to a particular challenge, or simply crying out for help. Service may be yet another form of prayer. In service we affirm something greater in those we endeavor to serve as well as in ourselves. For the artist, musician, actor, writer, or storyteller, his or her craft may well be a form of prayer. And of course, poetry is an exquisite form of prayer that draws us away from linear, ego-based thinking into the heart from which prayer most naturally erupts.

Moreover, I believe that conscious preparation, both logistical and psycho-spiritual, for the collapse of industrial civilization is a path of prayer. One can prepare out of fear, or one can prepare out of concern and compassion for loved ones, one's community, and oneself. Amid that prayer, one understands that one may not survive physically and that survival alone is not necessarily the ultimate intention behind preparation. As emphasized in *Sacred Demise*, a chaotic future is an initiation replete with lessons for expanding and deepening the soul. Preparation should be a kind of ritual procession in which we walk toward the future with awareness, wisdom, discernment, prudence, openness, and a willingness to proceed even though we do not know what the future holds, but knowing that preparation is the work we must do in spite of the uncertainty of outcome.

The prayer of preparation is an opportunity to live consciously, holding the opposites of the present with which we are familiar and the future with which we aren't. Reminiscent of Noah building an ark, we may feel foolish, we may be scorned by others, and we may doubt the soundness of what we are doing, but we prepare nevertheless because like Noah, we have no way of knowing the end result. In fact, it is the *process* of preparation that matters as much as the *product* of our efforts. In that process, we have opportunities for extraordinary teaching moments through collaborating with others, assessing what we need and do not need, and of course, working with and alchemizing all of the dark emotions. Accordingly, the collapse of industrial civilization and the end of life as we have known it becomes not the worst thing that could possibly happen to us, but rather, a heartfelt, conscientious spiritual practice.

CONFRONTING AND CONTEMPLATING
(Writing answers to these questions or drawing images in relation to them in a journal is highly recommended.)

1. As you contemplate life in a chaotic world, what are your greatest fears? Explain.

2. How are you currently coping with these fears?

3. In what ways are you providing service? Are you serving in a manner that puts you in contact with things you fear? If so, what is that like? If not, take some time to journal about how you could do so and what that might look and feel like.

4. Have you had the experience of surrendering to your fears by working directly with them through breathing exercises, meditation, creating artistically, musically, or in other ways that allow you to express and engage with your fears? If so, take time to journal about your experience.

5. Being grounded as we face our fears is very important. Many activities provide grounding: walking; gardening; working with materials such as stone, clay, earth, metal, or wood; and of course, deep breathing. Take some time to journal (or express artistically) how you ground yourself in the face of fear. If you do not have experience with this, experiment with various options. A number of grounding exercises may be found in the Appendix of this book.

6. What forms of prayer or ritual have you found helpful in the face of fear? Record words or images about these in your journal. You may also want to write a poem about this. Feel free to experiment with new prayers and new rituals as you work with your fears.

7. As you engage in conscious preparation for the future, in what ways do you experience that process as a spiritual practice? Again, feel free to write about this in your journal or create images.

Chapter 12: From Despair to Impassioned Inspiration

When despair for the world grows in me
and I wake in the night at the least sound
in fear of what my life and my children's lives may be,
I go and lie down where the wood drake
rests in his beauty on the water, and the great heron feeds.
I come into the peace of wild things
who do not tax their lives with forethought
or grief. I come into the presence of still water.
And I feel above me the day-blind stars
waiting with their light. For a time
I rest in the grace of the world, and am free.

~Wendell Berry~

Life begins on the other side of despair.

~Jean-Paul Sartre~

An Italian proverb states that a person who lives by hope will die by despair. Americans for nearly three centuries have lived by hope, and as noted above, our current President centered his campaign around it. It is as if since our inception as a nation we have, by whatever means necessary, warded off despair in favor of hope, and I believe that if we as a people were to abandon the shallow sense of hope we insist on maintaining, we would be driven to the depths of our despair regarding the current state of our planet.

About one year after Barack Obama became President, I noticed on one radical left website the words "the 'hopium' is wearing off." While the majority of Americans believe that Obama is a better President than George W. Bush, Jr., it has now become painfully obvious that Obama's leadership has offered little divergence from the policies of the Bush administration. In the throes of what can only be described honestly as the Second Great Depression, Americans suffering from a deluge of unemployment, foreclosures, bankruptcies, loss of health insurance and retirement savings have not yet fully confronted their despair. They pretend that a return to unlimited growth and delirious consumerism is possible and even likely in the long term, but all the while, just beneath the surface of that chimera, the demon of despair is growing increasingly restless and ominous.

The Value of Despair

Despair moves us to confront existential questions, and let's remember that that big word isn't just a philosophical term but directly refers to our existence. Existential questions are questions of meaning and purpose—questions about the human condition such as: Why do the innocent suffer? Why do those who commit brutal acts so often go unpunished? If there is a God, why do these things happen? Why am I here?

Despair also brings us face to face with an emptiness that is at our core, regardless of how fulfilled and serene we feel. And while some theologians would assert that the emptiness is a God-shaped void that only religion can fill, I would argue that the emptiness cannot be filled by anyone or anything because it is a fundamental reality of the human condition. However, I hasten to add that the pain of the void can be minimized in a variety of ways.

Citizens of industrial civilization have attempted for centuries to fill the void by cherishing the delusion of unlimited growth, the dogma of unbridled progress, the creed of consumerism, the sanctity of the family, the piety of organized religion, the intellectual rigor of obtaining advanced degrees, and of course, the use of substances to obviate or medicate the sensation of emptiness. As civilization continues to deteriorate, and as fewer and fewer options for filling the void are available, the masses will be brutally confronted with their own despair. When the people, things, and activities that have provided meaning for them throughout their lives no longer exist, we are likely to witness madness and suicide on an unprecedented scale. I state this, dear reader, not to incite fear, but to prepare us for a milieu of chaos resulting from a pandemic of meaninglessness as nearly all of that which has provided meaning for so many is swept away.

What is more, I realize that anyone reading these words may be at times overwhelmed with despair. This is difficult to avoid when contemplating the scale of horror that humans have inflicted on the planet in terms of wars, resource depletion, environmental devastation, and innumerable forms of injustice and brutality. Unless one lives a hermetically sealed life, one encounters these realities daily.

When I first published *Sacred Demise,* I was afraid that it would be reviled at worst and virtually ignored at best. While it is true that it did not and will not become a best-seller, I have been astounded at the book's success and the comments I have received from readers. Consistently they report that *Sacred Demise* profoundly lowered their level of despair by catalyzing a sense of meaning and purpose in their lives. In most cases, readers completed the book, or re-read it, and took away a palpable appreciation of the demise and what is truly sacred about it.

As I engage with collapse-aware individuals and communities throughout the world, what I consistently hear is the profound alienation they feel in a world unraveling. We all have personal wounds that evoke despair, but as Greenspan notes: "Despair grows not only out of our personal wounds, losses, and disappointments, but also out of our needs for community and a shared sense of meaning—spiritual necessities for which we harbor a profound and aching, though largely unconscious, nostalgia."

She also notes that often our personal despair will not let up until we confront our despair for the world. You may be familiar with Joanna Macy's despair and empowerment workshops, designed to help people face their despair and create community with others who are engaged in similar work. Macy believes that despair is to be trusted because it is a natural, visceral response to a planet in crisis inhabited by beings who are committing suicide.

Beyond Contemporary Psychotherapy

Generally, the psychotherapy profession does not address despair for the world. In fact, if you were to walk into a therapist's office and say that you feel grief and despair for the world, you are likely to be labeled depressed, paranoid, phobic, or pathologized in some other way, presented with myriad reasons why your despair is unwarranted in a world so full of glorious potential, and probably asked to consider taking an antidepressant. It is likely that unless you consult a therapist who is fully informed regarding the coming chaos, you will need to find support from other individuals similarly informed and share your feelings about the future with them.

Joanna Macy speaks to this directly:

> But because of the individualistic bias of mainstream psychotherapy, we have been conditioned to assume that we are essentially separate selves, driven by aggressive impulses, competing for a place in the sun. In the light of these assumptions, psychotherapists tend to view our affective responses to the plight of our world as dysfunctional and give them short shrift. As a result, we have trouble crediting the notion that concerns for the general welfare might be genuine enough and acute enough to cause *distress.* Assuming that all our drives are ego-generated, therapists tend to regard feelings of despair for our planet as manifestations of some private neurosis.[48]

This is precisely why in recent months I have begun a Transition Counseling practice, which some people have called "Collapse Coaching," that offers people an opportunity to share with me their feelings about the future and receive support and practical input regarding emotional preparation. I believe that increasingly we will need this kind of coaching in our communities as the wheels fly off of a civilization dependent on cheap fossil fuels for its operation and the illusion of endless growth and consumption for its motivation.

When we do not acknowledge despair, it reinforces our tendency toward numbness, the preferred "feeling state" of most citizens of modern culture. If we remind ourselves that *emotion* has the word *motion* in it, and if we consciously allow the despair, yes even dialog with it, asking it what it wants from us, we may find that it is indeed an ally.

In reality, despair presents us with an opportunity to enhance our sense of meaning and purpose. As Greenspan states: In a chapter entitled "From Despair to Faith" in *Healing Through The Dark Emotions,* Greenspan states, "Despair is faith's darker handmaiden. There is no faith without doubt and despair, just as there is no good without evil, no day without night. To be authentic, faith must be all-inclusive—encompassing Auschwitz as much as it encompasses paradise."

If you bristle at the word *faith,* feel free to replace it with *meaning, purpose, inspiration,* or some other word.

The soul is extremely comfortable in the territory of despair. For this reason, we need to trust our despair and allow it to guide us to the transformation that is waiting to happen within us. We also need to remember that we feel our despair in the context of a world that is withering and a species that is rushing headlong toward extinction. Our personal despair and the wider story of despair cannot be separated. This does not mean that we stay stuck in blame and abdicate personal responsibility where it should be claimed. What it does mean, however, is that suffering is both personal and collective, and that the latter is larger than our personal egos. It may be that despair is a catalyst not only for our personal transformation, but also for our species.

Thus arises another opportunity to remind us all that service in the world is often an excellent antidote to despair. Service can give our lives meaning and help place our personal story in the context of the larger story of a civilization that has reached its growth limits and is currently in demise. Unlike the growth of civilization, the soul's growth is boundless. In fact, the more we acknowledge our limitations of material growth, acquisition, and control, the more expansive our souls are likely to become, and service frequently enhances the process.

In *Healing Through The Dark Emotions,* Miriam Greenspan offers a number of exercises for working with despair. One of those focuses on connecting one's own pain to the pain of the world. This exercise will be explained at the end of this chapter in the "Confronting and Contemplating" section.

Giving Despair to Nature

Yet another tool for soothing our despair is to follow the example of Wendell Berry in his beautiful poem which opens this chapter. In it he states that when despair for the world grows in him, he consciously enters nature and allows it to comfort him so that for a time he can rest in the grace of the world and experience himself as free. Yet it is not only comfort he receives but the "peace of wild things." But how can "wild" be synonymous with "peaceful"? Isn't "wild" unpredictable and therefore anxiety-producing? Actually, what may be the most effective antidotes to despair are the aspects of life and nature that are wild, unpredictable, capricious, even dangerous. Think about it: Is not part of our death-like despair the lack of wildness? Bill Plotkin states in *Nature And The Human Soul* that "Something in us is truly wild and wants to stay that way through our entire life. It is the source of our deepest creativity and freedom."

I want to underscore Wendell Berry's advice. I am blessed to live in the foothills of the Rocky Mountains in Boulder, Colorado. Recently, I have committed to journeying twice monthly up into the mountains and spending sacred time in some isolated place there. It may be as short as one hour or as long as an entire day. While I have taken many extended trips into the mountains earlier in my life, having lived at the foot of Pikes Peak in my late-twenties, I now journey into the mountains more contemplatively and for shorter periods of time.

My intention when taking these short trips is exactly the same as Wendell Berry's. I go in order to "rest in the grace" that is there. It is a comforting, soothing, inspiring, and restorative experience. However, without exception, grief comes, whether I invite it or not. It is quite simply, ever-present these days as I allow myself to become intimate with nature--and I give my grief to the earth. Sometimes I do it by lying face down on the earth and sobbing. Sometimes by standing with my back pressed firmly against a towering pine tree until I burst into laughter. Sometimes by sitting in the soil and sifting it tenderly through my fingers as my tears flow.

Part of me realizes that it is only a matter of time until the lush landscape into which I have immersed my body and soul will be destroyed by climate change. Another part of me is also keenly aware of the earth's magnificent history of regenerating herself. The very elements of nature in which I revel on these journeys are remnants of the earth that have been destroyed in eons past. Perhaps in a million years, the landscape in which I sit that may be destroyed in my lifetime, will metamorphose into another lovely landscape or other elements that will provide comfort and revitalization for some other member of the earth community.

Somehow, when I return from my short mountain getaways, I am buoyed; I feel some distance from my despair for the world, and I am renewed in body and soul. It is as if I have spent hours communing intimately with a dear friend. Eros swells and fills by heart and body. And even as I return to the low-intensity urban community in which I live, my friend remains in my heart. She is still up there in the mountains, and I can return to her, but more importantly, she is in my body, and I take her with me as I do the work I came here to do. Even if she is made extinct, she is within *me*, and her palpable sacred presence within *cannot* be made extinct. I am exhilarated by her effervescent, wild fecundity, and my despair recedes. I feel my wildness; industrial civilization has not killed it because my wildness inspires me to find meaning in the madness of a collapsing world. And it compels me to write these words and to invite you to immerse yourself in *your* wildness because when you do, it will be impossible to be driven by despair.

CONFRONTING AND CONTEMPLATING
(Writing answers to these questions or drawing images in relation to them in a journal is highly recommended.)

1. In your journal, write or draw everything you know about your despair. Are there words or images that accompany it? Are there times of the day when it is more apparent than at other times? How does it feel in your body?

2. As we have noted in this chapter, despair raises issues of meaning as it confronts us with life's greatest questions and an emptiness within, which I have asserted is part of the human condition. Take some time to write or draw about how you attempt to fill the emptiness. How does that work or not work? What gives your life meaning? How do certain people, things, or activities bring meaning to you?

3. What would give meaning to you in a collapsing, chaotic world where many of your current resources or routine activities may no longer exist? Take some time to journal about this.

4. In *Healing Through The Dark Emotions,* Greenspan suggests a number of exercises for working with despair. Reminiscent of Carl Jung's process of active imagination, Greenspan includes an exercise on talking with despair.

She writes: "In a place where you will not be disturbed, in a state of meditation or relaxation, or just in your ordinary waking consciousness, ask questions of your despair: *What do you want of me? What are you asking of me?"*

"Some common answers to these questions: Change your daily habits. Eat better. Exercise more. Breathe deeply. Take better care of yourself. Speak your anger to your spouse. Grieve your losses. Change your idea of who you are…." These are only a few of the answers that might arise as you ask despair what it wants from you.

5. What do you know about your wildness? Is it with you? Do you feel it? How do you express it? If you don't know much about it or you don't feel it, why is that? Where is it hiding and why?

6. If you are not already a member of a heart and soul group or some group where emotional and spiritual preparation for a chaotic world can be freely discussed, consider starting one. What feelings arise as you consider doing that?

7. What actions are you taking in the world to minimize your despair? Are those actions serving that purpose?

Chapter 13: From Anger to Anguish: Anger As a Mindfulness Practice

Messsenger

My work is loving the world.
Here the sunflowers, there the hummingbird —
equal seekers of sweetness.
Here the quickening yeast; there the blue plums.
Here the clam deep in the speckled sand.

Are my boots old? Is my coat torn?
Am I no longer young, and still not half-perfect? Let me
keep my mind on what matters,
which is my work,

which is mostly standing still and learning to be
astonished.
The phoebe, the delphinium.
The sheep in the pasture, and the pasture.
Which is mostly rejoicing, since all ingredients are here,

which is gratitude, to be given a mind and a heart
and these body-clothes,
a mouth with which to give shouts of joy
to the moth and the wren, to the sleepy dug-up clam,
telling them all, over and over, how it is
that we live forever.

~ Mary Oliver ~

In some spiritual and psychological circles we frequently hear unambiguous proscriptions against the emotion of anger. The taboo originates to some extent from a focus in those circles on ascendance, transcendence, and an aversion to descent. From that perspective, people on a spiritual path are supposed to be kind and play nice all the time. The insistence on "rising above" anger is no doubt another manifestation of disavowing soul and the body, preferring instead to distance oneself from the messy foibles of living in a body and having a complex repertoire of emotions.

However, in many indigenous traditions, anger is not experienced with the same suspicion one finds in Western spiritual circles. While ancient teachings regarding anger do not condone aggression, they do not unequivocally assume that feeling the emotion of anger will lead to hostility or violence. In fact, they tend to revere anger as an innate human emotion which may be utilized on behalf of the earth community without inflicting harm. Ancient teachings often include practices for "uploading" the raw emotion of anger to higher chakras or physiological energy centers on behalf of preserving boundaries or protecting the innocent—both of which are characteristics of the non-aggressive warrior.

Anger is one of the Five Stages of Grief articulated by the death and dying researcher, Elisabeth Kubler-Ross. As I noted in *Sacred Demise*, in the context of those stages, anger shows up in reaction to a loss. First we feel shock and denial then move into anger which may include frustration, anxiety, irritation, embarrassment, and shame. Subsequently, we move into bargaining, depression and grief, followed by acceptance and re-investment in our lives. As Kubler-Ross emphasizes, none of the stages is neatly detached from the others. We tend to move through them fluidly, with each stage somewhat blurring into the next stage or containing remnants of the last one.

The Anger Epidemic

In the process of preparing emotionally to navigate the coming chaos, it is crucial to examine each stage of grief, to note where we have been in the process, to look at where we are in the moment, and to honor each emotion along the way. Many people today are stuck in anger because they have not allowed themselves to move through it into mindful grieving. In fact, I believe that the United States, and many nations throughout the world, are currently mired in anger. In 2009, author and spiritual teacher Caroline Myss, stated in her article "An Epidemic of Global Anger":

> We are a community of nations on fire with anger. And we are
> getting angrier by the day. Whether we look at the increase in
> uprisings occurring around the world or at the escalating tension
> brewing in America, what is becoming more apparent is that we
> are witnessing a rapidly increasing rate of global anger, so much
> so that it qualifies as an epidemic.[49]

As noted above, many Americans are enraged at their government. Some who have been researching the demise of the current paradigm and understand the self-destructive aspects of corporate capitalism, the limits of economic growth, and the unsustainability of a civilization dependent on fossil fuels feel angry because their leaders refuse to acknowledge what is so. As their minds have been awakened, so have their emotions, and anger has been part of the process. But as they have come to understand that industrial civilization itself is collapsing, they are likely to have stopped wanting to repair and improve it and have begun to entertain a larger picture of how they could join with allies in constructing a new paradigm and a new culture.

It is likely that for these individuals, anger metamorphosed into deep grief or despair, as a feeling of powerlessness to "fix" civilization set in. Implicit in the emotion of anger is the sense that something can or must be done to alter the adversity that has evoked anger. As one comes to understand the inevitability of the unraveling and the futility of attempting to prevent it, one may in fact experience a sense of relief that collapse is beyond control and proceeds in its own way, in its own time. One grasps that our mandate as a species is to move *with* the demise, not against it, and find within the unraveling a greater purpose than the one civilization has offered, which may actually facilitate our proceeding with the work we came here to do. At that point, even though we may carry some residue of denial or anger, and even though our willingness to see what is so puts us directly in the path of deep grief, the embrace of our purpose and our role in the collapse process is in itself a re-investment in our lives and in the well being of the earth community.

However, the individuals I have just been describing do not comprise the vast majority of those in the United States or the world who are fixated in anger because those individuals are also fixated in denial. One cannot move through the Five Stages of Grief if one does not move beyond denial. Refusing to see what is so guarantees that the journey through the stages will not occur. So whether one is an enraged Muslim suicide bomber or a vitriolic white, middle class Tea Party enthusiast, one's emotional state and behavior belie an inordinately diminished perspective of reality, resulting in a desperate need for rancorous scapegoating---in other words, fixation in anger.

The Mary Oliver poem which begins this chapter is about loving the world, which in part means reveling in the kind of sensual delight of nature mentioned earlier in this book—that is, "becoming accustomed to savoring that which is momentous, concealed within bare bones simplicity." It also means a profound gratitude which the poem describes as "mostly rejoicing, since all the ingredients are here." The world has given us stupendous gifts which Oliver says causes her to "stand still and learn to be astonished."

But does our gratitude for the world mean that we should never be angry about the injustice or the self-destruction and eco-side its inhabitants have perpetrated upon each other and the earth community? Certainly not, but deep connection with our purpose in the world provides perspective that buoys us and allows us to keep moving forward when the magnetic pull to become fixated in anger may feel irresistible.

Anger and Life Purpose

When we are intimately familiar with our purpose, we understand that the world is not paradise, it is not a vacation resort, and it is not a place to which we have come to live in perpetual bliss. Rather, the world is comprised of both the magnificent wonderment and extraordinary beauty depicted by Mary Oliver, as well as the horrors engineered by a species which may be about to become successful in its incalculable attempts to commit suicide.

Author and spiritual teacher, Marshall Vian Summers, writes in his book *Greater Community Spirituality:*

> *Be without judgment of the world. If the world were a perfect place, you would not need to come here. If the world were a place that functioned harmoniously, without friction or conflict, this would not be the place for you....The world is your place to work and to give. Its pleasures are small but real. Its pains and difficulties are great. The world cannot give you what you seek, for what you seek you have brought with you from beyond the world.*[50]

That which we have brought with us from beyond is none other than the "something greater" to which I have been referring throughout this book—the "I that is not I." Summers refers to it as Knowledge, and others use terms like *the sacred, spirit, the Self, the divine within.* I believe that the more intimately familiar we are with the "I that is not I," the less we expect from the world, and the more we are willing to serve the world in order to imbue it with the sacred. Loving the world, as Oliver names it, is not about sentimental emotion, but about a commitment to the work we came here to do which, by definition, serves the earth community.

As stated in Chapter 6, I believe that a chaotic world will be, among other things, an angry world, especially in the initial stages of the demise. In a December, 2009 article, "America The Traumatized"[51], Adele Stan argues that a series of events that occurred in the first decade of the twenty-first century have made us a PTSD nation---and that was before the BP oil disaster of 2010. Until we understand trauma and post-traumatic stress, the need to blame the traumatizing event or person(s) who inflicted it is exceedingly compelling. When we do grasp the magnitude of trauma and its consequences, we come to understand how futile our rage is in the face of the deluge of horror.

I write these words some two months after the BP Gulf of Mexico cataclysm. Am I angry as I witness this eco-atrocity? Am I enraged at the lies of BP with regard to its prior knowledge regarding the safety of the Deepwater Horizon rig? Am I livid when I hear the stories of people who tried to warn the corporation that its bypassing of standard international safety regulations would result in catastrophe? Does white hot rage pulse through my body as I witness BP's CEO, Tony Hayward, taking a yachting trip in the midst of the disaster and begging to "get his life back" as the entire world lays the blame for this debacle at his door and as the entire planet is now in the path of the destruction visited upon it by a multitude of corporations and CEOs of BP's and Tony Hayward's ilk? Am I incensed when I see millions of people immersed in an epic blame-fest, pointing fingers and mouthing incessant sentences beginning with "they shoulda, coulda, woulda"?

The answer to all of those questions is a resounding "yes," *and* from the moment the catastrophe was first made public, I realized the probable scope of it, and I saw the word *t-r-a-u-m-a* writ large all over it. What purpose at this point will my anger serve? How could I be seduced by the assumption inherent in my anger that the there is a possibility that the situation can be remedied? In my opinion, the BP oil disaster of 2010 is nothing less than 100 Hurricane Katrinas in slow motion. It is an unfathomable game-changer— perhaps *the* tipping point in humanity's destruction of this planet. As I witnessed countless animals dripping and dying from disgusting quantities of crude oil resembling raw sewage suffocating their bodies; as I consider that perhaps 40-50% of the sea floor of the Gulf of Mexico may now be covered with petroleum; as I reflect on the spread of the spill into other oceans and the death of plankton and the ultimate devastation of the food chain; as I consider the economic devastation of a section of the country that comprises about 20 percent of the nation's Gross Domestic Product; and as I speculate that perhaps the entire Gulf Coast region may eventually become uninhabitable, I see, hear, and feel nothing but trauma. In fact, if the entire population of the United States were not already suffering from post-traumatic stress disorder, it is now.

Mindful Anger

Yet what I have personally discovered about my anger over the years is neither that I shouldn't have anger nor that I should discharge it whenever I feel like it, but rather, to approach my anger mindfully. A stellar article by Holistic Psychologist, Jennifer Franklin, Ph.D., entitled "Mindfulness In Practice: Anger Management,"[52] defines mindfulness this way: "To be mindful is to be conscious, more awake, more informed about how one lives one's life. Being more mindful, therefore, allows us to make more awake or informed choices in every moment. Our words and actions would be more mindful if we were more awake or conscious in those moments when we choose them." According to psychotherapist Richard Pfeiffer, Ph.D., quoted in the article, anger is a neurological response process that essentially prepares us to fight or flee.

In the first section of this book, "Building Your Internal Bunker," we explored options for creating more mindfulness within ourselves. Meditation is, of course, one of the principal tools for strengthening mindfulness, even if the meditation is not the specific technique called "mindfulness meditation." It is important to remember that mindfulness isn't just about becoming mindful of the world around us, although that generally accrues from a meditation practice, but rather, mindfulness is about being mindful of ourselves. It helps us become centered observers of our own process.

For example, Dr. Franklin's article offers the classic example of road rage and how it can be handled mindfully instead of reactively:

> When you exercise mindfulness, you exercise non-reactivity or the capacity to stay centered, grounded, and unshaken in response to a stimulus. Now, don't confuse non-reactivity with non-feeling. Let's use road rage as an example. You're driving, and someone cuts you off, and in response to being cut off you flip the driver the bird. You've just behaved reactively.
>
> Contrast that with what non-reactivity would look like in that scenario: You are cut off by the driver, and rather than focusing your attention on the event itself, you focus it on you. You focus it on the sensations you are feeling in your body, most likely a fast heart rate, perhaps a tightness in the chest, or constricted breathing. Then you shift your attention to your breathing, sending the breath into the parts of your body that are feeling the anger—your heart, your chest—wherever it is for you. In the time it took you to do this exercise, you never even thought about flipping the driver the bird because you were too busy focusing on your reaction; that driver has probably gone on his or her merry way by now. This is non-reactivity.
>
> Non-reactivity allows us to feel all of our feelings but not react to them. We feel them until we organically feel something else or until we decide mindfully, with awareness and choicefulness, that either we want to focus on something else or we want to act.

Is The Earth Angry?

As I sit with the BP disaster, other emotions course through my body—deep, deep grief; fear, despair, and helplessness, and I have to wonder about the emotions of the earth itself. And since I believe that Gaia is a living, breathing organism, I must correct my use of "the earth itself" and state unequivocally that I believe *she* must be very, very angry. Within the past two years prior to the BP disaster, we have witnessed what many believe is an unprecedented number of natural disasters. Although officials from the U.S. Geological Survey insist that the number of earthquakes has not increased in recent years, many question that conclusion. Is Gaia "working through" her Five Stages of Grief? And if she is angry, what might she do next?

Perhaps those questions feel too anthropocentric to the reader, so I refer to the natural process of homeostasis which is "the ability of a system or living organism to adjust to its internal environment to maintain a stable equilibrium."[53] When a system is out of balance, some internal process attempts to adjust the imbalance and return it to a state of balanced functioning.

In a 2008 interview with C-Realm Podcast, Albert Bartlett, emeritus professor of physics at the University of Colorado at Boulder and author of *The Essential Exponential for Our Planet*, stated, regarding population and unlimited growth, "If we don't stop it now, then Nature will stop it through a big die-off." Bartlett argues that population and economic growth spell annihilation for the planet if humans do not radically change their ways of occupying our planet.

One might argue that if Bartlett's theory is so, it is all a matter of simple physics and that speaking of earth's anger is pure anthropocentrism. Yet the distinguished doctor of medicine and biophysics, James Lovelock, who penned the book *The Revenge of Gaia*, argues in that work, as he does in many places, that humans have created out-of-control global warming and climate change which are now wreaking revenge on our species. Lovelock too may be indulging in rampant anthropocentrism, but if the earth itself has conscious self-awareness, both Bartlett and Lovelock may be onto something.

While we cannot validate with certainty earth's anger, we can certainly attest to our own in the face of humanity's devastation of the ecosystems. And while I do not concur with some in the field of psychology who argue that anger isn't really a fundamental human emotion but a kind of mask for other feelings such as fear and grief, I do believe that in the case of our anger toward members of our species who are committing ecological suicide, it is crucial that we connect with our grief and terror regarding the state of the planet and the dire consequences of industrial civilization which we are now beginning to experience.

In the short term, anger may be useful in motivating us to act—to prepare for the coming chaos, to help raise the awareness of others, and to inspire others to prepare, but if we allow ourselves to fully grasp the calamitous reality of the future into which we are moving, I believe that our anger will soon be eclipsed by fear, grief, and despair. For this reason, in this book I have devoted more attention to those emotions than to anger.

In an angry, chaotic world, it will be important for us to read the deeper emotions that underlie the rage we are likely to see erupting in society and in our communities. We will need to fortify ourselves emotionally and logistically from the collateral damage that myriad wounded-animal outbursts from others could inflict upon us, and even more importantly, not allow our egos to succumb to the momentary pleasure our own indulgence in rage might afford. At the same time we validate the rage our fellow humans feel, our compassion must penetrate the vitriol and understand the shipwreck that any human soul might become after years of sailing the waters of dogged denial and unwarranted faith in the American dream. If you are reading these words, it is likely that you have awakened from the dream or are in the process of doing so. Millions more never have and never will. How will we hold all of our emotions in the face of the rage that their sense of betrayal will evoke in them? How will we go on loving the world?

CONFRONTING AND CONTEMPLATING
(Writing answers to these questions or drawing images in relation to them in a journal is highly recommended.)

1. In your journal, describe in detail everything you know about your anger. Creating a symbol for this may be helpful, but it is important to be able to articulate your knowledge of your anger, how it feels in your body, when it gets triggered, and how you respond to it.

2. When you see or hear other people expressing anger, what happens inside you? How do you take care of yourself in an angry environment?

3. What do you hate about the world? What angers you, sickens you, scares you, and what feeds your despair about living on this planet?

4. Ponder Mary Oliver's poem at the beginning of this chapter and write about what you love about the world.

5. Does your work cause you to "stand still and learn to be astonished"? If so, explain? If not, what kind of work might facilitate that response?

6. Re-read Jennifer Franklin's quote on mindfulness and anger in this chapter. Practicing mindfulness in the face of any emotion is tremendously useful. We can be mindful of ourselves in the midst of anger, grief, fear, despair, and joy. For one day, commit to practicing mindfulness in the context of all emotions—your own and those you see expressed. How do you do this? Pay attention to your body's reactions; pay attention to your breath, and as you notice the emotions emerging from within and that you witness in the world, breathe into them. Really notice what is happening inside of you. Feel free to journal about it if you like.

Chapter 14: Cultivating Compassion Amid Chaos

If you want others to be happy, practice compassion. If you want to be happy, practice compassion.

~ Dalai Lama~

Compassion is the ultimate and most meaningful embodiment of emotional maturity. It is through compassion that a person achieves the highest peak and deepest reach in his or her search for self-fulfillment.

~Arthur Jersild~

When compassion fills my heart,
free from all desire,
I sit quietly like the earth.
My silent cry echoes like thunder
throughout the universe.

~Rumi~

Let's get loose
With
Compassion,

Let's drown in the delicious
Ambience of
Love.

~Hafiz~

When I contemplate preparing on any level for navigating a chaotic world, the quality of compassion is not the first thing that leaps to mind. Instead, I sense the need for discernment, discrimination, self-sufficiency, cooperation, perseverance, and stealth. Yet I suspect that the Long Emergency will test our compassion beyond anything we can now imagine. Consequently, it will confront us repeatedly with decisions about priorities regarding our survival and the survival of others.

A number of definitions of compassion have been captured in this quote from Wikipedia online:

> Compassion is an emotion that is a sense of shared suffering, most often combined with a desire to alleviate or reduce the

suffering of another; to show special kindness to those who suffer. Compassion essentially arises through empathy, and is often characterized through actions, wherein a person acting with compassion will seek to aid those they feel compassionate for.

Compassionate acts are generally considered those which take into account the suffering of others and attempt to alleviate that suffering as if it were one's own. In this sense, the various forms of the Golden Rule are clearly based on the concept of compassion.

Compassion differs from other forms of helpful or humane behavior in that its focus is primarily on the alleviation of suffering.

Some scientific studies suggest that people who consciously practice compassion produce higher levels of the anti-stress hormone DHEA and lower levels of the stress hormone, cortisol. Overwhelmingly, people who practice compassion report that they feel happier and more at peace.

In less chaotic times, it is easier to practice compassion when we are likely to have less contact with suffering people. In a collapsing world where we encounter misery more often, it may be much more challenging to express compassion. For example, if one person in your neighborhood has lost their job and is deeply anxious because they cannot find another job, you feel your heart going out to that person, and you may want to share food with them, suggest contacts you know who might be able to help them find a job, or take up a collection in the neighborhood to help them pay their utility bills. However, if twenty people in your neighborhood have lost their jobs and if some are struggling with depression, one or two have attempted or committed suicide, and two or three other families are shattered by domestic abuse, you may soon feel overwhelmed. As a result, you may begin experiencing another aspect of compassion which is compassion fatigue.

What will make a chaotic world chaotic is not just the wheels flying off of industrial civilization, but the wheels flying off of individual lives and families. Anyone reading these words who happens to survive and remain reasonably intact emotionally, will be surrounded with people who are mired in various stages of post-traumatic stress disorder. In some cases it may be dangerous to engage with them as they may become violent. In other cases, they may be severely depressed, disoriented, hysterical, or even psychotic. Children and the elderly will be especially vulnerable in a collapsing world because services for them will probably be non-existent, and they may be abandoned by desperate relatives who are so distressed that they feel incapable of caring for any dependents. As is always the case in any natural disaster, tens of thousands of pets will be abandoned and left behind to fend for themselves. In summary, millions of innocent beings will be casualties of the chaos, and anyone who is not is likely to be challenged emotionally, mentally, physically, and spiritually beyond anything they can now imagine.

Being Compassionate Yet Protecting Oneself

So how does one maintain compassion at the same time one needs to protect oneself physically and mentally? How does one offer assistance and support without becoming overwhelmed, burned out, or risking bodily harm? Decisions now unthinkable about who lives and who dies may have to be made. Physically and mentally intact individuals will need to determine when it is appropriate to help and when it isn't. How then does one remain compassionate and hold these bone marrow realities in one's body at the same time?

I have no simple answers to these questions. Here again, we are confronted with realities far greater than the human ego and the rational mind. Perhaps we have no way of knowing the answers until we are in the middle of the chaos. What I do know is that every person in the kinds of situations I've been describing and which the collapse of industrial civilization is likely to manifest will need to have built a very strong "internal bunker" as discussed in Chapter One of this book in order to persevere. Spiritual practice as well as emotional alchemical adeptness will be crucial.

One reason I have included extensive material in this book regarding human emotion is that compassion grows out of nowhere but the fertile ground of human suffering. Compassion cannot be created intellectually by reading books or listening to lectures about it by spiritual teachers. We *feel* compassion because we have felt the depths of our own anguish. Human suffering creates empathy in the sufferer unless the psyche of the sufferer has become overwhelmed, in which case, the psyche may shut down and become numb, violent, or may dissociate. Empathy is the capacity to feel with the suffering of another person, and industrial civilization has often been commandeered by individuals who have no capacity for experiencing empathy or who, if they have the capacity, have buried it deep in the psyche in the name of profit, progress, and self-gratification. Consequently, compassion is not valued or freely expressed in modern culture. In fact, to even speak the word results in being labeled a "bleeding heart" or a "touchy-feely" personality. If you Google the word "compassion," you will sooner or later find a website on "pity politics"—one indication of the inability to distinguish between compassion or feeling *with* the suffering of others, and pity which results from a top-down perspective of feeling sorry *for* someone.

For me, compassion is not an all-or-nothing emotion which I either feel one-hundred percent or don't. I feel degrees of compassion depending on the situation, persons involved, and my own emotional state. We cannot manufacture the emotion; something in us has to be moved sufficiently in order to experience it. Other emotions can obscure our compassion. For example, if one is angry or terrified, one may not be as easily moved to compassion as at other times.

Equally important is the ability, in some instances, to distance oneself from compassion if one is feeling overwhelmed. Compassion fatigue is real, and if the emotion is not carefully managed, it can lead to burnout, numbness, bitterness, or other reactions that paralyze us or prevent us from navigating chaos skillfully.

Anyone who is committed to the path of becoming a "warrior of vulnerability" is very likely to feel compassion intensely as collapse accelerates and the unraveling becomes more dire. The more consciously self-aware of our own suffering we are, the deeper we are likely to feel compassion, and the more sincerely it is likely to be experienced by those for whom we feel the emotion. This is why we cannot muster compassion within ourselves in response to moral or religious teachings about it. No matter how much we may intellectually know that we "should" feel it, it must erupt from our hearts and bodies in order to be authentically demonstrated.

Another way of saying this is simply that commitment to the path of becoming a warrior of vulnerability and practicing emotional alchemy is not only personally transformative but socially revolutionary. Allowing the soul to descend into the dark emotions with conscious intention to heal our broken-ness not only makes restoration of one's own psyche possible, but can radically alter how we perceive and meet the suffering of the entire earth community.

Michael Dowd, author of *Thank God for Evolution*, emphasizes that compassion is an aspect of our integrity as are responsibility and accountability. It means "stepping into the shoes of those we have harmed, and then making amends—while cultivating compassion for ourselves and others."[54] In the culture of industrial civilization we have been programmed to compete and to be "right." In fact, compassion is often considered anti-integrity. Any suggestion of adopting the perspective of a perceived adversary is considered disloyal, spineless, or naïve. It is assumed that if one has any "self-respect" at all, one will not kowtow to the enemy.

Compassion Makes Us Vulnerable

Yet we must question the notion of "self-respect" when the compassion-phobic tell us that that emotion threatens it. Again, I refer to the Jimenez poem at the beginning of Chapter One which confronts us with the question of who or what the self is. My human ego or personal mind adamantly insists that I have rights and that I must be vigilant and defend myself against anyone or anything that is a threat to my ego. From that perspective, projection, blame, paranoia, greed, attacking or belittling the other is "necessary" for my survival. The human ego is not that far removed from the reptilian brain which operates primarily from a fight-or-flight landscape. What distinguishes the human from the non-human is our ability to operate from conscious self-awareness to access the sacred Self and in the process, have the capacity to distinguish between it and the ego.

As Alexander Solzhenitsyn reminds us in *The Gulag Archipelago*:

 If only it were all so simple! If only there were evil people
somewhere insidiously committing evil deeds, and it were
necessary only to separate them from the rest of us and destroy
them. But the line dividing good and evil cuts through the heart
of every human being. And who is willing to destroy a piece of
his own heart?

A pivotal aspect of compassion is the visceral experience of knowing, when we view any member of the earth community that is broken, that there but for the grace of something greater, go any one of us. What is called for is allowing the heart to be broken open, then adopting a warrior sensibility that is willing to defend and protect that which is suffering.

Our compassion and willingness to intervene on behalf of the suffering may be enormously challenged in a chaotic world. We may find ourselves unwilling to open to people who in the past may have criticized or shamed us for preparing for a chaotic world. Deliciously tempting will be the ego's favorite line: I told you so. Likewise, we may find ourselves resistant to comforting the formerly wealthy, entitled, and arrogant who stand before us broken and impoverished. The ego will argue mercilessly that they have gotten exactly what they deserved, and that they do not merit our compassion.

Yet as anyone knows who is reading these words, there is no guarantee that any of us will survive. However, if we do, we are likely, sooner or later, to require the compassion of others whether we are struggling to survive illness, injury, loss of loved ones and all things familiar, mental exhaustion, hunger, or thirst. A collapsing world is likely to be a profound equalizer in which the cliché "we are all in this together" will take on an entirely new meaning.

Compassion is a skill that evolves from practice. None of us is perfectly compassionate. On some occasions, we are skillfully compassionate; on other occasions, our attempts are woefully inadequate. However, it is essential that part of our preparation for the future be the conscious practice of compassion which must issue from a feeling in the heart, translated into meaningful, skillful action on behalf of a broken, withering earth community.

CONFRONTING AND CONTEMPLATING
(Writing answers to these questions or drawing images in relation to them in a journal is highly recommended.)

1. Think about the people in your life who currently chide you for taking the collapse of industrial civilization seriously. Perhaps you have endured months or years of their ridicule. Perhaps they have even called you mentally ill. Now imagine a scenario in which they have lost everything, have become destitute and in need of food, water, and shelter. They come to you and ask you for help. What is your gut response? What emotions do you feel in your body as you think of this? What does your ego want to say to them? Write about this in full detail. Do not minimize your feelings. The purpose of this exercise is not to "be nice" but to be truthful. Don't focus on the practicalities of whether you have help to give them, but simply on what your ego feels as you hear their request.

2. Imagine that you are approached for help by a formerly wealthy white male corporate CEO who has lost everything including his family. He is destitute, wearing torn clothing, has lost 50 pounds, is disheveled and dirty, hungry, and thirsty. As the former CEO of one of the top weapons corporations on earth, he has colluded in the murder of millions of people. His industry has also been responsible for the destruction of incalculable numbers of acres of the Amazon rainforest. He is on his knees weeping and begging for your assistance. As you imagine this scenario, what do you feel? What does your ego say? Again, write about this scenario in full detail.

3. Choose one person in your life who you believe has harmed you. It could be in more recent times, or it could be much earlier in your life. Write in your journal the details of how you think this person harmed you. What did they say or do? Pay attention not only to the details of their actions and words, but especially to your feelings about these.

   After you have written about this in detail, put aside your journal and make sure you will not be distracted. Sit in a comfortable chair and close your eyes. Take several deep breaths—inhaling as slowly and deeply as possible and exhaling as deeply and slowly as possible. Then begin to breathe normally. Now think about this person who you think harmed you, and pretend for a few moments that you *are* that person. Move into their perspective. Imagine yourself as that person, seeing you. Imagine them being interviewed and being asked to give their opinion of you. What would they say?

   Now come back from your visualization experience and write about what happened in your visualization in your journal. Did you at any time during the visualization or during your writing notice any feeling of compassion for that person? If so, write about that. If not, don't worry or try to manufacture compassion. Just move on.

Now or after sitting with this exercise a couple of days, write in your journal, an apology to this person. DO NOT JUSTIFY YOUR ACTIONS IN ANY WAY. Share with them the extent to which you have entered their perspective and the extent to which you see and feel what they saw and felt. This is not about "getting to the truth" but rather entering into their perspective. Take as much time as you need to complete the letter, but COMPLETE IT.

Now write in your journal what it was like, from beginning to end, to do this exercise. Some people would encourage you to actually send this letter of apology to the person. I do not feel a sense of urgency about this. From my perspective, what matters most is that you entered into the perspective of the other person, even if just for a few moments. If later on, you want to actually apologize to the person, that is your choice. What is most important, I believe, is thoroughly engaging in the process of this exercise.

4. Think about someone in your life who has harmed you or who you think has harmed you. While it is important to acknowledge the harm, take some time to think about how the harm done by this person has in some way, helped you. What did they "teach" you? What were the gifts in this experience to you?

5. Think about the person in the last exercise or another person who has harmed you. What is your "shared suffering"? How have you both suffered in similar ways? What aspects of suffering do you both have in common? Write about this in detail in your journal.

6. How do you take care of yourself to protect yourself from "compassion fatigue"? In what situations are you vulnerable to it? What happens when you don't protect yourself? What happens when you do?

Chapter 15: Courage—Compassion Embodied and Fulfilled

I have come into this world to see this:
the sword drop from men's hands even at the height
of their arc of anger
because we have finally realized there is just one flesh to wound
and it is His - the Christ's, our
Beloved's.
I have come into this world to see this: all creatures hold hands as
we pass through this miraculous existence we share on the way
to even a greater being of soul,
a being of just ecstatic light, forever entwined and at play
with Him.
I have come into this world to hear this:
every song the earth has sung since it was conceived in
the Divine's womb and began spinning from
His wish,
every song by wing and fin and hoof,
every song by hill and field and tree and woman and child,
every song of stream and rock,
every song of tool and lyre and flute,
every song of gold and emerald
and fire,
every song the heart should cry with magnificent dignity
to know itself as
God:
for all other knowledge will leave us again in want and aching --
only imbibing the glorious Sun
will complete us.
I have come into this world to experience this:
men so true to love
they would rather die before speaking
an unkind
word,
men so true their lives are His covenant --
the promise of
hope.
I have come into this world to see this:

the sword drop from men's hands
even at the height of
their arc of
rage
because we have finally realized
there is just one flesh
we can wound.

~ Hafiz ~

I want to begin the chapter by noticing how much courage is required to pick up this book and read it up to this point. The fact that you are even drawn to read this book, let alone the possibility that you may resonate with its contents could put you at a distinct advantage in a chaotic world because it demonstrates the extraordinary quality which is the focus of this chapter.

The origin of the word *courage,* whether in ancient or modern languages, is related to the heart. If traced far enough, we see that *courage* and *core* are also related. From this we can deduce that courage for the ancients was not primarily synonymous with bravery, as some dictionaries indicate, but was connected with emotion that originates from the heart. Curiously, in word etymology, we don't find *mind* or *thought* used as synonyms for *core.* Humans seem to have sensed from the earliest times that the heart is the core of who we are as humans and that it is from our core that courage comes forth.

Courage Is Not Heroic

This suggests that courage cannot be manufactured or even learned. It can be instilled neither by military boot camp training nor by role models of courage. Nor is courage a heroic attribute. I define heroic as the notion that something or someone can and must prevail, no matter what.

The hero is an archetype or universal theme in human consciousness, and ancient mythology is filled with tales of the hero and the heroic. One aspect of spirit obsession is heroism, the culture of the United States of America being a poster child for it. Heroism is attended by competition, and in heroic cultures, what matters most is winning; losing and loss are not tolerated.

Heroism has been useful during some aspects of American history such as the Great Depression and World War II when the country adopted a "we can" attitude in facing unprecedented challenges to its values and economic status. More recently, however, the nation has foolishly persisted in clinging to this attitude in the face of the collapse of industrial civilization, refusing to name the present unraveling as such and persevering in the delusion that a "we can" mindset will reverse ghastly unemployment numbers, the economic devastation rendered by a gangster financial system, energy depletion, and massive environmental cataclysm around the planet, the Gulf Oil Disaster being only one of thousands of examples.

Mythopoetically speaking, the hero is paradoxically redeemed when he can admit defeat and allow his fall from triumph to transport him into transformation. It is then that he discovers his sacred Self and his greater purpose in the world. This motif has been replicated innumerable times throughout history, and in the twenty-first century, industrial civilization is now playing out the early chapters of the all-too-familiar story. My work for the past decade has been about assisting our species in choosing defeat in order to find its rightful and most salutary place in the earth community.

The Courage-Compassion Connection

The previous chapter focused on compassion, but that quality has no value without courage. A heroic culture perceives compassion as passive and cowardly, yet courage is the irrevocable, unequivocal outcome of compassion because compassion by definition leads to action. That does not necessarily mean that if one feels compassion for another, one must immediately take action to alleviate the suffering of the other. In some instances, that would not be humanly possible. For example, I feel compassion for the dolphins mercilessly decimated by the Gulf oil disaster, but I cannot personally rescue them. What I might be able to do is help fund an organization that is assisting the dolphins or volunteer with it.

Compassion will literally *drive* us to act, but we must be discerning about how, when, and where we act, not only to avoid compassion fatigue and a misallocation of energy, but because it is important to act in accordance with one's higher purpose. For example, I feel compassion for the homeless who are suffering in a plethora of ways, but I may not possess the talents and skills to assist them that someone else has who feels that their purpose is to work with the homeless. Likewise, that person may not be drawn to writing and teaching as I have been for most of my life.

Moreover, what we are "drawn to" is not the only criteria. Yet another archetype that all humans possess is that of the warrior. In modern cultures, "warrior" has become synonymous with "warmonger," "macho," and "having balls." For the ancients, a warrior was someone who defended and protected the community. While it may be tempting to call a soldier fighting in Afghanistan or Iraq a warrior because he or she is perceived as protecting the community, these particular wars have revealed that what soldiers are "protecting" are the last remaining drops of oil and oil pipelines in strategic locations of the world, heroin trafficking which helps finance the war and the American economy, and the image of America as the most powerful nation on earth. We need only observe the unprecedented number of military suicides in these wars to notice the discrepancy between the warrior archetype and what passes for warriorhood today. Warriors in ancient times rarely took their own lives because they genuinely perceived their role as protectors of the community whose code of honor determined that they must either prevail over the enemy or die in the process of doing so.

Derrick Jensen frequently tells the story of the Native American Cheyenne dog soldier who in the heat of battle drove his picket pin, to which he was tied with a rope, into the ground and remained there until either he won or was relieved by another dog soldier or was killed by the enemy. Jensen asks the question to his audience, "Where will you drive your picket pin?" In other words, where will you stand your ground with those forces that are murdering the earth? When and where will you say "enough!" and not move?

Bill Plotkin states that "…when the warrior defends the life of her community, she thinks, feels, and acts on behalf of the entire biosphere, not merely the human dimension of it."[55] The modern "warrior" who enlists to fight for his/her country is not fighting for the biosphere; in fact, she or he may become profoundly victimized by the same toxic chemicals that are destroying it. Countless veterans returning from Iraq and Afghanistan have serious chronic health issues as a result of being exposed to things like depleted uranium and a host of toxic chemicals.

We can deduce from the experiences of modern-day "warriors" that they almost always feel trapped in a long-term military strategy that has nothing to do with victory but rather, with perpetuating the earth-annihilating agenda of industrial civilization. Like the Cheyenne dog solider, the Western soldier in Afghanistan or Iraq has essentially three choices for dealing with the trauma and absurdity of war, but the choices are far different from the picket pin scenario. He can desert and live in another country that is not his native land, he can commit suicide, or he can more vigorously engage in the barbaric behavior he has been ordered to carry out, becoming addicted to combat, and therefore decompensating into a brutally violent human being who is fundamentally unfit to return to civilian life. Recent movies such as "The Hurt Locker" and "Brothers" depict this tragic reality, pervasive among modern soldiers.

Authentic warriorhood is inextricably connected with compassion as this old Korean fairytale reminds us, offering many lessons regarding courage:

The Wife and The Tiger's Whisker

Once upon a time, a young wife named Yun Ok was at her wit's end. Her husband had always been a tender and loving soulmate before he had left for the wars, but ever since he returned home he was cross, angry, and unpredictable. She was almost afraid to live with her own husband. Only in glancing moments did she catch a shadow of the husband she used to know and love.

When one ailment or another bothered people in her village, they would often rush for a cure to a hermit who lived deep in the mountains. Not Yun Ok. She always prided herself that she could heal her own troubles. But this time was different. She was desperate.

As Yun Ok approached the hermit's hut, she saw the door was open. The old man said without turning around, "I hear you. What's your problem?"

She explained the situation. His back still to her, he said, "Ah yes, it's often that way when soldiers return from the war. What do you expect me to do about it?"

"Make me a potion!" cried the young wife. "Or an amulet, a drink, whatever it takes to get my husband back the way he used to be."

The old man turned around. "Young woman, your request doesn't exactly fall into the same category as a broken bone or ear infection."

"I know," said she.

"It will take three days before I can even look into it. Come back then."

Three days later, Yun Ok returned to the hermit's hut. "Yun Ok," he greeted her with a smile, "I have good news. There is a potion that will restore your husband to the way he used to be, but you should know that it requires an unusual ingredient. You must bring me a whisker from a live tiger."

"What?" she gasped. "Such a thing is impossible!"

"I cannot make the potion without it!" he shouted, startling her. He turned his back. "There is nothing more to say. As you can see, I'm very busy."

That night Yun Ok tossed and turned. How could she get a whisker from a live tiger?

The next day before dawn, she crept out of the house with a bowl of rice covered with meat sauce. She went to a cave on the mountainside where a tiger was known to live. She clicked her tongue very softly as she crept up, her heart pounding, and carefully set the bowl on the grass. Then, trying to make as little noise as she could, she backed away.

The next day before dawn, she took another bowl of rice covered with meat sauce to the cave. She approached the same spot, clicking softly with her tongue. She saw that the bowl was empty, replaced the empty one with a fresh one, and again left, clicking softly and trying not to break twigs or rustle leaves, or do anything else to startle and unsettle the wild beast.

So it went, day after day, for several months. She never saw the tiger (thank goodness for that! she thought) though she knew from footprints on the ground that the tiger---and not a smaller mountain creature---had been eating her food. Then one day as she approached, she noticed the tiger's head poking out of its cave. Glancing downward, she stepped very carefully to the same spot and with as little noise as she could, set down the fresh bowl and, her heart pounding, picked up the one that was empty.

After a few weeks, she noticed the tiger would come out of its cave as it heard her footsteps, though it stayed a distance away (again, thank goodness! she thought, though she knew that someday, in order to get the whisker, she'd have to come closer to it).

Another month went by. Then the tiger would wait by the empty food bowl as it heard her approaching. As she picked up the old bowl and replaced it with a fresh one, she could smell its scent, as it could surely smell hers.

"Actually," she thought, remembering its almost kittenish look as she set down a fresh bowl, "it is a rather friendly creature, when you get to know it." The next time she visited, she glanced up at the tiger briefly and noticed what a lovely downturn of reddish fur it had from over one of its eyebrows to the next. Not a week later, the tiger allowed her to gently rub its head, and it purred and stretched like a house cat.

Then she knew the time had come. The next morning, very early, she brought with her a small knife. After she set down the fresh bowl and the tiger allowed her to pet its head she said in a low voice, "Oh, my tiger, may I please have just one of your whiskers?" While petting the tiger with one hand, she held one whisker at its base, and with the other hand, in one quick stroke, she carved the whisker off. She stood up, speaking softly her thanks, and left, for the last time.

The next morning seemed endless. At last her husband left for the rice fields. She ran to the hermit's hut, clutching the precious whisker in her fist. Bursting in, she cried to the hermit, "I have it! I have the tiger's whisker!"

"You don't say?" he said, turning around. "From a live tiger?"

"Yes!" she said.

"Tell me," said the hermit, interested. "How did you do it?"

Yun Ok told the hermit how, for the last six months, she had earned the trust of the creature and it had finally permitted her to cut off one of its whiskers. With pride she handed him the whisker. The hermit examined it, satisfied himself that it was indeed a whisker from a live tiger, then flicked it into the fire where it sizzled and burned in an instant.

"What have you done?" Yun Ok cried, horrified.

"Yun Ok," the hermit said softly, "you no longer need the whisker. Tell me, is a man more vicious than a tiger? If a dangerous wild beast will respond to your gradual and patient care, do you think a man will respond any less willingly?"

Yun Ok stood speechless. Then she turned and stepped down the trail, turning over in her mind images of the tiger and of her husband, back and forth. She knew what she could do.

With regard to this story, let me hasten to add that in no way do I offer it as a moral prescription regarding anyone's relationship with a person suffering from post-traumatic stress disorder. I want to emphasize that it is a myth and is therefore meant to be interpreted symbolically. I have included it here because it speaks to the contrast between courage and heroism. The wife in this story demonstrates phenomenal courage motivated by love. In the process she becomes a spiritual warrior who because she is willing to be re-made by her initiatory experience, has the capacity to assist others in the transformation process.

Warrior and Killer Are Not Synonymous

In a chaotic world, killers may be a dime a dozen, but warriors are likely to be few and far between. Echoing the quote above by Solzhenitsyn, Joanna Macy reminds us that the line between good and evil runs through the landscape of every human heart. But in the Mahayana Buddhist tradition, the bodhisattva is the hero because that person is willing to use his/her wisdom to help liberate all of the earth community. The use of "hero" in this context is synonymous with warrior. As Plotkin explains, the ancient Shambhala warrior was seen as a person of great courage, both morally and physically, whose task would be to enter the realms of barbarian power and dismantle the weapons of domination. That warrior's weapons were compassion and insight which profoundly informed his courage.

Authentic emotional and spiritual preparation for navigating the coming chaos must necessarily involve training in a kind of Shambhala warriorhood in which we will be smitten with compassion, yet must be discerning enough to direct our compassion wisely in order to avoid compassion fatigue and preserve personal safety. It will require us to be physically, emotionally, and spiritually fit—to be stealthy and as Jesus taught, "wise as serpents and harmless as doves." The ability to "read" other human beings and listen with our hearts as well as our ears to the earth community will be crucial. There will be no place for hubris-based heroism in a chaotic world because heroism is likely to be personally dangerous and collectively useless.

Coming to us across twelve centuries is the Shambhala prophecy which emerged from ancient Tibetan Buddhism. The prophecy foretells of a time when all life on Earth is in danger. Great barbarian powers have arisen. Although these powers spend much of their wealth in preparations to annihilate each other, they have much in common: weapons of unfathomable destructive power, and technologies that lay waste our world. In this era, when the future of sentient life hangs by the frailest of threads, the kingdom of Shambhala emerges.

In her book, *Coming Back to Life* and in her workshops, Joanna Macy tells the story of the Shambhala:

> You cannot go there, for it is not a place; it is not a geopolitical entity. It exists in the hearts and minds of the Shambhala warriors. That is the term the prophecy used – "warriors." You cannot recognize the Shambhala warrior when you see him or her, for they wear no uniforms or insignia, and they carry no

specific banners. They have no barricades on which to climb or threaten the enemy, or behind which they can hide to rest or regroup. They do not even have any home turf. Always they must move on the terrain of the barbarians themselves.

Now the time comes when great courage — moral and physical courage — is required of the Shambhala warriors, for they must go into the very heart of the barbarian power, into the pits and pockets and citadels where the weapons are kept, to dismantle them. To dismantle weapons, in every sense of the word, they must go into the corridors of power where decisions are made.

The Shambhala warriors have the courage to do this because they know that these weapons are "manomaya." They are mind made. Made by the human mind, they can be unmade by the human mind....

So in this time, the Shambhala warriors go into training in the use of two weapons. The weapons are compassion and insight. Both are necessary, the prophecy foretells. The Shambhala warriors must have compassion because it gives the juice, the power, the passion to move. It means not to be afraid of the pain of the world. Then you can open to it, step forward, act. But that weapon by itself is not enough. It can burn you out, so you need the other — you need insight into the radical interdependence of all phenomena. With that wisdom you know that it is not a battle between "good guys" and "bad guys," because the line between good and evil runs through the landscape of every human heart. With insight into our profound inter-relatedness, you know that actions undertaken with pure intent have repercussions throughout the web of life, beyond what you can measure or discern. By itself, that insight may appear too cool, too conceptual, to sustain you and keep you moving, so you need the heat of compassion. Together these two can sustain us as agents of wholesome change. They are gifts for us to claim now in the healing of our world.

Many in the Tibetan lineage believe that this is the time of this ancient prophecy. If so, perhaps we are among the Shambhala warriors.

The functions of the warrior are intimately connected with those of the elder--- functions which will be explored in depth in a later chapter. Both the warrior and the elder are imbued with compassion, tempered by discernment in service of the community---standing guard on behalf of all other beings, both human and non-human. As in the story above, compassion compels us to take risks that require courage, and in the process, we are transformed into beings more capable of meeting others where they are, offering not heroism, but authentic healing.

CONFRONTING AND CONTEMPLATING
(Writing answers to these questions or drawing images in relation to them in a journal is highly recommended.)

1. This chapter opened with an acknowledgement of your courage in picking up this book and continuing to read it. What has challenged your courage since you began reading this book? How have you dealt with that? Write about that in your journal.

2. Think about a time in your life when you tried to be heroic. What happened? If you succeeded, how did that feel? If you failed, how did that feel? Explain this in journal writing.

3. Think about a time when your "defeat" proved to be advantageous, salutary, or in some way fortunate. What happened? What did you learn from the experience? Again, write about this.

4. What do you know about the compassionate warrior in you? (This is the place where compassion and courage meet in the non-heroic warrior.) How is it expressed? Explain this by writing in your journal. In what situations do you tend to lose compassion and become heroic? In what situations do you tend to lose the warrior and respond only with compassion?

5. Read the story of "The Wife and The Tiger's Whisker" at least two more times. Notice what grabbed you in the story. Write about that.

6. Write about an experience or event in your life when you have "driven your picket pin into the earth" and did not move. Remember, this is an act not motivated by being stubborn and clinging to one's position, but rather, standing one's ground on behalf of the integrity of the community. You may also want to create an image.

7. What acts of courage are you demonstrating or have you demonstrated in preparing for life in a chaotic world? This can be anything from having the courage to talk about it with others to relocating and building a sustainable homestead.

Chapter 16: The Joy of Mindful Preparation

The earth has disappeared beneath my feet,
It fled from all my ecstasy,

Now like a singing air creature
I feel the rose
Keep opening.

My heart turned to effulgent wings.
When has love not given freedom?
When has adoration not made one free?

A woman broken in tears and sweat
Stands in a field
Watching the sun and me
Trade jokes.

But never would Hafiz laugh
At your blessed labor
Of finding peace.

What do the dancing white birds say
Looking down upon burnt meadows?

All that you think is rain is not.
Behind the veil Hafiz and angels sometimes weep

Because most eyes are rarely glad
And your divine beauty is still too frightened
To unfurl its thousand swaying arms.

The earth has disappeared beneath my feet,
Illusion fled from all my ecstasy.

Now like a radiant sky creature
God keeps opening.

God keeps opening
Inside of Me.

~Hafiz~

Let's face it, preparing logistically or emotionally for the collapse of life as we have known it since arriving on this planet is not supposed to be fun. Certainly there are moments when we joke about it with trusted others as we stock our larder with food, water, medical supplies, and a host of other items we might wish to have stored for the Long Emergency. If we decide to relocate to a more sustainable part of the world, we may experience moments of excitement with family or friends who are accompanying us. If we are given to dark humor, there is no lack of fuel for that particular fire.

Yet, as we contemplate living in a chaotic world, joy is not the first emotion that leaps to mind. In fact, it is the one emotion that tends to get lost in the shuffle of preparation. We may "agonize as we organize" the logistics of navigating the future in terms of acquiring supplies, finding a sustainable location in which to reside, learning skills that will be necessary in a post-collapse world, building relationships with neighbors and community, planting gardens, raising chickens, or taking permaculture classes. Even our spiritual preparation is "work"—building an internal bunker? What, another preparation project?

However, as you dear reader may have discovered by now, while all of this requires effort, none of it has to be drudgery. For myself and for many of us who have been preparing for some years, the entire endeavor can, and I would suggest, *must* be imbued with joy.

As I dialog with countless conscious individuals engaged in preparing for the Long Emergency, without exception they tell me that if they could not create joy in their lives and balance preparation with play and creating beauty, they would probably give up because they would feel so much despair. Each person seems to have a unique way of experiencing joy, but in order for them to persevere, it has become a necessity in their daily routine, not a luxury. One man told me, "I eat some ice cream every night because it makes me happy." A woman said, "I get silly and goofy with my dogs every day because doing so brings me invigorating joy that revitalizes me and supports me to engage in another round of preparation."

Joyful and Mindful Preparation

Whether we actively practice a specific technique of mindfulness meditation or not, we are forced to become mindful in the process of preparing for the collapse of industrial civilization. One cannot be mindless and prepare consciously and intentionally at the same time. Yet even as we try on a plethora of "what if" scenarios in our minds, none of which are particularly pleasant, we can experience joy in preparing to navigate a chaotic world, and what is more, in the throes of that chaos, there very well may be moments of joy.

In Chapter 5, we considered the pleasure aspects of eros in relation to the world of the future in which thousands of things, experiences, and people that we now take for granted may become inexplicably dear to us in a milieu where our only contact with them may be in our memories. In that world, the tremendous losses we are likely to encounter will result in savoring and appreciating incredibly simple experiences and sensations, and doing so is likely to evoke deep feelings of joy.

Dominique Browning, author of *Slow Love: How I Lost My Job, Put On My Pajamas, And Found Happiness* states that "Slow Love is a way of being mindful, in whatever you are doing. It is a way of being open to the wonder and miracle of this world, falling open to it, and making sure you tap into that every day. It can be as simple as helping someone cross the street, enjoying the last bite of a farm fresh egg before heading to the sink, catching the sound of church bells, and really listening to their music."[56]

What speaks most audibly to me in Browning's prescription for contentment is that the more we lose in the future, the more crucial it will become to savor what we still have. "In the consumption society," writes Clive Hamilton, "economic growth can be sustained only as long as people remain discontented."[57] What is more, consumer society inculcates in us the belief that we are entitled to be happy. After all, it's written in the Declaration of Independence, right? All people are endowed by their Creator with the right to life, liberty, and the pursuit of happiness, yes? Actually, the original word Thomas Jefferson used in the Declaration was "property" not "happiness." Eventually, property was replaced with happiness, but even so, Colonial America did not perceive itself as entitled to happiness, nor did it perceive happiness as synonymous with accumulating worldly possessions.

A chaotic world will unequivocally test our capacity for experiencing a quality of happiness that I refer to as joy—the ability to access a treasure-trove of well being deep within ourselves that transcends our current conditions, whatever those may be. The end of the world as we have known it will shatter the happiness of many people, but at the same time, it may increase their joy. As author and death and dying counselor, Stephen Levine, notes: "The ironic thing is we have almost no contact with joy because of our obsession with happiness."

No matter how bleak the future may at times become, there will undoubtedly be moments of humor, laughter, and even giddiness. Part of supporting ourselves and our community in the Long Emergency will be creating moments or hours of joy when and where appropriate. These experiences cannot be contingent on sophisticated technology or even electricity. They will probably need to be simple, ingenious, and heartfelt.

In his 2010 article "(F)unemployment: Making The Best of It"[58], Vermont-based journalist, Frank Smecker notes that "With all this (f)unemployment going around, there is now more time to get out in the local community, relocalize, meet new people, foster new relationships, grow food together, find food together, restore landbases, take a break, hop on a bike, go swimming, watch the land come alive with animated life and then, resume community-based work."

While there is no "fun" in being without an income as expenses and debts pile up, like me, Smecker believes that employment as we know it will probably not exist a decade from now and that this time of massive unemployment creates space in our lives that allows us to prepare for a future of permanent unemployment.

No Gratitude, No Joy

In *Sacred Demise* I included a chapter on "Mirth-Making Amid Crumbling and Chaos" in which I focused on creating joy in the community. In the current chapter, I prefer to focus on creating joy within the individual psyche by practicing mindful living. A number of tools will be offered to assist the reader in this practice, and one of the most important, in my opinion, is the practice of gratitude.

Gratitude is an attitude of thankfulness and a sense of appreciation for what one has in the moment. It implies two things: Relationship and humility. The relationship aspect of gratitude means that when one feels grateful, there is something or someone or some force outside oneself to which one feels in some way indebted, as is obvious when one is grateful to another person for a gift or a kindness. In situations where one feels grateful for fortunate circumstances which don't directly involve another person, one is not grateful *to* anyone or anything but simply glad that things worked out as they did.

Even so, the very emotion or thought of gratitude implies that one is not oneself the origin of what one feels grateful for. I may say that it's "just the way things worked out," but I'm not responsible for "things" working out the way they did. Thus, I'm grateful for a particular turn of events. Nevertheless, a relationship with circumstances is implied, as is the reality that I am not in control of them but rather an observer. Of course, a sociopath like Joseph Stalin who said, "Gratitude is a sickness suffered by dogs" cannot experience gratitude because it requires empathy and the ability to appreciate oneself as a participant in the human condition. Gratitude is a state of mind that inherently recognizes interdependence with the external world whether it be other humans, nature, the sacred, or a combination of these.

In a time of colossal loss, which I anticipate a chaotic world will entail, gratitude for the ability to survive, to have food, water, shelter, companionship, reasonably good health, and the use of one's limbs and senses will be crucial. I imagine that a "glass half-full" perspective will soon supersede the "glass half-empty" outlook early on among those have understood and prepared in advance for the collapse of industrial civilization---especially those who have endeavored to prepare emotionally and spiritually. This has always been true in nations and societies experiencing collapse. In the most dire scenarios, being able to find one small thing every day for which one is grateful enhances resilience and the potential to survive. From the Nazi holocaust to the collapse of the Soviet Union to genocide in Bosnia or Rwanda, thousands of persecuted and displaced human beings have found solace and inspiration in gratitude.

Sacred Joy

In his extraordinary 2009 book, author and Director of The Institute for Sacred Activism, Andrew Harvey, writes in *The Hope: A Guide To Sacred Activism*[59] that seven types of joy are necessary in our lives as we navigate the death and rebirth of the current paradigm of industrial civilization.

**The Joy of Inspiration

This is the joy we find in mystical and ecstatic poetry, in beautiful music, in all of the arts, in meditation, and in being part of the transformation of consciousness in others. We may receive an inspiring communication that our presence or actions have made a difference in someone's life. Perhaps inspiration arrives in the form of a relationship with a child whose capacity for innocence, trust, or exuberance surpasses our own. It is important to remember that we can be inspired even in the throes of a chaotic world. In fact, we must be if we are to remain resilient and persevere.

**The Joy of Being in Nature

We have considered this form of inspiration in an earlier chapter, but in the melodious words of Andrew Harvey, "When I am inwardly tuned to the Beloved, all of Nature is revealed as radiant with the Presence; every stone and flea and squirrel and human being and the whole of Nature appears as a ceaselessly flowing epiphany of the Radiance."

In the above chapter on despair, I related my own experience of immersing myself in nature and allowing it to evoke all manner of emotion including "impassioned inspiration."

**The Joy of Sacred Friendship

The work to which we feel called in order to fulfill our purpose is an enormous act of friendship with the entire earth community. As we do that work, we need sacred friendships that sustain and inspire us. We need support and encouragement, and we need to offer it to our friends as well.

Extremely important in maintaining sacred friendships is the willingness to do our personal shadow work and own our part in the conflicts that will inevitably arise in any deep friendship. I have experienced that conflicts in friendships, while not pleasant to navigate, can ultimately bring forth joy for both parties as rough edges and disquieting feelings are dealt with honestly.

**The Joy of Sacred Friendship With Animals

Many readers of *Sacred Demise* were profoundly stirred by one chapter entitled "What The Creatures Can Teach Us." If we are serious about befriending the earth community, we must befriend other species. These may be household pets or creatures in the wild, but we can be certain that a world in chaos will become a treacherous if not impossible place for them to inhabit unless they are protected by us.

The joy of experiencing our own wild, animal self may be invaluable in a turbulent world, and it could at times become one of the few joys to which we have access.

**The Joy of Loving The Sacred With Heart and Mind

This is not about becoming religious or even abandoning atheism or agnosticism if one embraces those. I believe that an individual who identifies with either perspective can indeed appreciate the sacred and remain true to her disbelief. Since the word *sacred* simply means *set apart* or *reverently dedicated,* almost everyone identifies with an aspect of his/her life for to which these words apply.

The sacred to which Andrew Harvey refers has to do with the "something greater" that we have been considering throughout this book. The joy of loving the sacred means loving all manifestations of something greater wherever we find it, and particularly in other human beings. This means acknowledging the sacred in the other and allowing oneself to be humbled by it. In turn, Harvey suggests, "…you start to become more intimate and humble with others and to radiate increasingly toward them, in your ordinary life, the same sacred transparence."

**The Joy of Play

Here we encounter a concept I have repeatedly emphasized throughout this book and in all of my work and writings: the marriage of opposites. Preparing to live in a chaotic world, and of course navigating the Long Emergency, is very serious business, yet no matter how grave the conditions may become, we will undoubtedly encounter opportunities to play. These experiences are not likely to resemble the forms of play to which we are currently accustomed, but play will be an option, and play we must when we have the opportunity to do so. To be human is to play, and anything we can do with grace and respect that nourishes our humanity in a world unraveling will be blessedly life-affirming.

For some people, mindful preparation is not joyful, but it can be, and I believe that experiencing joy as we mindfully prepare may be more salutary than being driven by terror. We may not survive, but we will have had a good time attempting to do so, especially if we are not preparing alone and have the support of family or friends who join us in our efforts.

Take a moment to think about another person or family who is in total denial of the unfolding collapse. Perhaps they are living "normal" lives, unencumbered with concerns about the future. They work, play, watch TV, play video games, take vacations, enjoy summer barbecues and making winter snowmen. They sense intuitively that all is not well and that the future will be worse than the present, but they prefer to remain oblivious. They may even realize that some kind of preparation is necessary, but their attitude is simply: I'll deal with it when I have to.

Do they not appear to be "happier" than someone who is mindfully preparing for the future? Does not the person mindfully preparing "appear" to be less happy? From the outside, whose life looks more appealing? If we were to ask the "normal" family if they are happy, they would undoubtedly answer in the affirmative. If we asked them to tell us about joy in their lives, they would probably recount the kinds of activities I've mentioned above. If we were to ask the person or family mindfully preparing for the future to tell us about joy in their lives, we would probably hear very different definitions of the word "joy" from those given by the "normal" family. They might tell us that while they do not feel particularly joyful when they contemplate the future, they are finding meaning and perhaps even joy in mindfully preparing for it.

In a later chapter we shall consider the joyful task of creating beauty in the world. This chapter is intended to emphasize the need for integrating and accessing joy in our lives in the midst of a chaotic world. As we honor the necessity of joy in the human experience, let us notice that in the poem at the beginning of this chapter, Hafiz tells us that as a result of his ecstasy, "God keeps opening in me." He does not say that seriousness, piety, or devotion cause God to keep opening in him, but rather, ecstasy.

It is also important to notice that this chapter on joy concludes a section on becoming a warrior of vulnerability. We cannot consider joy without noticing that like the dark emotions, consciously feeling it increases our vulnerability and decreases our armoring. In situations of grief, loss, shame, disappointment, anger, frustration, and other unpleasant emotions, we tend to fortify the ego with a serious demeanor and an avoidance of humor. We naturally assume that aloof stoicism protects us, whereas opening to frivolity endangers us.

Joy, Vulnerability, and Healing

Feeling joyful does increase one's emotional vulnerability, and yet what we have considered so far in this book underscores openness to vulnerability and the capacity to consciously relax into our emotions as salutary choices even as we inhabit a volatile milieu. A chaotic world will no doubt present myriad opportunities to assess whether or not the tradeoff is worth the risk.

The mystics, such as Hafiz, were often deeply wounded people who had endured profound sorrow and loss in their lives. Their soul descent into the darkness rendered them capable of appreciating a full spectrum of emotions and moods, and they were able to hold uncanny opposites in one body, one heart. Through their ordeals, they learned viscerally that things are not always as they seem, and they developed the capacity to see more incisively into certain situations and discern the deeper reality of them. For those of us navigating the turbulent twenty-first century, on one level, the notion of a collapsing, unraveling, disintegrating world feels terrifying. But from the soul's perspective, informed by sacred joy, Hafiz asks and answers:

> What do the dancing white birds say
> Looking down upon burnt meadows?
>
> All that you think is rain is not.

CONFRONTING AND CONTEMPLATING
(Writing answers to these questions or drawing images in relation to them in a journal is highly recommended.)

1. List all of the ways in which you are preparing for living in a chaotic world. These would include: geographical location, shelter, food storage, access to water, medical supplies, livelihood, self-defense, community and family support. Perhaps you have made this kind of list many times, but it may be useful to do it again. As you have prepared or are preparing, have you encountered any moments of joy, lightness of heart, play, or humor in the process? Write about those in your journal.

2. As explained in Chapter 5 and again in the quote from Dominique Browning on "Slow Love," the losses of the collapse of industrial civilization are inviting us to slow down and savor those things in life which bring deep joy and pleasure. Since reading about this in Chapter 5 and again in this chapter, how are you practicing this principle in your life? Write in detail about your experiences with this. In other words, in this particular exercise, you are re-visiting Exercise 4 and 5 at the end of Chapter 5. The intention of the current exercise is to check in with yourself and notice your progress *or* fine tune it.

3. Experiment with "inflicting joy" in your world. Discreetly and appropriately spend an hour somewhere in your world creating laughter. For example, when a friend of mine takes his dog for a walk each day, he counts how many smiles the two of them "inflict" on the people they pass on the street. "Inflict" humor in the check-out line, at the post office, in the bank, on the job, or wherever you can appropriately do so.

4. What challenges do you notice around feeling and expressing gratitude? Right now, list 20 things in your life for which you clearly feel grateful. What do you experience as you list these?

5. Take some time to think about people in your life who have deeply influenced you, living or dead. You may like the way they influenced you, or not. Very often, the negative influences of people in our lives ultimately serve us in unanticipated ways. List 4 or 5 of these individuals. It may be very useful *for you* to write a letter of gratitude to them. You may choose never to send it, and of course, if they are not alive or if you are estranged from them, sending the letter is not an option. Nevertheless, choose one of these individuals and write a detailed letter thanking them for their influence in your life.

    If you feel the influence was positive, explain that specifically. If you feel the influence was negative, also explain that specifically and tell them how their negative influence was ultimately useful to you.

6. Choose 3 of the 7 Sacred Joys and write about how you experience them in your life. What evokes them? How do you engage in those joys? How do those joys energize you?

7. Take time to deeply contemplate the poem by Hafiz which opens this chapter. What lines grab your attention or move you emotionally? How is God or the Sacred, opening in you? Write about this in your journal.

Section IV

Elderhood at Any Age:
The Skillful Use of Inner Transition Tools

Chapter 17: Elders, Olders, Youngers, and Humanity's Next Rite of Passage

The ancient notion of the elders had less to do with political power and social leadership and more to do with healing and deeper knowledge. It used to be considered that each genuine elder had some form of healing to contribute to this world. An elder was a person who had survived the troubles of his own life and had gathered some wisdom from facing the darkness within as well as what troubled others.

~Michael Meade, *The World Behind The World*~

So it's interesting that in my elderhood, more than before, there's a physical sensation reflecting that. "When the heart breaks open, it can hold the whole universe." In that phrase is the major thrust of the work: redefining pain for the world as compassion, instead of pathologizing it as a sign of personal neurosis or personal failure.

~Joanna Macy, *Coming Back to Life*~

I live my life in widening circles
That reach out across the world.
I may not complete this last one
But I give myself to it.

I circle around God, around the primordial tower.
I've been circling for thousands of years
And I still don't know: am I a falcon,
A storm, or a great song?

~Rainer Maria Rilke~

As stated earlier, this book is not a manual of logistical preparation. Instead it offers specific tools for inner transition in preparation for navigating a chaotic world, but the use of any tool requires skill and practice. I recall being fascinated as a child with many of the tools in my father's workshop. I watched him use them and attempted to use them myself, sometimes successfully, and sometimes with great clumsiness. Occasionally, I even hurt myself by nicking a finger on a saw blade or inadvertently slamming a hammer on my thumb. Some of the tools I saw in my father's workshop I learned to use skillfully; others I never learned to use.

Emotional and spiritual preparation for the Long Emergency requires practice in order to skillfully navigate a world in chaos in which humans are likely to be psychologically tested and confronted with questions of meaning and purpose in unprecedented ways. We will become skillful using the tools in this book only as the soul deepens and emotional ordeals initiate us into elderhood.

The Deeper Meaning of "Elder"

Willingness to navigate darkness and "trouble" as Michael Meade and Malidoma Somé name it, and persevering until we arrive on the other side of it, are two of the hallmarks of maturing into elderhood. Yet it is crucial to understand that "elder" and "older" are not synonymous when considering soul maturity. We have all met "olders" who possess little if any wisdom, and we have met "youngers" who are filled with wisdom and profound knowledge.

Michael Meade reminds us in *The World Behind The World* that the indigenous notion of elderhood partially defines it as the ability to see seven generations down the line, which of course, means looking into the darkness. "Becoming an elder," Meade says, "involves learning to see in ways that go far beyond simple self-interest." Elders are deeply concerned with the well being of the youth which is why tribal elders supervise and carry out initiatory rituals. But beyond tending the youth, elders are the spiritual leaders of the entire community and agonize to attend to the tribe's constant need for healing and purification in order to keep it on a path that would preserve it intact forever.

An elder is an archetype as well as a literal person. Even if the role no longer exists, the archetype endures and emerges in some form in all societies. The role of a twenty-first century elder in a non-tribal society is different in terms of literal functioning but similar in terms of what the elder is asked to hold for the community. The culture of industrial civilization is delusional and unwilling, or in some cases, incapable, of seeing what is so. The elder must be willing to see, no matter what, and she must act accordingly. At the same time, the modern elder must be discerning about when to speak about the demise of civilization and how. Unlike the tribal elder, he will not be respected or acknowledged as a caring steward of the community and is likely to be tolerated at best or held in contempt at worst. Occasionally, those who resonate with elder consciousness or are in the process of becoming elders themselves will honor the elder's work and offer their support.

If you are reading this book, it is likely that you are drawn to it in part because, whatever age you may be, the elder in you is calling you to a particular role in which you may find yourself in a chaotic world. In the first place, if you understand that industrial civilization is collapsing and that the human race is transitioning across an evolutionary threshold in the process, that awareness in itself is an enormously significant aspect of elder consciousness. It demonstrates courage, wisdom, and a fundamental discernment of the current unfolding of world events.

It is likely that as collapse exacerbates, you will find yourself surrounded by a few others with strong elder consciousness and many more human beings who have absolutely no understanding of what is happening. You are likely to need every tool in this book and perhaps many more acquired from other places. You have every right to feel fear, sorrow, grief, despair, or any other unpleasant emotion in the throes of the unraveling because you are human, and it will be very important to treasure and not lose your humanity. At the same time, staying grounded and bonded to your sacred Self will be imperative.

For as long as you survive physically, you are likely to be perceived and mis-perceived by countless troubled souls around you as someone who holds a treasure that they do not yet know how to access within themselves. You may need to carefully guard against compassion fatigue or even being targeted by desperate individuals who are at a loss to understand your grounded wisdom and so may turn you into a target for their terror and frustration. You are likely to be challenged mightily in the midst of chaos and all of its attendant emotions to hold yourself and others in that milieu with compassion, wisdom, stealth, and grace. You will need to know when to guard your emotional boundaries and when to relax them—when to help and when to walk away—when to protect yourself and when to open up.

If these challenges sound super-human, they may be, and you may fail many times, but you are not being called to heroism. As I took great pains to explain in *Sacred Demise*, there is far more at stake here than your survival. We will all die at some point. What matters is that we know and are willing to do whatever it takes to fulfill our purpose and live from moment to moment with the question: Who do I want to be in the face of collapse? As well as the question: Am I willing to become a new kind of human being, and if so, what do I need to open to in order to become and help perpetuate that new species?

What Distinguishes The Elder?

In his 2009 book, *The Great Waves of Change: Navigating The Difficult Times Ahead*, which also offers a regimen of spiritual preparation for an unraveling world, Marshall Vian Summers emphasizes that "The very circumstances that people deny, reject, avoid, and are terrified of are the very circumstances that could redeem them, that could unite them within themselves and that could make them powerful and whole, effective and fulfilled."[60] And "Ultimately, the very circumstances that seem so threatening, overwhelming or disconcerting are the very circumstances that will enable your true gifts to come forward."[61]

As the unraveling intensifies, what distinguishes the elder from others who do not understand it is her willingness to be with what is so, to see incisively into the darkness, and to open to the collapse as a necessary evolutionary threshold. Thus Summers emphasizes that it is "so important to see what others cannot see, to feel what others will not feel and to do what others will not do."

And not only must the elder remain grounded throughout myriad Long Emergency scenarios, but as emphasized above, he must be willing to serve the broken bodies and souls around him. "Your spirituality will be about caring for people," Summers writes, "feeding people, serving people and taking care of the world around you."[62]

The first section of this book calls the reader to "build his internal bunker." Perhaps you have been pondering the coming chaos for some time and having read this book thus far, you are coming to understand why emotional and spiritual grounding are essential for navigating a world in demise. Perhaps now you understand why storing massive caches of food, water, medical supplies, and learning a variety of post-collapse survival skills are not enough.

Up to this point, I have not described possible scenarios, but overall, it might be useful to ask yourself how emotionally and spiritually equipped you are to deal with general scenarios such as: observing countless troubled or psychotic individuals around you; witnessing epidemic violence; being aware of untold numbers of physically ill human beings who cannot obtain healthcare; seeing a plethora of suffering children and elderly people who cannot care for themselves; sitting with people who are severely ill or dying; having to endure days of your own hunger or thirst; days or weeks of not being able to take a bath, shower, or brush your teeth; days or weeks of getting very little sleep, if any.

Where will your emotional and spiritual sustenance come from? Certainly not from your stored food or water catchment system or your solar oven. The emotional, spiritual, and possibly professional work you have been doing all your life may well have been preparing you for the future to which I am alluding. Or perhaps you feel you haven't been doing any work that adequately prepares you. Nevertheless, I believe that the tools in this book, if carefully applied, have the capacity to apprentice you as an elder in training.

Fortunately, at this time in our history, we have many role models for supporting our journey into elderhood: The late Thomas Berry, Miriam MacGillis, Vandana Shiva, Bill Plotkin, Michael Meade, Joanna Macy, Andrew Harvey, Marshall Vian Summers, Eckhart Tolle, Karen Armstrong, Riane Eisler, Alice Walker, Malidoma Somé, Sobonfu Somé, Richard Rohr, Thich Nhat Hanh, Pema Chodron, to name only a few. Our work is not to imitate or compare ourselves with them, but to utilize the wisdom they impart to support the calling we are answering in order to care for the earth community.

You didn't just fall out of the sky on the day of your birth for no reason, in random time. You came here at *this* time in order to experience the momentous events this book would prepare you for. Yes, this is the "trouble" you came here to get into, and as Michael Meade reminds us:

> When in the right trouble, we awaken to inner resources and
> draw upon what is second nature to us. When the common

solutions fail to help, we learn that we are carried by patterns beyond our usual awareness, by portions of eternity buried within from the very beginning. Trouble turns our lives upside down, but also inside out; so that the inclinations of the soul can be seen and known.[63]

CONFRONTING AND CONTEMPLATING
(Writing answers to these questions or drawing images in relation to them in a journal is highly recommended.)

1. Using the definition given in the first few pages of this chapter, think about whether or not you consider yourself an elder. Whether you do or don't should not be judged. If you do consider yourself an elder, write about why that is so. If you do not, what more in terms of descent, soul maturity, deep wisdom might you need in order to become an elder? Take plenty of time to ponder this question.

2. What do you know about your elder self? What are her strengths? What are his vulnerabilities? What are your experiences of doing the work of an elder in your world? How have you been received? How have you been rejected? What gifts do you bring to your community whether or not they are welcomed?

3. In the words of Marshall Vian Summers, in what ways do you see what others cannot see, feel what others will not feel and do what others will not do? What are the feelings you experience as you notice this? Write about this.

4. How are you grounding yourself in order to prepare yourself for the scenario described in this chapter regarding what a chaotic world may cause you to deal with? Write about this and be very specific. What tools are you honing and mastering in order to remain physically, emotionally, and spiritually grounded?

5. What tools in this book have you begun using, and what have been the results so far?

6. The Rilke poem at the beginning of this chapter echoes the perspective of a conscious elder who is beginning to realize her role which may at times feel confusing, disorienting, thankless, and at other times, incredibly fulfilling, meaningful, and rewarding. Take some time to ponder the poem deeply and write your reactions in your journal.

7. Think of an elder you know or work closely with. How does this person demonstrate his/her elderhood? What demonstrations of elderhood by this person inspire you, comfort you, reassure you? What demonstrations of elderhood by this person cause you to tremble, frustrate you, or challenge you in some way? What have you learned from this person? Be sure to include experiences that were not pleasant.

8. The following is a suggestion and only a suggestion: Rent the movies "The Road" and "The Book of Eli" and study the qualities of an elder that you witness in those movies.

Chapter 18: The Beauty and The Blight:
A Calling to Create

And this is what you can do too, maybe, if you live simply and with a lyrical heart in the cumbered neighborhoods or even, as Mozart sometimes managed to, in a palace, offering tune after tune, making some hard-hearted prince prudent and kind, just by being happy.

~Mary Oliver~

True beauty is woven through the heart of life and is ever engaged with forces of ignorance, darkness, ugliness and negativity; yet domination and power are not beauty's way. Beauty works from within these conflicts of forces, and her brightening may or may not appear. Where beauty seems absent, she is often hidden and still at work in the slow industry of transformation.

~John O'Donohue, *Beauty: The Invisible Embrace*

Everybody needs beauty as well as bread, places to play in and pray in, where nature may heal and give strength to body and soul.

~John Muir~

In the Confronting and Contemplating section of Chapter 16, we considered the possibility of "inflicting" joy on our world. This chapter suggests that "inflicting" beauty and creating art in a chaotic world may be restorative and may temper the consequences of unprecedented destruction.

Building upon Michael Meade's assertion that being in the right trouble allows us to discover inner resources and thereby experience authentic transformation, I offer the following Native American folk tale, told by Michael Meade in current time in *The World Behind The World*, but having been told for centuries by native peoples in North America. It is a tale of unraveling and re-making, as trouble and beauty travel together to unravel the old and weave something previously unseen.

The Unraveling and The Re-Making

Once upon a time, a story was told about an old woman and
a cave, and the story continues to be told today. Some people
said that the cave did not exist, nor the old woman, but the old

ones said that cave exists, and in that cave there's an old woman weaving a beautiful garment. She's making a trim for it, elegant and beautiful, in order to finish it. And because she wants it to be the best it can be, she's making it out of porcupine quills, and in order to weave them, she has to flatten them, and in order to flatten them, she has to bite them down with her teeth, and she's been biting down on porcupine quills for so many years—for maybe hundreds, maybe thousands of years that her teeth have been worn down to stubs that barely appear above the surface of the gums. And still she keeps biting down on the quills and weaving the trim of the garment.

She does it constantly and only once in awhile stops, and when she stops, she goes to the great cauldron that is on the other side of the cave, and when she goes to that cauldron, she stirs the soup that is in it—the soup that she has been making from all of the herbs, and all of the plants and grains and everything good that grows on the earth in this great cauldron. And if she doesn't stir it once in awhile, it will burn, and many things will turn out badly, so she stirs it, and because she's so old and tired from all that she's been doing, she moves very slowly over to the cauldron, and stirs the thing very slowly. And while she is stirring the cauldron, the black dog that is also in the cave goes over to the garment that she has been weaving and unravels everything that she has done so that when she finishes stirring the soup that has everything in it, she has to begin the weaving of the garment all over again.

Now some people say that black dog is the cause of all the trouble in the world, and if that black dog would just stop interrupting the weaving of the old woman of the world, everything would be fine, but the elders say, if that black dog ever stops unraveling things, if this world ever loses the trouble that is in it, and the garment is completed, then that will be the end of the world and everything in it. That is to say, it is the unraveling that keeps everything going. It is the trouble that keeps the beauty being made. It is the taking apart that causes the old woman to begin making the world again, over and over again.

I cannot help but notice that from time to time, the old woman, the Great Mother, must stir the cauldron. If she doesn't, its contents could burn, and things could turn out very badly for her children. Lurking about her cave is the black dog of trouble, without which things cannot be unraveled or beauty re-created time and time again. It is, in fact, the stirring and the unraveling that keep the world going and being re-made when it must be. I also notice that the woman is an elder, and that she is biting down on the porcupine quills. In Native American symbolism, the porcupine is sometimes seen as a being that moves mysteriously between two worlds. Structurally, the external tip of the quill is a barb that protects the animal, and at the base, the quill is snagged causing it to catch on things like thread. Therefore, it is likely that she is using her teeth to smooth the snagged edge, taking charge of that which feels mysterious and prickly to create an exquisitely beautiful garment. Unafraid of trouble, in fact relying on it for the unraveling, she stirs and weaves and re-creates.

I find enormous comfort in this story which reassures me that my personal trouble and that of the world evoke periodic stirrings and unravelings which must occur if the world is to be re-made and beauty created.

Caring For A Culture That Doesn't Care For Itself

The elder's job is to care for the culture, but when the culture refuses to be cared for or to abide within limits, an unraveling results. However, it is not only the aging person in the culture who cares for it. Alongside the elder is the poet, storyteller, artist, musician, and actor who create works of beauty. As noted above, these individuals "drag in the darkness" and tell us what is so and in the process, reveal what is unraveling and what must be remade.

Whether one considers himself an elder or not, one can do the work of an elder by continually creating beauty because creating beauty brings meaning and purpose to the culture. As the pot is stirred and the world unravels, we must continually ask ourselves, as this book has repeatedly suggested: Am I willing to be remade into a new kind of human being? What is my purpose and who do I want to be in the wake of the remaking?

Everyone reading these words is capable of creating beauty. One need not await the designation of an official title such as "musician," "poet," "artist." Anyone who grows a garden, cooks a delicious meal, parents a child, rescues an animal, stitches a wound, or offers a kind word and some food to a homeless person is creating beauty. Anyone who reads this book slowly and mindfully engages in the exercises herein is creating an extraordinary work of art: the cultivation of conscious self-awareness in the universe.

Many well-meaning individuals are busily engaged in attempting to save the world through remarkable activist endeavors. In *The Hope: A Guide To Sacred Activism*, Andrew Harvey clarifies that activism is not about saving the world because, in fact, the world doesn't want to be saved. Rather, the work of the activist/elder/healer is about bringing consciousness, kindness, compassion, relatedness, and yes, beauty to a chaotic world. In the words of *The Hope*, these are "spaces of grace" in which we are willing to utilize our gifts in service of the remaking of our world.

If the Long Emergency proves to be as physically, socially, economically, and ecologically devastating as it appears it may, our world could become increasingly blighted and aesthetically distasteful. Beauty will be desperately needed, but the forms of it that we have the capacity to create could become dramatically limited. An extensive inventory of art supplies or musical instruments may not be accessible. Therefore, we may be compelled to re-think much of what we now believe constitutes creating beauty and respond accordingly. Undoubtedly we will be challenged to find beauty in small, simple, perhaps unexpected places—the occasional live wildflower, the human voice, sunlight beaming through a glass of water—and to create it with limited resources at our disposal.

Beauty Heals and Restores

Not only is the creation of beauty restorative and energizing, it is also healing. A 2010 BBC News article entitled "Singing Rewires Damaged Brain"[64] reports the findings of physicians who have been studying the repair of brain damage in stroke patients who could not speak. Whereas a stroke can cause disconnection between the two sides of the brain, "as patients learn to put their words to melodies, the crucial connections form on the right side of their brains."

The story continues:

> Dr. Aniruddh Patel from the Neurosciences Institute in San Diego, said the study was an example of the "explosion in research into music and the brain" over the last decade.
>
> "People sometimes ask where in the brain music is processed and the answer is everywhere above the neck," said Dr Patel.
>
> "Music engages huge swathes of the brain – it's not just lighting up a spot in the auditory cortex."

Beauty engages the right brain, not only in stroke patients, but in all humans who allow themselves to enter its domain. It transports us beyond the rational, linear thinking of the world of survival and problem-solving to the world of being—the world of soul.

What we love about beauty and what draws us into it is its revelation of both the visible and invisible worlds. Thus creating beauty in a chaotic world offers to that turbulent milieu elements of the mysterious, the sacred—the I that is not I. When I imagine living in a chaotic world, I sense that people will be starving for beauty because so few manifestations of the sacred will be present. Beauty has the capacity to transport us beyond the most horrific conditions into the source and meaning of our humanity, and in a world unraveling, I believe that our species will ache for all things beautiful. As John O'Donohue writes in his lovely book about beauty:

> Beauty dwells at the heart of life….To recognize and celebrate
> beauty is to recognize the ultimate sacredness of experience, to
> glimpse the subtle embrace of belonging where we are wed to
> the divine, the beauty of every moment, of every thing.

Beauty is the intersecting point where eros and the sacred converge. It evokes eros even as we consciously or unconsciously experience the sacredness it holds. But also informing the convergence of eros and the sacred is the woundedness we bring to our appreciation or our creation of beauty. Life in a collapsing world will not be as much about our own personal woundedness as the woundedness of the earth community and other members of our own species. All sentient beings may hunger for moments of grace and beauty, and in the words of O'Donohue, "Where woundedness can be refined into beauty a wonderful transfiguration takes place."[65]

Creating beauty is intimately connected with creating ritual. The word *ritual* literally means "to fit together," and it becomes an expression of art if it is given some thought ahead of time and a great deal of space in which to erupt spontaneously. Ritual is a form of conversation with the sacred in which we feel inspired by something greater and then express that inspiration, along with our gratitude for it, in specific acts within sacred space. The intention of ritual is to heal, to create beauty, to unite community, and to honor the sacred in the universe. Ritual serves to fit together what has been broken and to create wholeness. By incorporating objects from nature into the ritual, we invite the participation and blessing of the earth community and honor our relationship with it. Each time we engage in or create earth-based ritual, we heal more of our disconnection from our relatives in the earth community. In this process, as emphasized in Chapter 3, soul-based community has fertile ground for erupting, as it were, out of the earth, and more of our illusion of separation from each other is healed.

In an earlier chapter I referred to Maslow's hierarchy of needs. Our species has assumed for millennia that when our survival is threatened, only survival needs require our attention. Thus in troubled times, those activities or relationships that might feed the soul and fortify our self-actualization are cast aside: School budgets eliminate art, music, and drama programs; pets are dumped at animal shelters because they are "too much trouble" to care for; public works of art are neglected and allowed to decay; and many individuals, lacking discretionary income to attend concerts, plays, or visit art museums, hunker down and spend money only for the bare necessities of life. These are only a few examples of industrial civilization's assumption, tirelessly nurtured by the Puritan ethic, that the pursuit or enjoyment of beauty is a luxury, not a necessity. Civilization's paradigm teaches us to "eat our vegetables first," then we can have dessert—if our parents (political systems) have enough money to provide it for us.

A new paradigm grounded in the values of the human soul will likely be constructed by humans who have discovered that without nurturing their souls, life is really not worth living. These individuals will not only take great care to implement beauty in their homes and communities, but beauty will become an integral aspect of their daily lives because they are likely to be men and women who were able to find beauty in the horrific and cling to its sustaining power. They will have come to understand on a cellular level that life without beauty is no life at all. No doubt they will be profoundly informed and inspired by nature as they create unprecedented works of art, music, storytelling, poetry and other expressions of beauty.

Meanwhile, we must take great care as industrial civilization's collapse exacerbates, not to take the innumerable expressions of beauty in our world for granted. One of the first modern ecologists, Rachel Carson, reminds us how tragic it would be to do so.

> One summer night, out on a flat headland, all but surrounded by the waters of the bay, the horizons were remote and distant rims on the edge of space. Millions of stars blazed in darkness, and on the far shore a few lights burned in cottages. Otherwise there was no reminder of human life. My companion and I were alone with the stars: the misty river of the Milky Way flowing across the sky, the patterns of the constellations standing out bright and clear, a blazing planet low on the horizon. It occurred to me that if this were a sight that could be seen only once in a century, this little headland would be thronged with spectators. But it can be seen many scores of nights in any year, and so the lights burned in the cottages and the inhabitants probably gave not a thought to the beauty overhead; and because they could see it almost any night, perhaps they never will.

CONFRONTING AND CONTEMPLATING
(Writing answers to these questions or drawing images in relation to them in a journal is highly recommended.)

1. Ponder the story "The Unraveling and The Re-Making." What grabs your attention in the story? In the current stirring and unraveling that is occurring in the world, what is being stirred up and unraveled in you? Write about that. Also write about what is being re-made in you? What beauty is being created in the entire process?

2. At the end of Chapter 1, you were asked to notice how you are creating beauty in your world. Related to creating beauty is "dragging in the darkness." Do you sometimes "drag in the darkness"? What responses have you noticed when you create beauty or drag in the darkness? Has either one made a difference anywhere in your world?

3. Write (or draw) about one or more places in your life where, in the words of John O'Donohue, woundedness has been refined into beauty. An experience such as this would naturally include a story. Write or draw the story. Who are the characters? What happened? What was the resulting beauty that evolved from the refinement?

4. Consider creating a poetry salon in your home or some safe space where you invite friends to bring poems to share. Encourage people to memorize and speak the poem they share instead of reading it. Allow plenty of space and time for people to speak. The intention is to provide sacred space for soul to be expressed spontaneously. Make clear that the intention is to share poetry and not conversation at this point in the gathering. This sacred time of speaking poetry from the heart is in itself a powerful ritual. After poems have been shared, you may want to encourage conversation, followed by a potluck and perhaps the playing of musical instruments or singing together.

    You may want to begin this gathering with a brief ritual to create sacred space and set an intention and tone for the event.

Chapter 19: Beyond Survival

It is not up to you to determine the outcome. It is up to you to prepare for the future and to live fully in the moment—eyes wide open, paying attention, being responsible and exerting yourself appropriately.

~Marshall Vian Summers, *The Great Waves of Change: Navigating The Difficult Times Ahead*~

I have fought the good fight, I have finished the race, and I have remained faithful.

St. Timothy, New Living Translation, 2007

As the reader knows by now, I am not a survivalist. I have never believed that the prime objective in preparing for the Long Emergency is to remain alive. None of us is enthusiastic about death, but we will all die. To deny this fact and focus primarily on survival is to embrace the heroic perspective and, in my opinion, miss the point.

I've stated in this book and in many other places that the human race is committing suicide. What is also true is that most citizens of industrial civilization secretly believe they will never die, and while they may give lip service to the inevitability of death, they act as if they are entitled to live forever. As a culture, we are horrified by death, refuse to talk about it, whitewash it with liturgical platitudes and convince ourselves that we must "move on" as quickly as possible. Meanwhile, we inflict death on ourselves and the earth community with our lifestyles. Only children playing war games or cowboys and Indians behave with such destructive obliviousness to death.

One reason I have so rigorously emphasized life purpose in this book is that, from my perspective, purpose not survival *is* the point. Moreover, one cannot make both survival and purpose a single priority. At some point, one will be forced to choose one over the other. One may choose to remain alive over fulfilling one's purpose, and that will bring forth one kind of result. Or one may choose fulfillment of purpose over survival, and that will manifest a different outcome. In current time we are rarely forced to choose which priority we will embrace, but I suspect that in a chaotic world, the dilemma will become more frequent, if not a daily occurrence.

In any event, this book has been written from the assumption that fulfillment of purpose is the fundamental underpinning and motivation for preparation, particularly emotional and spiritual preparation. I believe that when a chaotic world gives us very few reasons to persevere in it, our sense of purpose can provide the meaning that bolsters perseverance when perhaps all else has failed.

Some people tell me that emotional and spiritual preparation is unnecessary for them, if not a waste of time. They argue that they will worry about how to deal with particular situations when the situations occur and that no matter how much they might prepare, future situations will be different from anything they could possibly prepare for. In fact, I find some truth in this argument, yet some of the same folks who make it are folks who regularly engage in practicing logistical preparation. They may work out daily, organize weekend war games in the mountains, make excursions to large discount supply houses to purchase preparedness items, or spend hours at the target range improving their marksmanship. Yet they may not grasp that logistical crises cannot be fully prepared for, anymore than emotional or spiritual crises can be.

What is also true is that practice, whether logistical or emotional, is never wasted. In this book I have emphasized the need for emotional and spiritual warriorhood, and of course, warriors do not prepare for battle *in* battle, but long beforehand. Combat troops are trained to deal with myriad hypothetical wartime scenarios which they may never encounter, yet their training may be extremely valuable and applicable in very different wartime scenarios. Thus, I believe that working and applying all of the exercises in this book, perhaps several times, may provide superb training for the emotional and spiritual crises we are all likely to encounter in the Long Emergency.

Spiritual preparation for the future includes an acknowledgement that our efforts to navigate a chaotic world with the rational mind and human ego are inadequate. We must therefore strengthen our connection with the sacred Self which enhances our capacity for inner listening, discernment, awareness of our environment, and willingness to adapt. A working relationship with the sacred Self prepares us to determine when we should allow a situation to unfold, and when we should take charge of it. As the relationship strengthens, so also does the equilibrium necessary for navigating the troubled waters of holding other opposites such as feeling compassion vs. maintaining boundaries.

Just as we will sometimes fall short in our logistical preparation, we will certainly fall short in preparing emotionally and spiritually. The well-trained solider is never prepared for crawling through a battlefield lined with dead bodies. Nor is he prepared for witnessing the horror of innocent civilians, particularly children, lying dead in pools of blood. In fact, these are examples of the kinds of incidents that, witnessed repeatedly, drive soldiers in combat to suicide and produce post-traumatic stress disorder in veterans.

Making Friends With Death

I believe that navigating a collapsing world will entail constant observation of various forms of death—the death of infrastructure, the death of abundance, the increasing absence of goods and services that we now take for granted, the death of institutions, the disappearance of employment and shelter, the increased scarcity of food and water, the death of landscapes, and yes, the literal deaths of people and animals. The collapse of industrial civilization and the lifestyle it has provided is a catastrophic death of a paradigm and a way of life. While we may look ahead to the ultimate blessings unleashed by this death, it will nevertheless be traumatic to live through the magnitude of losses it will manifest.

If, however, we can begin now to make friends with death, as the Buddhist tradition has taught for thousands of years, we may be better prepared emotionally and spiritually to navigate a civilization dying on myriad levels. Likewise, a willingness to inhabit a milieu of death could provide a paradoxical psychological advantage.

Some survivors of special forces combat training acknowledge that they are trained to approach incredibly dangerous situations with the attitude that they are "already dead." That is to say, the odds of survival are so small that they consider themselves as good as dead. As a result, it is as if they have no life to lose and are "free" to carry out their mission to the fullest extent.

In some sense this attitude reflects that of the person who is profoundly clear about his or her ultimate purpose—who understands that the magnitude of one's life purpose dwarfs physical survival in a world where both are constantly under siege. In other words, because we will all die, what matters most is not survival, but whether or not we remain committed to fulfilling our purpose, even if we do not or cannot fulfill it.

Following "Hospice Workers for The World," a chapter near the end of *Sacred Demise*, I included a number of exercises for confronting and contemplating one's own death. I hope that the reader will feel free to participate in those because they are extremely valuable; however, the intention of this chapter and this book is different. My emphasis here is on the importance of grasping how much more momentous one's life purpose may be than physical existence itself in a collapsing, chaotic world. Intimate familiarity with one's purpose not only informs the preparation process but shifts priorities from those designed to merely augment survival to those that include the fine tuning of skills related to fulfilling one's purpose as collapse intensifies.

More simply put, the essential question is not: How can I survive the collapse of industrial civilization? But rather: Why am I here, right now, in this place, at this time, experiencing the end of the world as I and my species have known it?

CONFRONTING AND CONTEMPLATING
(Writing answers to these questions or drawing images in relation to them in a journal is highly recommended.)

Take plenty of time to complete these exercises by thinking deeply about them and writing or drawing *detailed* responses in your journal.

1. As you contemplate living in a chaotic world, a world of collapse and loss, even as you envision such a world, what do you feel passionate about?

2. What are the talents, skills, and gifts that you have discovered and developed within yourself over the years that you passionately want to offer to the world in the preparation process and as you and others navigate the coming chaos?

3. When you are no longer on this planet, what do you want to have contributed that will endure long beyond your physical presence here?

Chapter 20: Preparing For Not Knowing

Certainty

Certainty undermines one's power, and turns happiness
into a long shot. Certainty confines.

Dears, there is nothing in your life that will
not change - especially your ideas of God.

Look what the insanity of righteous knowledge can do:
crusade and maim thousands
in wanting to convert that which
is already gold
into gold.

Certainty can become an illness
that creates hate and
greed.

God once said to Tuka,

"Even I am ever changing -
I am ever beyond
Myself,

what I may have once put my seal upon,
may no longer be
the greatest
Truth."

~ Tukaram ~

Some months ago during our weekly local heart and soul group meeting, one member began talking about how important it is that we prepare for the unknown. I was intrigued by this notion because her comment did not describe any particular scenario. It simply suggested preparing for uncertainty. But of course, such a comment immediately evokes the question, "How does one *prepare* for uncertainty?" We may know how to prepare for famine, for lack of water, for the absence of healthcare, and for extremes in weather patterns, but how do we prepare for the unknown?

Quantum Physics, Ancient Wisdom

Biologist David Suzuki, commenting on the discovery in quantum physics that at the most elementary level of matter, nothing is certain and can only be predicted statistically, states that, "If there is no absolute certainty at the most elementary level, then the notion that the entire universe is understandable and predictable from its components becomes absurd."[66]

Whether we take the standpoint of quantum physics and Werner Heisenberg's Uncertainty Principle[67] or the standpoint of ancient Buddhist tradition which teaches that human existence is by definition uncertain, the physical universe, while operating within the parameters of certain laws, is replete with surprises. Moreover, if it is fundamentally uncertain in relatively stable times, it can only be wildly uncertain in chaotic times.

I believe that the only way of preparing for the unknown is to become as resilient as humanly possible. On the one hand, this is in part an intellectual and emotional process, but even more so a spiritual practice, meaning that becoming resilient is greatly enhanced by experiencing oneself as related to the earth community and the unfolding of events within it. Unquestionably, people tend to become more resilient when they assume that there is meaning in their predicament, even if that meaning may not be obvious at the time. Conversely, a sense of separation from the community of life and the inability to find meaning in life's challenges foster fear and a need to control outcomes. However, a sense of relatedness with the universe supports flexibility as well as a willingness to adapt.

I have little doubt that in a chaotic world resulting from the collapse of industrial civilization, the ability to become resilient will be nothing less than a matter of life and death. That means that one must be mentally and spiritually prepared for all options, including one's own death and including options which one cannot even presently imagine.

For thousands of years, ancient spiritual traditions and indigenous wisdom have taught humans how to develop an attitude of resilience in the face of adversity. In the Hindu tradition we see the devotee Arjuna on the battlefield of life being counseled by Lord Krishna—a conversation which became the sacred text, the Bhagavad Gita. Similarly, the Buddhist tradition has taught the impermanence of life and the necessity of being "comfortable with uncertainty" as "things fall apart," the titles of two recent books by Buddhist teacher, Pema Chodron. In Native American tradition and other indigenous traditions, warriors and holy men and women are taught how to shapeshift or take on the appearance of other life forms in order to avoid danger or carry out their appointed missions.

Coming to terms with and living in harmony with the uncertainty principle is about becoming resilient. The dictionary defines resilient as: *The capability of a strained body to recover its size and shape after deformation caused by compressive stress; an ability to recover from or adjust easily to misfortune or change.*

I can think of no quality more urgently needed in the Long Emergency than resilience. Perhaps not overnight, but certainly within a short space of time, a way of life we now take for granted will no longer exist. The dizzying changes that result will be attended by confusion, anxiety, grief, and a disorienting lack of grounding.

The 4 A's of Resilience

Everything written in this book has been included in order to enhance the reader's physical, mental, emotional, and spiritual resilience because Rule Number One in navigating the coming chaos is to apply the principle of resilience at all times. Therefore, I would like to offer four specific guidelines for practicing resilience.

1. *Anticipating*—The origin of the word comes from a Latin expression which means "to take care of ahead of time" or "to take possession beforehand." This means that we practice being observant. We cannot anticipate every event or challenging situation, but we can minimize a significant amount of adversity by being conscious and paying attention. Because we are human, some situations cannot be anticipated, but the fact is, most can if we are alert and observant.

2. *Assessing and Allowing*—Some circumstances compel us to take immediate action, but many more do not. In the majority of cases, we need to breathe and take our time to assess the situation and allow actions and events to unfold. Assessing and allowing require discernment which is never infallible but engages the intuition, as opposed to the rational mind operating on its own, in order to inform our bodies and emotions about what might be the best course of action. Going forward, we are more fully equipped to take action.

   How do we develop discernment? It develops within us organically as we build our internal bunker using the tools offered in Chapter One.

3. *Acting*—Unless we need to make a split-second decision, we listen deeply to our bodies and feelings, assessing the situation as much as possible, and then we take action. Our actions should be compassionate, non-judgmental, and based on an intention to heal, harmonize, and protect.

4. *Adapting*—When we have done all we can to act with discernment and integrity but circumstances out of our control prevail, we must adapt accordingly. This applies to individual events that occur in a chaotic world, as well as the overall process of unraveling.

Currently, everyone reading this book is likely to be engaged in activities in their community which may help minimize the devastation of industrial civilization's collapse. For example, individuals working in the Transition, permaculture, or localization movements are certainly endeavoring to make their communities secure in terms of food supply and self-sufficient in terms of energy supply. However, no matter how much a community has prepared for collapse, some aspect(s) of it will take its residents by surprise in which case, they must adapt accordingly.

Emotional resilience in the Long Emergency cannot be overemphasized, nor can spiritual grounding. We can learn much from individuals and communities who have survived shorter emergencies in the past such as the Great Depression, the Nazi holocaust, protracted ordeals of genocide, ethnic cleansing, and other forms of persecution. One of the most important realities their stories reveal is that on countless occasions, they were only able to persevere because of their sense of being sustained by something greater. We cannot navigate the coming chaos unless we develop strong relationships with other human beings *and* with the sacred Self.

All experts on resilience tell us that the more we know about ourselves, the more resilient we are likely to become. This does not mean that we must spend all of our time being narcissistically pre-occupied with ourselves, but rather, that utilizing and expanding our inner transition tools will increase resilience and our ability to support others in the face of adversity.

Knowing and Not Knowing

Despite the caution against certainty in the lovely poem by Tukaram which opened this chapter, and while much of the chapter has emphasized the value of *un*-certainty, I do not wish to diminish the importance of knowing—and especially *knowing* that one knows. To distinguish between the folly of certainty and the inestimable value of knowing, we need to return to our consideration of the "I that is not I."

The demand for certainty is based on the human ego and its principal ally, the rational, linear-thinking mind. This mind demands answers and outcomes; it craves the security of knowing what will happen next and how. It cannot tolerate not knowing or sitting with mystery. Moreover, the more a civilization built on the rational, linear-thinking mind and the human ego deteriorates, the less useful will be our insistence upon certainty. In fact, *certainty* based on separation from the earth community and the sacred Self gave birth to industrial civilization and its legacy, and it cannot serve as the prime source of knowing in the milieu of a new paradigm.

In *The Great Waves of Change*, Marshall Vian Summers distinguishes between rational mind certainty and Knowledge, his term for what I name the sacred Self. Of this he writes, "While your mind, your intellect, does not know what will happen next, Knowledge within you is responding to the signs from the world….Therefore, fundamental to your preparation is building a relationship with Knowledge…."[68] Continuing this distinction between certainty and knowing, Summers states:

> Now at this great threshold, you will have to read the signs
> very carefully and very objectively, both from what the world is
> telling you and from what Knowledge within you is indicating,
> in order to begin to navigate a changing set of circumstances,
> a changing set of situations—navigating the troubled waters
> ahead.[69]

In other words, we are most resilient when we understand that the ego-based, rational mind cannot and does not know what will happen, at the same time that we are drawing upon our relationship with Knowledge, the sacred Self, the divine within, or whatever we prefer naming the "I that is not I" to inform us on a cellular, bone-marrow level what is so. I cannot think of a more apt description of the spiritual practice that the collapse of industrial civilization entails for every human being who desires to remain awake and find every imaginable facet of meaning in it. In other words, as we anticipate navigating the coming chaos, it may be that the most essential preparation of all will be preparation for not knowing exactly how the collapse of industrial civilization will unfold, even as we consciously cultivate an intimate relationship with the sacred Self within us which knows exactly where we need to be and what we need to be doing as the world with which we are familiar increasingly unravels. Or as Marshall Vian Summers emphasizes:

> You do not know how it is going to turn out. But how it is going
> to turn out really does not matter because you are here to serve
> the world, and you serve the world without requiring a result.

CONFRONTING AND CONTEMPLATING
(Writing answers to these questions or drawing images in relation to them in a journal is highly recommended.)

1. Think about a time in your life when you were very certain about the outcome of a particular situation but later discovered that the outcome was very different from what you were certain would happen. In your journal, explain how you were affected by this experience. What did you learn from it?

2. What is it like for you to abide with uncertainty, particularly around issues or events that are very important to you? What happens in your body, emotions, and rational mind? What mental messages are activated during uncertainty? Write about this in your journal.

3. What is your experience with becoming resilient? Have you become more resilient in recent years? If so, write in detail about what happened. How did resilience develop in you? If resilience is a problem for you, write about that as well explaining why you think it is so challenging. What might happen if you were to become more resilient?

4. For one week, make a conscious effort to practice the "Four A's of Resilience" A key to practicing these principles is to record your experience with doing so in your journal. Explain exactly what happened as you focused on practicing the "Four A's".

5. What are the emotional qualities that you personally need to strengthen in order to become more resilient? Be specific and also write about how you might begin developing these qualities using some of the tools you have received in this book.

6. Do you have a personal sense of the difference between "knowing" with your rational mind and knowing on a cellular level? Write about a time when you felt the difference. What did it feel like in your body and how did it feel emotionally?

7. At this point in your life and at this point your reading of this book, what is your relationship with Knowledge, the sacred Self, something greater? Please write in detail about this.

Chapter 21: The Next Culture:
A New Paradigm Erupting From Ancient Wisdom

If one does not look into the abyss, one is being wishful by simply not confronting the truth....On the other hand, it is imperative that one not get stuck in the abyss.

~Robert Jay Lifton~

When faced with a radical crisis, when the old way of being in the world, of interacting with each other and with the realm of nature doesn't work anymore, when survival is threatened by seemingly insurmountable problems, an individual human—or a species— will either die or become extinct or rise above their limitations with an evolutionary leap. This is the state of humanity now, and this is its challenge.

~Eckhart Tolle~

This is a time when courageous experimenting is required for humanity to make it through to the next century. Even more, this is a time for courageous experimenters to come together in community....Supporting a healthy and diverse ecology of sustainable microcultures could be the smartest insurance that any predominant culture could carry. As the ship of state goes down, the once proud protagonists may eventually come knocking at your door. When they come, you can smile kindly and say, "Hello. Welcome to the bridge. What are you feeling?"

~Clinton Callahan, *Directing The Power of Conscious Feelings: Living Your Own Truth*~

This chapter is about the next culture that humans have the opportunity to create, and I owe my use of the term "next culture" to psychologist, Clinton Callahan, who for decades has studied the devastating effects of a culture of emotional numbness on the humans who inhabit it, and who has experimented tirelessly with countless approaches to healing those wounds. He has proven himself a "warrior of vulnerability" and an elder who has helped initiate innumerable individuals into the sacred circle of conscious emotional awareness.

Callahan's work gives us a glimpse of what a culture might look like in which people relate *to* their feelings and to each other *through* feelings. Callahan also uses the term *archearchy* to describe a culture that is not dominated by the masculine principle or the feminine, but by both. As he says in *Directing The Power of Conscious Feelings*, it is a new and truly sustainable culture, oriented more toward being present and being with, and less toward consuming, owning, having, going, and doing."

Clinton Callahan has laid out the kind of emotional skills that humans must cultivate in order to create the next culture, and I believe that these skills are unquestionably related to our connection with the sacred Self, for they are, in fact, developed in relationship with soul. A commitment to cultivating next-culture emotional skills is likely to produce warriors of vulnerability who will live their lives very differently from the typical citizen of industrial civilization.

Moreover, as warriors of vulnerability commune with each other in a multitude of ways for a variety of purposes, the possibility of birthing a new culture becomes increasingly realistic. New models for meeting the needs of the individual and the community evolve as optimum emotional and spiritual functioning is cultivated. This is not to say that conflict will vanish or that our species will become impeccably harmonious in its interactions overnight. What it does mean, among other things, is that humans who have attended to emotional and spiritual preparation for living in a chaotic world may have an edge over those who previously insisted that only logistical preparation mattered.

Creating a New Story

We hear much about abandoning the old story and writing a new one, but what does that mean? Both Thomas Berry and Brian Swimme have taught exhaustively the need for a new story and have also offered a clear definition of it. In Swimme's many writings and lectures regarding the conscious self-awareness of the human species, he emphasizes that when we come to understand that our function as a species is to become consciously self-aware of the universe and its infinite functions, we will understand and live a new story. "The human," he says, "is the space created in the universe process for hearing and celebrating the stories of the universe that fill the universe."[70] In this regard, I personally have found Swimme's "Powers of The Universe" lecture series invaluable as a rational, yet soulful, explanation of our emergence from and our eternal relatedness with the universe.

Thomas Berry in *The Sacred Universe* echoes Swimme's words:

> We recognize that in every aspect of our being, we are a
> subsystem of the universe system. More immediately, we are a
> subsystem of the Earth system….Our human role is to enable the
> universe to reflect on itself in a special mode of consciousness.[71]

In order to compose the new story, Berry says that humans must become "present to the earth in a mutually enhancing manner." This requires an intimate connection with the earth community as described by Plotkin and others in this book. Specifically, Berry states:

> I believe we must return to a sense of intimacy with the Earth
> akin to that experienced by many indigenous peoples in earlier

times. This can be done through our new story of the universe, which is now available to us through empirical inquiry into the origin, structure, and sequence of transformations through which the Earth has come to its expression at the end of the twentieth century. We have finally realized that our modern knowledge reveals a universe with a psychic-spiritual and physical-material dimension from the beginning…Once we appreciate this transmaterial dimension of the universe, we will be able to understand that the human story is inseparable from the universe story.[72]

If Swimme and Berry are correct, a new cosmology of the universe and our relationship with it will be required in order to write and live a story that is authentically new and unequivocally divergent from the story of industrial civilization. Happily, a number of endeavors by humans in current time are embodying the new story and hold promise for bringing it to fruition.

Movements That Feed My Optimism

Presently, as I observe the rapid unraveling of the current paradigm and the institutions that have evolved from it, I notice four movements that inspire optimism in me regarding the creation of a new culture. Those movements are: Permaculture, Transition, The Business Alliance for Local Living Economies (BALLE), and Slow Money. (Resources and contact information on each of these may be found in the Appendix of this book.) This is not to say that other movements devoted to collapse preparation are irrelevant because they undoubtedly serve purposes that complement the four movements mentioned here.

Permaculture

In 1970 an Australian ecologist and university professor, Bill Mollison, after years of observing nature and the patterns of beings inhabiting it, developed a design system which he first applied for the purpose of creating sustainable agriculture. Later, Mollison and his student, David Holmgren, came to understand that permaculture principles could be applied in myriad aspects of life. Today, without realizing it, many people practice certain aspects of permaculture, such as organic gardeners, land use planners, recyclers, and of course, countless indigenous people.

Permaculture ethics are comprised of essentially three main concepts: Care of the earth, care of people, and the notion of fair share—that is, use only what you need and share the rest. Permaculture principles are guidelines for designing gardens, homes, using land, and even how to live our lives sustainably, resiliently, and in harmony with nature. Most people learn the basics of permaculture by taking a class which focuses on its principles and how to apply them.

Transition

In 2005, Rob Hopkins was teaching a permaculture class at the Further Education College in Kinsale, Ireland when he began contemplating the myriad ways permaculture could be applied for creating sustainability in local communities. Later Hopkins moved to Totnes, England and there, spread the concept further among its residents. With an eye to creating "Transition Towns" or totally self-reliant communities, the Transition movement spread virally, so that by 2010, it now has established itself in over 300 communities around the world. However, to fully understand the movement and its significance, it is necessary to read and study Hopkins' 2008 *Transition Handbook.*

Hopkins message confronts the reader with the reality that if certain changes are not made and made very quickly, the planet and the human race may not survive. He favors a gradual transition into voluntarily choosing to live sustainably over being forced to do so by a cataclysmic unraveling. Hopkins also emphasizes that the changes must begin and flourish at the local level, not globally. True to the principles of permaculture, he argues that smallness of scale on every level is the parameter in which Transition must function.

In the *Handbook,* Hopkins organizes the Transition model according to three simple but incredibly significant categories: head, heart, and hands. Head simply refers to the necessity of acquiring information and understanding regarding the state of the world in terms of energy depletion, environmental devastation, and economic growth, or what some call the "Three E's." Heart pertains to the psychology of change and how we are spiritually and emotionally affected by the unprecedented challenges presented by the Three E's. Heart also addresses our spiritual and emotional preparation for Transition on a global scale. Hands refers to re-skilling or learning old skills that are new for us but that may help sustain us as the myriad systems of industrial civilization fail. These might include canning, carpentry, herbal medicine, and beekeeping, to mention only a few.

Small Transition groups or initiatives, have sprung up across the United States and in numerous other countries and are burgeoning into powerful community forces working toward food security, energy independence, re-skilling, and overall sustainable living.

Business Alliance for Local Living Economies (BALLE)

In 1987 the Social Venture Network, a community of some 400 North American businesses was founded, and in 1988, New England Businesses for Social Responsibility emerged in an effort to promote socially responsible business practices. Judy Wicks, owner of Philadelphia's White Dog Café, joined with other business owners in 2001 to form BALLE.

BALLE has now established more than 80 networks across the U.S. and Canada, involving over 22,000 entrepreneurs. Its focus is on rebuilding local and regional food systems and local and regional economies.

BALLE's website describes its network mission in this way:

> At its core, BALLE's work is about community empowerment.
> BALLE networks of local businesses are working at the
> grassroots level to reconnect eaters with farmers, investors
> with entrepreneurs, and business owners with their employees,
> neighbors and ecosystems.
>
> BALLE's mission is to catalyze, strengthen and connect
> networks of locally owned independent businesses dedicated
> to building strong local living economies. Its services are
> designed to facilitate the development of community networks
> of independent businesses, to guide networks through various
> stages of development, to synthesize and communicate the
> best network development ideas and practices, and to build the
> larger movement for local living economies.[73]

Echoing the principles of Permaculture, according to BALLE's website, it seeks to:

- Focus on local first—producing, buying, and selling locally

- Increase self-reliance—which increases local resilience and increases community security and strengthens the local economy

- Share prosperity—by understanding that quality of life depends on the equitable distribution of resources

- Build community—by connecting producers with consumers, lenders with borrowers, and investors with entrepreneurs

- Work with nature—by creating design systems in harmony with it

- Celebrate diversity—which fosters resilience, innovation, and peace

- Measure what matters—not just economic growth but quality of life

Slow Money

Woody Tasch, author of *Inquiries Into the Nature of Slow Money: Investing As If Food, Farms, and Fertility Mattered*, left a career in investing and philanthropy to found the Slow Money Alliance. Similar to the three movements above, Slow Money is dedicated to:

- investing in small food enterprises and local food systems;

- connecting investors to their local economies; and,

- building the nurture capital (as opposed to venture capital) industry.[74]

What is nurture capital? According to Tasch, soil fertility, carrying capacity, sense of place, care of the commons, cultural, ecological and economic health and diversity, nonviolence—these are the fundamentals of nurture capital, a new financial sector supporting the emergence of a restorative economy. Slow Money's goal is "a million Americans investing 1% of their assets in local food systems within a decade."
At the Slow Money website, the following principles are enumerated, and readers are asked to sign them in order to become part of the network:

> I. We must bring money back down to earth.
>
> II. There is such a thing as money that is too fast, companies that are too big, finance that is too complex. Therefore, we must slow our money down—not all of it, of course, but enough to matter.
>
> III. The 20th Century was the era of Buy Low/Sell High and Wealth Now/Philanthropy Later—what one venture capitalist called "the largest legal accumulation of wealth in history." The 21st Century will be the era of nurture capital, built around principles of carrying capacity, care of the commons, sense of place and non-violence.
>
> IV. We must learn to invest as if food, farms and fertility mattered. We must connect investors to the places where they live, creating vital relationships and new sources of capital for small food enterprises.
>
> V. Let us celebrate the new generation of entrepreneurs, consumers and investors who are showing the way from Making A Killing to Making a Living.
>
> VI. Paul Newman said, "I just happen to think that in life we need to be a little like the farmer who puts back into the soil what he takes out." Recognizing the wisdom of

these words, let us begin rebuilding our economy from the ground up, asking:

* What would the world be like if we invested 50% of our assets within 50 miles of where we live?
* What if there were a new generation of companies that gave away 50% of their profits?
* What if there were 50% more organic matter in our soil 50 years from now?

Next Culture Options and "Inadvertent" Spirituality

You may argue that the four models of next culture explained above are only a few of the plethora of options available or perhaps not yet envisioned, and you would be absolutely correct. I offer these four because they embody the synthesis of logistical strategizing with spiritual awakening. Models such as these cannot be implemented without regard for the soul consciousness that makes them functional. Nor can spiritual models that disregard the necessity of becoming informed about the state of the planet, localization, re-skilling, community building, and constructing economies of scale, offer a real-world, grounded relationship with the sacred Self.

Although the founders and members of next-culture movements may not call themselves "spiritual" and may even bristle at the word because they identify with an atheist or agnostic perspective, their work is informed, inspired by, and imbued with a sense of something greater than their own well being—an unambiguous hallmark of the sacred Self.

Spiritual Activism

In 2009 I was blessed with an advance copy of Andrew Harvey's *The Hope: A Guide to Sacred Activism.* Until then, I had not encountered anyone endeavoring to integrate activism with a spiritual path. At about the same time, Andrew discovered my book, *Sacred Demise,* and we began a series of heartwarming conversations about the similarities in our work and our vision of the future. In *The Hope,* Andrew writes extensively about "networks of grace" which are imaginal cells of people working, meditating, inspiring, and acting together on changes or causes with which they feel called to engage. They could organize according to profession, or a kind of service about which they feel passionate, or around the sharing of skills. In my 2009 review of *The Hope,* I called it an "unprecedented marriage of activist passion and spiritual ardor"—a marriage long overdue in the modern world and exquisitely timed for the current milieu.

Andrew Harvey was profoundly influenced by his mentor and friend, Father Bede Griffiths.

Some months before Griffiths' death in 1993, Harvey spent many hours with him and listened as the aged monk spoke freely of the evolutionary threshold on which he believed humanity stood at the end of the twentieth century.

Once More, The Evolutionary Threshold

A new kind of human was/is trying to be born, according to Griffiths—a human that is both human and greater than human. In that birth, he believed, lay the potential for the emergence of a species that honors and respects the earth community and that relates to its own and all other species with compassion and justice. Never inhibited by church polity, Griffiths perceived the earth community and humanity's place in it in much the same way as did the late Father Thomas Berry, who referred to himself as a "geologian," that is, an earth scholar as opposed to a religious scholar. Moreover, Griffiths did not perceive the birthing of a new humanity as passive or painless. Rather he insisted that it would have to manifest first as an immense crisis or series of crises which he called "a cauldron of chaos."

As I reflect on Andrew's work and my own, I feel increasingly passionate about the reality that emotional work and the cultivation of a spiritual path travel together and need each other and that this psycho-spiritual perspective must inform all efforts to prepare for navigating the coming chaos. For in the cauldron of which Griffiths speaks—yes, in the same cauldron that the old woman weaving in the cave frequently stirs---lay the ingredients for a new kind of human being and the next culture.

Each of the movements highlighted in this chapter express myriad aspects of ancient and indigenous wisdom. They exemplify the living out of a new story, the fundamental elements of which are: A profound awareness of our chemical and spiritual union with the earth community and our "marriage" to our local communities; the honoring of place and the desire to nurture it economically, environmentally, and spiritually; a baseline belief that there is enough for everyone, and that we should use only what we need and share the rest. They hold a perspective of interdependence with the earth community and with other humans, while maintaining independence from systems that degrade self-sufficiency and foster the belief that some politician, political party, or savior can provide solutions from afar. Implicit within them is an abiding assumption, even if not consciously expressed, that the sacred is everywhere present and that it must inform all elements of the new story we create together.

As the second decade of the twenty-first century dawns, we journey together to write, sculpt, play, paint, dance, sing, plant, harvest, dream, and pray a new story. Those individuals who have allowed themselves to know the full truth of the collapse of industrial civilization and have divested their lives and energy from the old story are living a new version of the ancient archetype of exodus: escaping, journeying, and generating a new culture, and in this case, perhaps even a new species.

Contemporary poet, Alla Bozarth-Campbell has captured the soul of our journey in this extraordinary illumination:

Passover Remembered

Pack nothing.
Bring only your determination to serve
    and your willingness to be free.
Don't wait for the bread to rise.
Take nourishment for the journey, but eat standing.
Be ready to move at a moment's notice.
Do not hesitate to leave your old ways behind –
    fear, silence, submission.
Only surrender to the need of the time –
    love justice and walk humbly with your God.
Do not take time to explain to the neighbours.
Tell only a few trusted friends and family members.
Then begin quickly, before you have had time
    to sink back into old slavery.
Set out in the dark.
I will send fire to warm and encourage you.
I will be with you in the fire, and I will be with you in the cloud.
You will learn to eat new food
    and find refuge in new places.
I will give you dreams in the desert
    to guide you safely to that place you have not yet seen.
The stories you tell one another around the fires in the dark
    will make you strong and wise.
Outsiders will attack you, and some follow you
    and at times you will get weary and turn on each other
    from fear, fatigue and blind forgetfulness.
You have been preparing for this
    for hundreds of years.
I am sending you into the wilderness to make a new way
    and to learn my ways more deeply.
Some of you will be so changed by weathers and wanderings
    that even your closest friends will have to learn your features
    as though for the first time.
Some of you will not change at all.

Some will be abandoned by your dearest loves
  and misunderstood by those who have known you since birth
  who feel abandoned by you.
Some will find new friendships in unlikely faces,
  and old true friends as faithful and true
  as the pillar of God's flame.
Sing songs as you go,
  and hold close together.
You may at times grow confused
  and lose your way.
Continue to call each other by the names I've given you
  to help remember who you are.
Touch each other,
  and keep telling the stories.
Make maps as you go,
  remembering the way back from before you were born.
So you will be only the first of many waves
  of deliverance on the desert seas.
It is the first of many beginnings –
  your Paschaltide.
Remain true to the mystery.
Pass on the whole story.
Do not go back.
I am with you now and I am waiting for you.

CONFRONTING AND CONTEMPLATING
(Writing answers to these questions or drawing images in relation to them in a journal is highly recommended.)

1. 1. Take plenty of time to reflect on, write or draw about, the above poem by Bozarth-Campbell. How does it speak to you personally? How does it engage your heart? I suggest keeping this poem in a prominent place and reading it at least once weekly. It may offer us profound comfort and inspiration as the coming chaos intensifies.

2. Write about your responses to the four movements mentioned in this chapter. What is your familiarity or involvement with them? Write about other related movements that you feel will be significant in creating the next culture.

3. Write a detailed description of what you want the next culture to look like. Unleash your mind and heart to imagine how that culture might be structured in terms of food supply, transportation, health care, economics, housing, education, energy, cultural expression, and spirituality. How do you envision your role in making this kind of culture happen?

Appendix

Additional Resources

Body Scan Exercise for Grounding

By Phylameana Lila Desy[75]

Note: *Bedtime works fine for people who don't fall asleep easily, but for those who tend to fall asleep quickly upon hitting the pillow, sitting upright in a chair is probably best. Basically this exercise is a body scan which can be helpful in becoming more fully aware of how your body feels.*

Aside from the body scan helping to bring the body/spirit connection to balance it is also an excellent tool in identifying physical stresses and upsets. Pain can be so overwhelming in one part of the body that the rest of the body gets neglected. The body scan is an exercise in assembling the larger hurts alongside the minutest details of stresses that you may have overlooked within your body.

Be prepared to be amazed at the discoveries that you will make about your body during this process.

For example: A headache may get temporary or permanent relief by altering the focus down to the feet, although this depends on the severity of the hurt you are experiencing in your head.

Besides getting better grounded by doing the following body scan exercise, another benefit is that sometimes painful hurts are often miraculously lifted from us while the body scan is being done in order to help bring our awareness to the less obvious.

Grounding Exercise: Body Scan

Bring your thoughts from busy mental chatter downward by focusing on your feet. Don't rush this process. Take your time moving from each part of your body. Also, you don't need to touch yourself, just allow your mind to switch focus from wherever it is. Begin with your feet and move upwards.

Notice the soles of your feet, your toes, in-between your toes, the top of your feet, the back of your ankle.

Do they feel hot? or cold? Do they hurt? Are they numb? Do you feel your blood circulating through them? Are they feeling tired?

Don't judge how they feel - just notice how they feel. Wiggle your toes. How does that feel?

Once you have a made a strong connection with your feet you may then move your attention upwards to your ankle... then switch focus to your lower legs, onto your knee caps, behind your knees, your thighs, and so on.

Keep reminding yourself not to rush.

***Allow yourself to breathe** throughout the scanning process, especially as you come to any areas of discomfort (stressed muscles, soreness, etc.) or at any spot that feels like there may be an energy block.*

Once you have moved through your torso and up to your neck, drop back down to your fingertips, move your attention to the hands, up your arms and shoulders, returning your attention once again to your neck before finishing up with your focus on face and scalp.

ADDITIONAL EXERCISES AND PRACTICES

Tai Chi video meditation exercise
http://www.ehow.com/video_2357216_tai-chi-meditation-exercise.html

Breathing Relaxation guided video exercise
http://www.youtube.com/watch?v=-j5Z4E2wkh4

Mindfulness Meditation with Jon Kabat-Zinn
http://www.youtube.com/watch?v=3nwwKbM_vJc

Mindfulness Stress Reduction and Healing with Jon Kabat-Zinn
http://www.youtube.com/watch?v=rSU8ftmmhmw

Practicing Presence, by Eckhart Tolle DVD
http://www.amazon.com/Practicing-Presence-Spiritual-Teacher-Practitioner/
dp/1894884450/ref=sr_1_6?s=dvd&ie=UTF8&qid=1281801442&sr=1-6

Suggested Meditation Technique from Marshall Vian Summers in *The Great Waves of Change*
(Appendix)

A FEW RECOMMENDED READINGS

Sacred Demise: Walking The Spiritual Path of Industrial Civilization's Collapse, by Carolyn Baker:
www.carolynbaker.net

Healing Through The Dark Emotions: The Wisdom of Grief, Fear, and Despair, Miriam Greenspan:
http://www.miriamgreenspan.com/

The Bridge at the Edge of the World: Capitalism, the Environment, and Crossing from Crisis to Sustainability, James Gustave Speth: http://www.thebridgeattheedgeoftheworld.com/about-the-book.php

 Requiem for A Species: Why We Resist the Truth About Climate Change, Clive Hamilton: http://www.clivehamilton.net.au/cms/index.php

The Great Waves of Change, Marshall Vian Summers, available from New Knowledge Library:
http://www.newknowledgelibrary.org/

Perseverance, Margaret Wheatley

The Dream of Earth, Thomas Berry

The Great Work: Our Way Into The Future, Thomas Berry

The Sacred Universe: Earth, Spirituality, and Religion In The Twenty-First Century, Thomas Berry

Evening Thoughts: Reflecting On The Earth as Sacred Community, Thomas Berry

The Hope: A Guide To Sacred Activism, By Andrew Harvey

Nature and The Human Soul, Bill Plotkin

The Vanishing Face of Gaia: A Final Warning, James Lovelock

Sky Above, Earth Below: Spiritual Practice in Nature, John P. Milton

Confronting Collapse, Michael C. Ruppert

We Need Each Other: Building Gift Community, by Bill Kauth and Zoe Alowan

Madness at The Gates of The City: The Myth of American Innocence, by Barry Spector

The Earth Path: Grounding Your Spirit In The Rhythms of Nature, By Starhawk, Google Books online

The African Cosmological Wheel and Its Application, Malidoma Somé
http://www.schoolofwisdom.com/african_philosophy/the-african-wheel/

RECOMMENDED VIEWING AND LISTENING

Earth and The American Dream DVD

The Powers of The Universe, Brian Swimme DVD

Finding Your Life Purpose, Eckhart Tolle DVD

The Great Story, Thomas Berry DVD

The Work That Reconnects, Joanna Macy DVD

Books and CDs by Malidoma Somé, initiated teacher of the Dagara tribe of West Africa
http://www.malidoma.com/cms/

Books and CDs by Pema Chodron
http://www.shambhala.org/teachers/pema/biography.php

RECOMMENDED TRAININGS AND WORKSHOPS

Sacred Demise: The Heart and Soul of Transition, with Carolyn Baker
Carolyn@carolynbaker.net

Genesis Farm Earth Literacy and Transition Culture Training
http://www.genesisfarm.org/index.taf

Institute For Sacred Activism Training—Andrew Harvey
http://www.andrewharvey.net

Miriam Greenspan Workshops on Healing Through The Dark Emotions
http://www.miriamgreenspan.com/

Bill Plotkin Trainings and Workshops
http://www.natureandthehumansoul.com/newbook/programs.htm

Michael Meade Workshops and CD's
http://www.mosaicvoices.org/

TRANSITION CULTURE RESOURCES FOR THE MYTHOPOETIC HEART

RECOMMENDED POETRY

Love Poems From God, compiled by Daniel Ladinsky (contains poetry from mystical poets such as Rumi, Hafiz, Kabir, and Mira)

The Soul is Here For Its Own Joy: Sacred Poems From Many Cultures, translated by Robert Bly

Books and Audio Readings of Rumi, by Coleman Barks
http://www.colemanbarks.com/

Poetry of Mary Oliver (available at Amazon and local bookstores)

Poetry of David Whyte (available at Amazon and local bookstores)
http://www.davidwhyte.com/

Books and Audio Poetry of John O'Donohue
http://www.johnodonohue.com/

A Year With Rilke: Daily Readings From The Best of Rainer Maria Rilke, by Joanna Macy (available at Amazon and local bookstores)

RECOMMENDED STORYTELLING

Michael Meade
http://www.mosaicvoices.org/

Carolyn's Favorite Inspirational Music

Well-Tempered Clavier, Book I, by J.S. Bach

Suite Bergamasque, by Claude Debussy

Bill Douglas and the Ars Nova Singers
http://www.billdouglas.cc/

Carlos Nakai, Indian Flute
http://www.rcarlosnakai.com/

Peter Kater
http://www.peterkater.com/site/index.php

Olatunji Drumming
http://www.olatunjimusic.com/

CAROLYN'S FAVORITE ART

Michelangelo, Jan Van Eyck, Albrecht Durer, Johannes Vermeer, Vincent Van Gogh, Claude Monet, Edouard Manet, Salvador Dali, Frida Kahlo

Hopi Painting and Silver Craft by Michael Kabotie
http://www.kabotie.com/

Navajo Paintings by R.C. Gorman
http://rcgormangallery.com/

Guatemalan Textiles and Paintings
http://www.artemaya.com/index.html

UNDERSTANDING AND CREATING RITUAL

The word *ritual* originally meant "to fit together." It has been practiced throughout the history of the human species as a means of connecting with something greater than the human mind and ego. It acknowledges that humans are interdependent with the earth community and that from time to time, we need to remind ourselves of how we "fit together" with it. Additional purposes for creating ritual might be to facilitate healing; to bless or honor an event, a person, or an endeavor; to celebrate or give thanks for something received or accomplished.

In early human history, ritual was ubiquitous and deemed an essential part of human existence as humans were exceedingly aware of their interdependence with the elements and forces of nature. The more industrialized our species has become, the more disconnected we find ourselves from our relationship with the ecosystems.

The most powerful rituals are those in which the intention is to feel and express our connection with the earth. In such rituals, earth elements such as soil, fire, water, rock, plants, smoke, feathers, and other sacred objects from nature are used to reconnect us with the non-human world.

I believe that conscious ritual must be an integral aspect of navigating the coming chaos and creating a new culture. I highly recommend becoming familiar with the practice of ritual and sharing it with one's community.

One of the most useful resources for understanding and creating ritual is the book *Ritual: Power, Healing, and Community*, by Malidoma Somé, which explains the intention and creation of ritual. Also helpful is an audio CD by Malidoma entitled "Elemental Ritual" which can be ordered at his website at www.malidoma.com.

However, it is important to remember that ritual cannot be learned from reading a book. There are no formulas. The most powerful rituals erupt spontaneously from our hearts and from the earth. The more we practice ritual, the more comfortable we become with it, and the more mindful we are likely to be of our interdependence with the earth community. In this way, ritual becomes an art form, which is appropriate, since ritual and art are deeply connected. Revering and utilizing ritual will be essential as we navigate the coming chaos of a world unraveling.

ABOUT THE AUTHOR

Carolyn Baker, Ph.D., manages Speaking Truth to Power at www.carolynbaker.net. She is the author of *Sacred Demise: Walking The Spiritual Path of Industrial Civilization's Collapse, U.S. History Uncensored, and Coming Out of Fundamentalist Christianity*. A former psychotherapist, she conducts Sacred Demise workshops nationally and maintains an ongoing coaching practice. She has written numerous articles on earth-based spirituality and humankind's current crisis in consciousness. She lives and writes in Boulder, Colorado.

ENDNOTES

(Endnotes)

1. Clive Hamilton, *Requiem For A Species: Why We Resist The Truth About Climate Change*, 2010, p.222.

2. James Howard Kunstler, The Long Emergency, 2005, Grove/Atlantic.

3. James Gustave Speth, *A Bridge At The Edge of The World: Capitalism, The Environment, and Crossing From Crisis to Sustainability*, 2010, p. 234.

4. John Michael Greer, "Waiting For The Millennium: The Limits of Magic": http://www.energybulletin.net/node/53150

5. Clive, Hamilton, *Requiem For A Species*, p. 219.

6. Thomas Berry, *The Great Work*, 1999, p. 1.

7. Brian Swimme, "The Powers of The Universe": http://www.brianswimme.org/store/default.asp

8. Vaclav Havel, quoted in *A Bridge At The End of The World*, p. 200.

9. Clive Hamilton, *Requiem For A Species*, p. 210.

10. James Gustave Speth, *A Bridge At The Edge of The World*, p. 1.

11. Financial Crisis Suicide Numbers Mounting http://www.huffingtonpost.com/2008/10/14/financial-crisis-suicide_n_134453.html

12. Writing Therapy: http://en.wikipedia.org/wiki/Writing_therapy

13. Bill Plotkin, *Soulcraft*, 2003, pp. 195-196.

14. Memorizing Poetry: http://matthewkoslowski.com/2009/11/25/memorizing-poems/

15. Meditation, Yoga Might Switch Off Stress Genes: http://www.washingtonpost.com/wp-dyn/content/article/2008/07/02/AR2008070200973.html

16. John O'Donohue, *Beauty: The Invisible Embrace*, p. 94.

17. John Davis, Overview of Ecopsychology, http://clem.mscd.edu/~davisj/ep/ecopsy.html

18. Plotkin, p. 178

19. Ibid., p. 179

20. Raymond De Young Home Page: http://www-personal.umich.edu/~rdeyoung/

21. Your Soul's Work: http://yoursoulswork.com/Introduction.htm

22. Michael Meade, A Light Inside Dark Times Lecture Series, Mosaic Multicultural Foundation, 2008 at http://www.mosaicvoices.org/

23. Soul and Spirit http://www.realitysandwich.com/soul_and_spirit_soul_8

24. Copernican Revolution: http://en.wikipedia.org/wiki/Copernican_Revolution

25. Thomas Berry, *The Great Work*, p. 78.

26. Michael Meade, *The World Behind the World*, 2008, p. 94-95.

27. *Meeting The Shadow*, 1991, p.11

28. Malidoma Somè website: www.malidoma.com

29. *The World Behind The World*, p. 136-137.

30. *Peak Everything*, New Society, 2007

31. World Socialist Web: http://wsws.org/articles/2010/apr2010/pewr-a23.shtml

32. Surprising Reasons Why Americans Are So Lonely http://www.alternet.org/vision/146623/the_surprising_reason_why_americans_are_so_lonely%2C_and_why_future_prosperity_means_socializing_with_your_neighbors

33. Marshall Vian Summers, *Great Waves of Change: Navigating The Difficult Times Ahead*, 2009.

34. Liberation Economics: "Making A Living Through Living Your Purpose": http://transition-times.com/blog/2010/04/29/liberation-economics-making-a-living-through-living-your-purpose/

35. Post Peak Living: http://www.postpeakliving.com

36. Skill Share Network: http://www.skillsharenetwork.org/

37. "Sacred Economics" in Reality Sandwich, 2010: http://www.realitysandwich.com/sacred_economics

38. Vermont Commons: http://www.vtcommons.org/journal/2010/04/vermont-vox-pop-%E2%80%9C-call%E2%80%9D-collapse-carolyn-baker-interviews-hancock-vermont%E2%80%99s-kathleen

39. George A. Bonanno, The Other Side of Sadness: What The New Science of Bereavement Tells Us About Life After Loss, 2009, p. 199.

40. Michael Dowd, *Thank God For Evolution: How The Marriage of Science and Religion Will Transform Your Life and Our World*, 2009, p. 165.

41. Miriam Greenspan, *Healing Through The Dark Emotions: The Wisdom of Grief, Fear, and Despair*, 2003.

42. The Relentless Promotion of Positive Thinking Has Undermined America: http://www.alternet.org/health/143187?page=3

43. Beyond Depression: When Grief Doesn't Go Away: http://www.msnbc.msn.com/id/8050024/

44. Post Peak Living: http://www.postpeakliving.com

45. Imagining Life Without Oil and Being Ready: http://www.nytimes.com/2010/06/06/us/06peak.html?ref=us

46. Response to Imagining Life Without Oil: http://blueskyday.com/2010/06/06/reponse-the-the-peak-oil-story-in-the-new-york-times/

47. Miriam Greenspan, Healing Through The Dark Emotions, p. 196.

48. Joanna Macy, Working Through Environmental Despair, *Ecosychology*, Roszak, Gomes, & Kanner, eds., (Sierra Club 1995).

49. An Epidemic of Global Anger: http://www.huffingtonpost.com/caroline-myss/an-epidemic-of-global-ang_b_310209.html

50. Marshall Vian Summers, *Greater Community Spirituality*, p. 15.

51. America the Traumatized: How 13 Events of the Decade Made Us the PTSD Nation:http://www.alternet.org/news/144791/america_the_traumatized:_how_13_events_of_the_decade_made_us_the_ptsd_nation

52. Mindfulness In Practice: Anger Management: http://www.opendoortherapy.com/mfa_series_1to3.pdf

53. Homeostasis: http://en.wiktionary.org/wiki/homeostasis

54. Michael Dowd, *Thank God For Evolution*, p. 186.

55. Bill Plotkin, *Nature and The Human Soul: Cultivating Wholeness and Community in A Fragmented World*, p. 360.

56. From Fast Track to Slow Love: http://planetgreen.discovery.com/home-garden/draft-from-fast-track-to-slow-love-an-interview-with-dominique-browning.html

57. Clive Hamilton, *Requiem For A Species*, p. 71.

58. (F)unemployment: Make The Best of It: http://carolynbaker.net/content/view/1716/1/

59. Andrew Harvey, *The Hope: A Guide to Sacred Activism*, 2009.

60. Marshall Vian Summers, *Great Waves of Change: Navigating The Difficult Times Ahead*, 2009, p. 101.

61. *Ibid*, p. 155.

62. *Ibid*, p. 101.

63. *The World Behind The World*, p. 44.

64. http://news.bbc.co.uk/2/hi/8526699.stm

65. *Beauty: The Invisible Embrace*, p. 181.

66. David Suzuki, *Sacred Balance: Rediscovering Our Place In Nature*, 2007

67. http://en.wikipedia.org/wiki/Uncertainty_principle

68. *Great Waves of Change*, p. 34.

69. *Ibid*, p. 34-35.

70. Brian Swimme, *The Hidden Heart of The Cosmos: Humanity and The New Story*, 1996, p. 66.

71. Thomas Berry, *The Sacred Universe: Earth, Spirituality, and Religion In the Twenty-First Century*, Columbia University Press, 2009, p. 95

72. *Ibid*, p. 94

73. BALLE Network Services http://www.livingeconomies.org/network-services

74. About Slow Money http://www.slowmoneyalliance.org/about.html

75. Exercise for Grounding: http://healing.about.com/cs/grounding/a/bodyground.htm

CPSIA information can be obtained at www.ICGtesting.com
Printed in the USA
LVOW111251210812

295285LV00004B/72/P